COMMON SENSE
IN PROJECT
MANAGEMENT

PAUL A. TEDESCO

THOMSON
™
COURSE TECHNOLOGY
Professional ■ Technical ■ Reference

ISBN: 1-59863-175-6

Library of Congress Catalog Card Number: 2005911171

Printed in the United States of America

06 07 08 09 10 PH 10 9 8 7 6 5 4 3 2 1

Publisher and General Manager, Thomson Course Technology PTR:
Stacy L. Hiquet

Associate Director of Marketing:
Sarah O'Donnell

Manager of Editorial Services:
Heather Talbot

Marketing Manager:
Heather Hurley

Acquisitions Editor:
Mitzi Koontz

Marketing Coordinator:
Jordan Casey

Project Editor:
Sandy Doell

PTR Editorial Services Coordinator:
Elizabeth Furbish

Interior Layout:
Shawn Morningstar

Cover Designer:
Mike Tanamachi

Indexer:
Kelly Talbot

Proofreader:
Marta Justak

Thomson Course Technology PTR,
a division of Thomson Course Technology
25 Thomson Place
Boston, MA 02210
http://www.courseptr.com

THOMSON
COURSE TECHNOLOGY
Professional ■ Technical ■ Reference

Gifford Pinchot was my inspiration for writing this book. The initial ideas came from his books and classes on intrapreneuring.

Gezinus Hidding, professor at Loyola University in Chicago, willingly spent many hours reviewing the topics and presentation for their project management concepts.

Donald J. Geldernick identified, requested, and coordinated a group of people with management and project management experience to review the book and perform the initial editing processes. He was an immense help in finding a publisher for this book.

Brian Vanderjack, one of the project leaders I taught, calls often to let me know how he is applying and extending the concepts contained in the book.

Michelle Small, one of the project leaders I taught, provided many insights along the way.

Finally, this book is dedicated to my wife who was subjected to long hours of my absence as I toiled through many revisions.

FOREWORD

There are 75 books about project management in the Bibliography of Paul Tedesco's presentation here. Only eight of them significantly touch on a portion of his process. Although most of them have much to offer, none approaches the uniqueness of Paul Tedesco's *Common Sense in Project Management (CS-PM)*.

Many reviewers note that CS-PM embodies many concepts they want to use during projects but can't because they are thwarted by strictly defined project charters and the rigid controls of change review boards.

CS-PM gives us a new way to add value, eliminate useless tasks, and empower developers—and all of this comes through careful planning as we simultaneously develop and discover new value potential.

You do not have a learning curve or a replacement cost for the project management (PM) processes that you currently use. You use the same PM software you have now and learn the CS-PM process by applying the steps described here.

There are many new and different types of project management within the field of systems development. Tedesco's new book and process employ the best features of a number of them including Feature-Driven Agile, Xtreme Programming, and Scrum, along with traditional modern process-driven project management.

You move fast and lean without sacrificing quality. Common Sense in Project Management uses all of the aspects of your current project management tools and processes.

CS-PM documents issues that are not always documented in other project management processes. You mitigate risks and raise new issues that better support your company and create competitive advantages. CS-PM better enables us to communicate status to teams and keep records required by government agencies.

You gain the immediacy and speed of Scrum, Xtreme Programming, and Agile Methodology but retain the process-mapping Work Breakdown Structure that allows adequate documentation and Sarbanes-Oxley record keeping compliance.

With CS-PM, you overlay your existing process and use any software or techniques you are currently using, including linear waterfall, spiral, and incremental, or any combination of development processes.

CS-PM easily maps to Microsoft Project, Accenture Foundation One, CA/AllFusion Process and Project Management, Niku/ABT Workbench, Visible Analyst Workbench, Rational Unified Process (RUP), and Lotus AVM methodology.

CS-PM easily synchronizes to these Data and Process Modeling tools: CA/LBMS, Bachman Analyst, ERwin and BPwin, Visible Analyst Workbench, and Silverrun Technologies.

This is the value of Paul Tedesco's book: Sponsors empower project managers to discover new market values. They support faster-to-market delivery of value. Faster-to-market means more organizational harvesting of unanticipated new discoveries. This team value mining is a lot like the activities of wildcat oil drillers. They are always ready to seize a new opportunity.

We need faster-to-market value-added components. And we need to enable these processes early.

Each workday morning, the team meets to evaluate progress and new value propositions. They decide what to add, what to eliminate and what to defer or transfer. This process is similar to the way we resolve any risk mitigation or change management assessment.

It is critical to implement these adaptive value propositions and increase the use of tools that speed communication and work product delivery.

You augment these tools by increased use of e-mails and group messaging, server-based data sharing, cell phones that are answered, and text messaging. All forms of communication need to be logged or saved in folders according to their usage type. You perform this automatically, reducing administrative overhead associated with many methodologies.

Paul is a controlled wildcat, and this country was built on oil wildcat risk takers and cattle roughriders. We need the kind of enterprise executives who will support these risks in order to avoid the ultimate risk: oblivion.

Tedesco's new CS-PM processes can easily overlay existing process management tools for developing all sorts of new value: software development, product development, best practices (ala, CMMi and ISO 9003), engineering, manufacturing, construction, and process re-engineering.

Paul's technique treats undiscovered value by rescuing new discoveries in progress so as to add the value immediately, rather than suffer more opportunity losses.

The team identifies and applies new value early as it is discovered during the building stages. This is how an organization can survive and thrive, by not passing over the value that lies under-utilized. This is the ultimate value discovered during the process of developing a project.

—Donald J. Geldernick,
manager of the contributing editors who helped Paul improve his book

ACKNOWLEDGMENTS

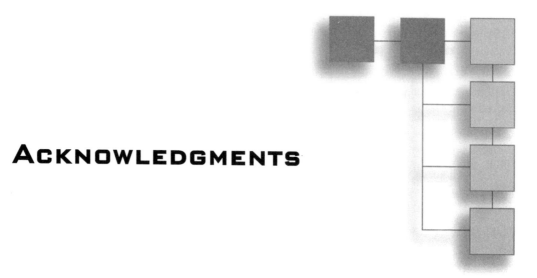

Many people have contributed to *Common Sense in Project Management*. This group includes all of those who worked with Paul Tedesco and Donald Geldernick in preparing the book for review. I thank each and every one, even if I don't mention you by name.

Donald Geldernick, Senior Project Manager/Consultant
IBM Global Services (former)

Vicki Brand, Global Medical Services Training Manager, formerly Project Manager
Shared Application Services
Abbott Laboratories

Dr. Gezinus J. Hidding
Associate Professor, Information Systems and Business
Loyola University of Chicago

Gillian Downey, Technology Project Manager
Bank of America
Jack Leary, Senior Vice President, Project Management
Milano, Inc.

Phillip Ejisimukwu, Oracle DBA and Applications Consulting
Accenture, now PAE, Inc.
pejisim@paeconsult.com
Gerry Quest, HR Manager for IT & Engineering Consulting
Sargent & Lundy

Dusan Kolesar, Systems Project Developer
Northern Trust

Dennis McDermott, National Director Risk Management and Quality Assurance
Computer Science Corporation (CSC)

Vicki Thom, Office and Computer Supervisor
Flo Products

Frank Underwood, Director/Project Manager
British-American Consulting (Ret)

Jack Nicholas, Associate Dean, Graduate School of Business
Loyola University

Josef Robey, Sr., Multimedia Engineer/IT Training Manager
CA, Universities (MI & Benedictine) & United Airlines

Don Jacobs, Organization and Communication Consultant
Archelon, LCC brokerage
Unocal executive (ret.)

Many thanks to the following Special Help Contributors:

From DePaul University: Dr. Helmut Epp, Rita Mack, Professors Terry Steinbach and
Jane Cleland-Huang, and Robert W. Starinsky also of the Tradewinds Group.

And especially to independent DBA technician Bobbi Foster and Will Pierce, University of
Illinois (ret.), for their very laborious proposal preparation contributions. And to author
Dr. David Langum of the Cumberland School of Law, Samson University, Birmingham,
Alabama, for his encouragements.

Additional thanks to Richard Costa, ICON Resources, Inc. for support service.

About the Author

Paul A. Tedesco was a project leader for over 40 years for some very advanced applications of artificial intelligence to both engineering and business applications. He has worked in and consulted for many of the Fortune 500 companies. He sits on the board of Cognitor, Inc., a company that applies artificial intelligence in the customer resolution management market. He also sits on the board of directors of SRC Technologies, Inc., an artificial intelligence company.

Mr. Tedesco began his career managing the application of artificial intelligence to the field of engineering for a department of Western Electric, a department that was later transferred to Bell Laboratories, now Lucent Technologies. He held many positions managing projects with several different companies. He was a project manager for Air Products and Chemicals, implementing a project management control system.

He later was a project manager for Amoco Chemicals, now BP, or British Petroleum. At that time, he was introduced to Phased Project Planning, the project management control system used by NASA to create the first Apollo space shots. He extended the concepts to include his prior project management experience.

He managed projects and project groups at Blue Cross and Blue Shield of Illinois where he was able to extend business benefits through the use of artificial intelligence and technical architectures. At the City of Chicago, he managed project leaders and controlled systems, including payroll, personnel, budget, building inspection, licensing, revenue, and water. He later returned to Illinois Blue Cross and Blue Shield to run a systems audit project. In all of these companies, he performed managerial tasks and acted as what is now called an *intrapreneur*.

He worked as an independent, managing projects for companies that include Ameritech (now a part of SBC), The National Association of Blue Cross and Blue Shield Plans, Combined Insurance (now AON), Kraft, International Minerals and Chemicals, Cap Gemini America, The American Medical Association, and other companies.

He formed several small companies, including Cognitor, Inc., Management Video Training, and others. He is now working with a group studying how to make projects work better. The group is called "Value Driven Project Leadership" and includes professors from Loyola University and National-Lewis University. The group also includes a number of consulting companies.

Contents

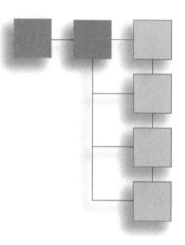

PART IV: INNOVATIVE PROJECT MANAGEMENT WITH BEST PRACTICES   205

INTRODUCTION

In *Common Sense in Project Management*, you will learn ways of creating systems projects on schedule and within budget while providing a high return on investment (ROI). "What?" you say. "Your project teams will turn projects into massive profit generators? Shouldn't this be the next goal for the Chief Information Officer?"

If you can implement projects on schedule and within budget and add value, won't that create many benefits for a company?

Note

Projects add value to a corporation when they extend the products that a corporation can sell, make products better fit a customer's needs, or simply reduce the cost of implementing a project. This provides a high return on investment, getting lots of value from a low investment.

You will learn to run projects that complete the tasks assigned while introducing new products, processes, and services. You enable your company to grow and profit, thereby increasing your corporate ROI.

You will run your projects inside of corporations because corporations provide many supportive facilities and benefits, including networks of supportive suppliers, a depth of proprietary technology, many personnel resources, and marketing clout. You incorporate ideas in your projects to simplify the task of creating and moving ideas from concept to a profitable reality.

Systems projects are normally humdrum with a known start, known process, and known goals. Here are some of the negatives that keep information service projects from adding value to the corporation:

1. Your information service projects do not normally create profit.

2. You only support understood needs and do not investigate to add new functionality or profitability.

3. You, as information service personnel, have little cooperation from your business departments.

4. You do not know all the business department needs, and with insufficient communications, you will have difficulty understanding any new business department needs.

5. You do not fully understand corporate goals, which makes it difficult for you to be a profit center in the corporation.

Some Barriers

Here are some of the barriers to implementing projects on schedule and within budget. It is very difficult for you to see into the future or to determine future business or systems needs, so you will not identify the business functions that are needed by your business. Your business is probably partially satisfied by small incremental advances, or by purchased systems.

Your companies need to change for your projects to create more of a profit. The chart on the following page demonstrates why change is necessary.

Currently, corporations must change to fit purchased systems. These purchased systems are only temporary fixes for corporations. Purchased systems perform very standard functions and cause corporations to lose some of their business competitive advantages. Yet, purchased systems could provide the best of business alternatives.

When you improve your communications and combine your innovation among systems, business, and management, you help corporations to create combined business and technical competitive advantages. Future business products and business and technical requirements can be created by using and extending existing system functions.

Your innovation supports corporate future needs. Your innovation helps improve your system delivery processes. Your innovation closes the gaps among the customer, senior management, business management, and systems. Your intercommunication supplies important information normally lacking within systems projects.

You simplify your iterative implementation using standard project methodologies. Your early communication and innovation provides the necessary documentation for both understanding and supplying the information needed for development methodologies. You identify and correct problems early through your documentation.

You will use corporate systems, while incrementally adding new features through existing software or creating new architectures that are better able to support future business. You satisfy customers, senior management, business departments, and technology requirements through new features.

Your innovation in big organizations is difficult, but *Common Sense in Project Management* (CS-PM) can help you succeed. You need a few passionately dedicated individuals or small groups who begin to discover advantageous business, technology, and architecture elements, thus helping you enhance corporate goals. You gain business and technical competitive advantages. You may even satisfy the needs of your information-hungry decision-makers.

Note

Intrapreneur is defined in Chapter 1, "How Innovation Happens in a Project."

High I.T. Project Failure Rates (for Decades)
- **Standish Group - Chaos 2002**
  - *23% of Projects Fail Altogether*
  - *49% of Projects Over Budget, and/or Late*
  - *28% of Projects Succeed*
- **Department of Defense Software Projects**
  - *29% - Paid for, but not delivered*
  - *46% - Delivered, but not successfully used*
  - *20% - Used, but extensively reworked or abandoned*
  - *3% - Used after changes*
  - *2% - Used as delivered*
- **KPMG study**
  - *62% of IT projects overran budget by more than 30%*

Project failure statistics.

Common Sense in Project Management (CS-PM) can be used by *intrapreneurs* to implement projects. Many concepts of CS-PM are an extension of intrapreneuring. As Gifford Pinchot said in his book, *Intrapreneuring*:

> Consider what happened as we moved from the Agricultural Age to the Industrial Age. The United States remained a major agricultural producer despite the industrial revolution, but the way we grew crops changed. Today, a larger and larger portion of agricultural value is created by industrial means. Farm labor has become a tiny part of a giant complex of industries that make tractors, agricultural chemicals, fuels, veterinary medicines, and rubber boots. A similar change will occur in the industrial sector as we enter what is called the Information Age. The information explosion will not eliminate industrial production in the United States, but it will change how it is done and change the factors that produce industrial success.

In our competitive world, innovation is becoming as important as productivity. We must find new ways to use information for business. Invention is the first step in creation and innovation. From invention, new needs are turned into business successes. New information needs to create competitive business technical advantages and business successes.

The business advantage from the information explosion encourages businesses and technical partners to form and create new business advantages. Critical business and critical technology issues drive business enhancements. Innovative project managers and their teams build highly profitable solutions. These managers create geometrically increasing benefits. Business advantages are created through a high level of design reuse, tool creation, and system reuse.

In *Common Sense in Project Management*, I integrate these concepts and show how creative projects are constructed, the responsibilities of the different participants, and the internal structure of the project. Finally, I demonstrate the types of information gathered and how that information is used within the project.

How to Read This Book

Reader's Guide—How to Read This Book	Executive Management	Business Manager	IT Executive	Project Managers	Developers	Construction Managers	Pharmaceutical Development Managers	Product Development Managers	CMMi/ISO 9000	"Best Practices" Improvement
Foreword	X	X	X	X	X	X	X	X	X	X
Introduction	X	X	X	X	X	X	X	X	X	X
Chapter 1	X	X	X	X	X	X	X	X	X	X
Chapter 2		X	X	X	X	X	X	X	X	X
Chapter 3				X	X	X		X	X	X
Chapter 4	X	X	X	X	X	X	X	X	X	X
Chapter 5	X	X	X	X			X	X	X	X
Chapter 6		X	X	X	X	X	X	X	X	X
Chapter 7			X	X					X	X
Chapter 8	X	X	X	X	X	X	X	X	X	X
Chapter 9		X	X	X	X	X	X	X	X	X
Chapter 10		X	X	X				X	X	X
Chapter 11	X	X	X	X				X	X	X
Chapter 12	X	X	X	X	X	X	X	X	X	X
Chapter 13				X	X	X	X	X	X	X
Chapter 14				X	X	X	X	X	X	X
Chapter 15	X	X	X	X	X	X	X	X	X	X

Reader's Guide.

PART ONE

MANAGING INNOVATION THROUGH PROJECTS

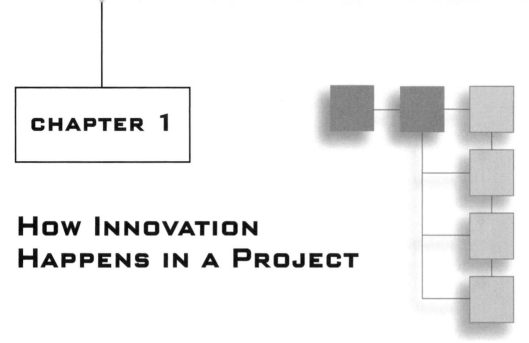

CHAPTER 1

How Innovation Happens in a Project

IT (information technology) hasn't come close to delivering the benefits businesses are looking for.

—Peter F. Drucker

In this chapter, you will learn to make your organization more competitive by delivering your projects, not just "on time and under budget," but with some extra added value that your customers will see and appreciate.

You can look at the tasks that you need to perform and find easier ways to complete them, or ways to simplify jobs that others need to perform. This is a part of innovation. You can add innovation throughout the project by replacing unneeded work tasks, such as adding pictures to a computer screen to capture information, with tasks that make the computer screen clear and easy to use. You can simplify production tasks by finding simpler ways of performing the task.

You will learn new concepts that are easy to adapt to your current management process because they don't really change the way you do business now; they simply add to it or simplify what you do.

You will find these new concepts easy to adopt because they are things that you do naturally, and you and your team members will constantly think, communicate, and negotiate. You will build a sense of ownership and commitment. Through this constant diligence, you will increase quality.

Our new innovation checklist introduces more quality checks and reduces the need for error repair later. You begin using the checklist by studying each task that needs to be accomplished. The following is an innovation checklist:

1. Define the business task or goal that is to be accomplished.

2. Define the business alternatives to accomplishing the business task.

3. Define the advantages and disadvantages of each alternative. This requires you to look into the future to best define the advantages.

4. Define the technology (or architecture) that needs to be in place to support each business alternative.

5. Define new business alternatives, tasks, or goals that could be supported by each technical alternative.

6. Select the best combination of business alternative and technical alternative to implement this task or goal.

Note

Think of an architecture as a set of design plans for building a house. Architecture can also be a set of design plans for building and maintaining a system.

Following the innovation checklist creates a continuing interplay and negotiation with the team members. Your negotiation interplay is between business and technical teams. These teams will learn and benefit from each other. Business people learn potential business applications of technology from the technical team. Technical people learn about business needs from the business people. Together your teams create new goals.

In this book, you will learn to use the Common Sense in Project Management (CS-PM) process improvement method. You can expect to provide customers with better products and services, and you can use CS-PM for software, products, process improvement, best practices improvement, construction, engineering, manufacturing, logistics, bioengineering and pharmacology.

Using Common Sense in Project Management, you add a specific series of steps to your existing project or process tools. When you use these steps, you will simplify your project, find alternative ways of implementing your project, and provide better product for your customers. I have included task lists in popular formats for project managers to add to their planning and scheduling tools.

Make Innovation a Part of Your Plan

Why do we need to alter the way that we implement projects? Companies have had high project failure rates for decades. This is documented by the Standish Group in their *Chaos Report*, which indicates that two percent of projects are used as first delivered.

The same report shows that 28 percent of information technology projects are successful. Other types of projects have a higher success rate. You can increase your project success rate by making a few simple changes.

You can increase project success rates by being innovative when you begin the project innovation for a known business project. I will show you how to use advanced technologies, architectures, teams, and negotiation to improve project delivery.

You will learn to incorporate new ideas in your projects, and you will deliver needed business benefits. Your team will discover and create new business. You will learn how to apply technical enhancements that improve your project and the delivery of your project.

In this chapter, I will explain how Common Sense in Project Management (CS-PM) works for a normal project. I will show you how you can use CS-PM to add new value to your project by using innovative approaches.

I will show you how to use team project techniques in a way that will enhance the methodology and tools that you currently use, and you will see that the innovative spirit helps ensure project success. I will show you how CS-PM allows a circle of discovery, innovation, and immediate implementation, which creates new business value, such as providing a business feature that increases the market value (price) of a product.

You will enhance your projects by using CS-PM to improve your development methodology. You will learn how to think about alternatives to what you need to accomplish. You will work with your team and constantly communicate in order to discover, identify, and immediately apply new knowledge to provide a better project outcome. You will have created what I call an extended advantage.

Note

A project is meant to deliver a specific business advantage. You will identify business and technical alternatives. You will also find new business that can be supported from the technical alternatives. This new business is the *extended advantage*.

When you use CS-PM, you will complete projects on time, within budget, and with added value. The extended advantage identifies critical business and technical work and creates newly discovered value.

Note

> When you review the project tasks, you will find some that can be skipped. It may not be necessary to complete these tasks. Other tasks will help the business to stay competitive or to become more competitive. These tasks are critical to the functioning of the business. I call these *critical business tasks*.

You will also have identified the technology that best supports the critical business tasks. These I call *critical technology*. You clearly define critical business and technology that needs to be created for the project, and you combine business and technology concepts. This combination helps uncover the interactions of the parts. You continuously modify and enhance the original plan to produce the final results.

Note

> Projects usually have a fixed charter or desired outcome. If you set a flexible project goal, you can add new benefits to the project as they are understood. As you add enhancements, you need to remember that the enhancements made should be beneficial to the business. These enhancements should also be used to shorten the project implementation.

Innovation Requires Flexible Project Requirements

Current projects have fixed project requirements. Fixed project requirements hold all the project participants to a tightly defined set of tasks or work breakdown structure (WBS). Instead, I use a flexible project charter that adapts to new discoveries of business or technical innovations through which you will learn to add new values as soon as possible after your discovery.

Note

> A WBS is a *work breakdown structure*. A recipe to make bread has a simple work breakdown structure. First, you gather the ingredients. Then you combine the basic ingredients. You wait for a specific event. You take some more actions, and finally you bake the bread. A complex work breakdown structure would be used for the construction of a building like the Sears Tower.

You start the flexible charter by determining the known requirements of the project. You will use these requirements to determine the tasks that are critical to the business, and you will learn to identify technology (or architecture) to enhance the project.

It is difficult for anyone to see very far into the future, but you will use concepts that will help you look to the future while working as a team. So a team, supported by many backgrounds, investigates and negotiates to define the flexible requirements, looks into the future, and helps uncover many critical business and technical alternatives. You will select the most important alternatives for further study. Your study will uncover hidden facts about the business and the supporting technology.

Column 1 of Figure 1.1 shows how you will start the flexible project charter. Column 2 shows how the alternatives found in Column 1 are studied to find the best way of creating the project. Column 3 completes the study started in Column 2 and defines the project requirements. Column 4 finishes the project, implements it, and operates the end product.

Managing Innovation Through Projects

Determine Project Requirements	Select Best Alternatives	Requirements Analysis	Design and Implement
•Determine Critical to Business / Technology •Determine Identify Business / Technology Alternatives •Determine Project Participants •Determine Business Department Personnel •Determine Senior Management Involved •Determine Customer Benefits •Select Immediate Implementation •Determine Reuse	•Determine Benefits to the Business •Determine Benefits of Technology (Architecture) •Determine Benefits of Each Alternative •Integration of Business and Technology Issues •Determine and Describe Benefits of the Combined Business and Technology	•Determine Specification Needs from Phase II Alternatives •Describe Requirements for Combined Business and Technology (Architecture) •Begin Description of System Parts •Write Use Cases for the Selected Items •Determine Possible Reuse	•Write the Specifications •Determine the Potential Problems •Determine How to Test •Write User Documentation •Code the System •Test the System (All Levels) •Implement the System •Operate the System •Review and Discover New Benefits and Alternatives

Figure 1.1 Managing innovation through projects.

Your project personnel in this flexible project perform a specific series of tasks. The tasks require their knowledge and expertise. The backgrounds of your team include both business and technology.

You will immediately use the technology (or architecture) to find new ways of implementing the required business functions while also supporting potential new business through the technology. Your team will discover and negotiate these concepts to form the flexible project.

The following steps indicate how your team members will use their knowledge to create and implement your flexible project. The team investigates the tasks identified in the project. In their study of alternatives, your business team members will define the tasks that are critical to the business while the technical members will identify the technical issues that are critical to the project.

When your team identifies a task that is critical for the business, that task is combined with a task that is now known to be critical to the technology. You want and need to complete these tasks as soon as possible. When your team has completed every critical task, you know that you can complete the project.

Because you addressed critical tasks first, you know that you have delivered a high level of value to the business. Tasks that are not as critical to the business (or the technology) will not necessarily be completed at the same time. So your team will concentrate on the essential targets of the business.

To complete the tasks, your team will combine business and technical tasks, and will create both business and technical opportunities. Your team implements each critical business and technical task (the tasks that have been combined) as early as possible. This means that other project tasks have not been implemented. Your team will implement tasks as early as possible and as often as possible.

Note

No implementation steps are skipped. Testing of concepts is performed as required, and quality control is performed as required.

You implement Common Sense in Project Management projects in cycles, putting the most critical tasks first. Once your team has implemented the first cycle of a cyclic project, it will discover that business and technology could have been satisfied in better ways. The end of each cycle provides an opportunity to correct some of the problems. When a cycle is completed, all the team members have new knowledge.

Note

Each project is divided into small tasks that can be implemented rapidly. The tasks that will provide the best value will be implemented first. Here value can be an increase in business, a simplification to the overall project, the addition of cost-saving architectures, or other things of value to the corporation.

For the next step, your team has new knowledge, which was extracted from a completed cycle. Your team reviews this new knowledge by sharing and incorporating their new ideas early. You will continue to negotiate new ideas, which will provide procedures, new or enhanced products, or improved system architectures.

You will continue to find new ways to provide better products for customers. Your team needs to determine the newest most important features that will make the corporation more competitive. These new important features will be implemented as early as possible.

Your team will continue to perform many project tasks as before. You will continue to initiate plans to control the testing of processes during requirements analysis, design, and implementation.

You will identify some new technical features. The new technology (or architecture) features can often add business opportunities. You will continue to negotiate between the team members to identify new requirements. Your team members need to include business personnel, senior management, system designers, architects, and even customers.

When your team performs the negotiation, you will simplify the project processes and the work breakdown structure (WBS) of the project, and you will be able to remove some of the business processes that are not critical to the business. You will also be able to use the technology or architecture to simplify some of the project steps.

When your team is working on implementing a project cycle, they need to find reusable procedures and tools. Your team will use "best practices" to find procedures and tools for reuse. These tools could have been created in other projects, in other cycles of this project, or within this project. Your team will study and find previous successes that can be used within this project.

You will address critical business and technical issues early in the project. You will work on critical business requirements that significantly add customer or process advantages. Your technical people will work on technical (or architectural) issues that are critical if they significantly add technical advantages or simplify the project.

Important Thoughts for Innovative Projects

Gifford Pinchot has said that innovation plays a very important role in business success. But innovation has not been a part of projects that create business information systems.

Some businesses use project control methods that prevent the discovery of new processes and features that satisfy new customer needs. Take, for example, the amount of time it has taken the old-line telephone companies to support the use of cellular phones. These companies have lost the opportunity to add benefits and competitive advantage based upon the cellular phone. Why?

Apply this example to your own business. You and your team learn about yourselves, your team, and your processes as you build solutions. When you see chances to improve products or product quality, it is at that point that you must add the new value; otherwise, the new value just sits on the shelf waiting for use.

When I manage innovations through projects, I use a very proactive process. I must constantly think, negotiate, and immediately add the discovered needs.

I have observed the project process for information processing for over 40 years, and the manner of projectizing information technology has not changed much in that time.

Software companies have applied rule-driven process control. But, unfortunately, old algorithmic rules deliver unusable product from the failed processes. This not only clouds our view of usable outcomes, but complicates our recognition of the successes.

A number of new project control methodologies have been developed and implemented over the years. Yet current project management methods, including spiral development, have not provided improvements. The innovative spirit, which makes any project management process effective, is lacking.

Current project management methods would be greatly improved by adding the innovative spirit, which would make project management more effective. I have added the innovative spirit to the process of running projects, which adds common sense to running projects. You can use a few common sense steps to make your projects successful.

As you continue to use the processes of CS-PM, you will begin to identify things that might be new business opportunities. For example, my team created a database system for a large, health care insurance claim administration system. The company did not want to purchase a database system, but I needed a database for my system, so consequently, my team designed and wrote a database system.

The database system was full featured, supporting both random accessing and ring processing. The database handled pricing information about doctors and hospitals. This database provided the doctor and hospital information that the state needed, and our company won the new business. So we created a new business opportunity.

Note

A random process for a database allows me to give key information and obtain the specific information that I want. So I could use the doctor identification to obtain the doctor charge information. But doctors have several procedures that they can perform so I need a way to look at all of the procedures that a doctor could perform. We used the ring structure to identify all the procedures for a doctor.

My management asked the initial questions about the potential capability of the database. I was able to define the new business opportunity only by working with the hospital payment department, and the doctor payment department. I did not have enough knowledge within my department or area of expertise to have created the new business opportunity. I used the expertise of the other departments to identify the needs for the new business opportunity.

When you started the project there was a specific, stated goal. As the project progressed, you identified new business opportunities. You create these opportunities to create business advantages, and you want to add these advantages as soon as possible.

When you add the advantages, you are adding value. At the same time that you are adding value to the project you are delaying or removing tasks that do not add value. By removing tasks that do not add value, you are removing clutter from the project. You are implementing processes that create business advantages. CS-PM makes it easier for people to create new business advantages and to remove clutter from projects.

Companies use several methods of rewarding the teams that go above and beyond the call of duty in implementing projects. Some companies provide bonuses for completing projects ahead of schedule. Some companies have created new departments to handle the new business opportunities; they often promote team members to run these departments.

Over a period of years, I have used many different project management processes. Regardless of the project management process I used, I was able to bring my projects in on schedule. I did this because I added the processes of CS-PM to the basic project management process.

> For example, in the same health care insurance environment, I managed the project that automated the payment of doctor claims. I identified all of the tasks that were critical to implementing the project. Several types of health care required a process that determined the amount of benefits remaining under the contract. I also combined payment and history capture functions into one process. Because the processes were similar, I incorporated all of these processes into one, thereby eliminating many separate tasks.

I found functions that were critical to implementing the project. I tested the payment theories for two types of health care processing, and I uncovered problems early in the process and changed the requirements to fit actual results. These simple changes allowed me to complete my project on schedule.

I will show you how to avoid the pitfalls of most projects. Here are the usual outcomes from projects that do not use the features of CS-PM. Projects continue to be delivered late, over budget, and not meeting critical business requirements. The Department of Defense studied 8,000 projects completed in 350 companies. Of those, only 16 percent are considered successful.

Note

Success can be measured by many standards. Meeting the bare minimum of usability and adequately supplying needed business processes is the lowest standard allowable.

Only about two percent of projects are used as first delivered. I will show you that managing innovation within projects increases the success of corporate systems and helps the systems to be used as delivered.

I will show you a cyclic project management process that is an enhancement to the spiral development methodology. Once you have completed a task, you will have new business and technical knowledge. You can use this knowledge to derive new business and technical benefits.

Negotiation Uncovers the Best of Alternatives

I will show you that the negotiation process, within a cycle, provides new, discovered benefits. In contradistinction to the spiral development methodology, when you manage innovation through your projects, you will systematically consider other advantageous requirements, which will make the overall project more successful.

The credit project team investigated other outstanding credit system requirements, questioned the system users, and found a better way of supplying needed credit information. The team negotiated requirement changes supplying credit information that was immediately available and did not require excruciating calculations. The changes made the project easier to implement and reduced the project time.

I will show you how to use technical functions and architectures to achieve successes. You will see that these technical functions and architectures are a basis for further project development. For example, with the health care project, we created functions that automatically wrote the program code (which shortened the time that programmers needed to write the system).

I will show you how to use many short implementation cycles. This will help you to avoid the problems of a large project that is constructed from the very beginning to the end. This is similar to the spiral development process. For example, in the health care project, we implemented system parts and uncovered problems in our design from early in the project. Correcting the problems early guaranteed that we would meet our target dates.

You will add innovation at each cycle of the project. This is a process missing from spiral development. You will add new value when an opportunity is discovered. After the first implementation cycle, the credit users immediately found new ways to use the credit information, so they changed their named requirements for the follow-on cycles.

When you build innovation into a project, you provide continuous upgrading of the product and continuously increase product benefits for the customer.

You will manage innovation throughout your projects, continuously increasing the effective innovation per dollar. I have implemented projects ahead of schedule, under budget, with few or zero defects, and have even added new business. For example, in the health care environment, I provided testing processes for two other groups and even handled new types of claims through our innovative processes.

You will have negotiation between business and development departments. Your negotiations will help to create a competitive advantage in the marketplace. Again, I helped the credit department speed up its credit extension process for customers who were standing at the cash register.

For example, your corporation could sell contracts to companies that would not buy without the newly created advantages. One such advantage was created through the design of a flexible database. Another advantage was the ability of a computer to understand the contents of a resume and match those contents to find the candidate best suited for a specific job. Ergo, you will make more money with less cost.

You will implement ideas and business requirements rapidly and cost effectively. You will use CS-PM to assist with some of your innovation requirements. I will show you how to keep potential innovations from languishing between conception and the marketplace. Managing project innovation reduces the risk that innovations will languish before commercialization. When I asked our health care business executives if they needed to handle combined doctor and hospital claims, they agreed, and we immediately determined how to implement these requirements rapidly.

There is currently little innovation in projects. Corporations usually formalize the project management process, making the project control paperwork the goal. Extraneous paperwork prevents innovation, causing the overall corporate goals to be lost. I will show you how to implement projects and satisfy stringent corporate requirements.

You can use information technology to solve many business problems and provide needed corporate benefits, but you need communication and innovation in almost every field to keep businesses competitive. Without communication and innovation, the businesses will not supply new competitive benefits.

For example, customer service has adopted information technology to assist customers in resolving problems with their products. Here are two examples from my recent past. I just spent four hours on the phone resolving a problem with a product. In the same week, I spent one hour on the Internet resolving a different problem. Which process was more effective?

Within large businesses, management sponsors need to support your projects for them to succeed. The corporate goals need to be known by your project participants so that decisions made by your team will conform to the goals of the corporation. For example, I described our corporate funding and timing needs to a project participant and together we found a way to satisfy both within the project.

Management sets projects goals, but the goals set by management should only be initial goals. Your team can change the goals to make the project simpler, to add flexibility to the project, to better support the customer, or just to be able to implement the project faster.

For example, when I implemented a project to control the inspection of buildings for a city government, I created tools that I could use to implement different types of inspections. The remainder of the overall system was implemented faster because of the tools that were created. When management set the goals for the project, they did not have complete knowledge of everything that could be accomplished in the project. Thus, when your team finds better ways of satisfying the corporate needs, they can refine the requirements to improve the project goals. So, as the project progresses, you will continue to negotiate to improve it.

One of the ways that your team can improve the project is to apply appropriate technology or architectures to it. These architectures will shorten the duration of the project. For example, I was involved in a project control system that was able to determine project overruns. When the end of the project was near, the team determined that the overrun calculations were not correct. I had used a decision table architecture, and so I was immediately able to support the new calculations.

Figure 1.2 shows how the combination of business requirements and architecture are used to create new business value.

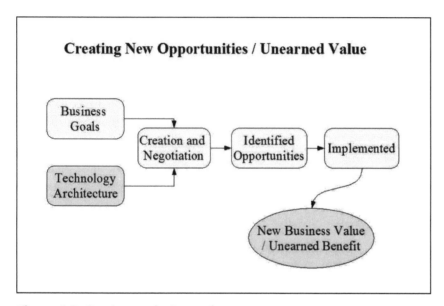

Figure 1.2 Creating new business value.

Creating and Discovering New Opportunities

Some corporations use the Rational Suite of products to provide several requirements definition iterations. If you do not use several requirements iterations, you can not use newly found project knowledge.

Note

A *project requirements definition* is where the content of the project is identified. The end result is a list of needs or requirements for the end product of the project. The functions of communicating, negotiating, and agreeing are used to arrive at the set of requirements.

You need to continuously communicate, negotiate, and agree with all of the members of the team throughout the development process. Consensus and communication about changes and newly discovered opportunities are the essence of managing innovation.

For example, in the large health care project, we discovered a new, technical, system control architecture. The architecture permitted us to divide the project into separate parts. Further, the architecture was fully tested at the end of the first part of the project. Then we used the architecture to simplify the remaining parts of the project.

You can simplify your project through innovation within the project. But you need to focus the innovation so that the energy spent on it is directed toward the end goal of the project. Focusing and releasing the innovative spirit for every company project provides a flood of innovation with many successful benefits. For example, focusing on simplifying a corporate budget process reduced the amount of time required for the company to respond to major catastrophes like tornadoes, floods, and major snow storms.

Your project managers need a substantial understanding of the business and of business issues. Project managers are able to identify critical business and technical issues only if they understand the business, and they also need to have some understanding of the technology involved in the project. Your project leaders will begin to learn these business and technical issues as parts of the project are installed. They will identify, combine, and install project parts early and often.

I will give you an example involving the successes in the credit department of a large retail company. They decided to use the innovative process to find a more successful way of implementing projects. They used the Common Sense in Project Management process throughout the project.

Their goal was to supply better customer credit information rapidly at the point of sale terminals and throughout the organization. I showed them how to innovate and how to manage the innovation throughout this project. The company chose the project manager.

I trained the project manager in the innovative processes of (CS-PM). I gave her samples of the process steps. I described past projects showing how I approached different problems.

Then I let her confront the problems in running the innovative project. When she made a mistake or asked specific questions, we would discuss the situation. In this way, she was able to learn from her questions or her mistakes.

She selected the different members of the project team. The project team consisted of business and technical personnel. Together, they identified the tasks they needed to complete the project. They identified critical business requirements.

Note

A business requirement is *critical* if it satisfies a customer need, keeps the company in business, or provides a business advantage over a competitor.

There is always more than one way to satisfy a need. The team identified the business alternatives that they felt would satisfy the need, and they also identified the technology that would be needed to support the business. The team identified different technology alternatives that could satisfy the needs. They then combined business and technology alternatives to find the alternatives that best satisfied the needs.

After the supporting technology is determined, there is an innovative task that needs to be performed. The team identified business advantages that had not previously been stated. These new business advantages could be supported by the selected supporting technology. The team studied over 300 requirements from the credit department to determine which needs could be combined with this project.

The project leader determined the advantages that could be implemented early. She created the project plan for each step of implementation using knowledge about the parts that could be implemented early. For example, she identified that an existing data structure and software could be used to implement a major part of the system early. The project team implemented this data structure part within a month of the start of the project.

The project leader followed the waterfall development methodology for each early implementation step. The project team continued implementation of parts throughout the project. In the end, they completed the project six months ahead of the initial schedule. The schedule had been prepared using the Estimax tool.

Note

Here is a quick review of the steps that the project leader followed. The project leader formed the project plan using both business and supporting technology. The project manager began by selecting the project team. The team investigated the system architecture (technology) and business at the same time.

You need to follow this example. Your team will contain both business designers and technicians from the start. Your advantage is that the project manager will have a full understanding of both business and technical aspects of the project. In the example the project used the waterfall development methodology and used Estimax, a function point analysis tool, to create the project estimate.

Note

You need to plan using both business and technology needs. If only business needs are used then the needs and benefits of the technology will not be available to simplify the project.

Many system projects analyze business and ignore technology. Many other projects define the end goal and ignore the architecture and/or technology that would simplify the project. You need to include both business and technology issues in your project.

I have seen the consequences of ignoring technology in the design of a system. The result is that the business structure becomes the system structure. In most systems project management processes, the initial teams generally only contain business system designers. Spiral and waterfall development methodology generally support only the business or end goal tasks of the requirements and only contain systems designers.

Here is how I see systems being developed today. This also fits the required set of steps for a standard development methodology. The designers design a major part of the project. The designers write the requirements and the specifications for the developers.

Developers then produce the system following those specifications. The result is that the system structure looks like the business function. As soon as the business changes, the system structure must be sacrificed to support the business changes. I have also seen how this process keeps innovative solutions from being used.

Note

When innovative solutions are not used, it becomes harder for businesses to compete.

Here are the advantages that I see from the large retail organization example mentioned earlier. The project leader used a technical architecture that supported the business, yet the technical architecture did not follow the business structure. The technical architecture provided business opportunities not previously expressed.

I have designed CS-PM so that the innovative project plan overlays and fits into any standard project control processes. In fact, any methodology can be used and overlaid with the additional WBS tasks.

Many innovative project management tasks precede tasks of a standardized project. For the waterfall development methodology, a large part of the CS-PM tasks would be completed before any development.

I have used a cyclic project structure that supports uncovering knowledge within projects. The spiral development methodology more closely follows the cyclic process of an innovative project. I have provided the mechanism so that some technical development is completed before designers have released specifications for application development.

When I run major projects, I organize the technical structure at the same time that business tasks are identified. In the case of the large retail organization, the team constructed the support structure for the system at the same time that the business design was being created. This approach works well in the innovative project management process.

Considering Technology and Business Together

In the innovative project process, you will add development technicians and designers at the same time. Here is an example that shows the power of the CS-PM concept and shows the time frame for the process. At the credit division of the retail company, several technical developers were added at the same time that designers were added. Technical developers created the technical system architecture, while designers consulted with credit business personnel.

Figure 1.3 indicates just how the business and technical functions are combined.

In the credit application, the project manager had all the designers and developers visit one of the company's credit central locations. Seeing credit central provided both the technical and business members of the project team with a business understanding. It also added to a common understanding between the business people, the business systems team, and the technical systems team.

When you begin your project, remember that site visits help with team building, with communications, and with creating an atmosphere that allows negotiations. Through the site visits, the credit central personnel came to know systems personnel, and vice versa. Systems personnel learned how the business was run.

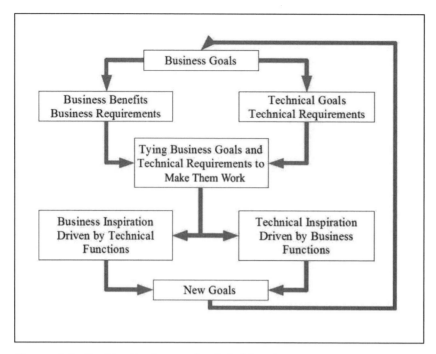

Figure 1.3 Combined business and technical functions.

The credit central personnel and systems personnel gained a mutual knowledge of the operation. When the systems personnel had ideas, they communicated freely with the credit central personnel. When the credit central personnel had ideas, they communicated freely with the systems personnel. The ideas would enter into a negotiation process and some form of the ideas (innovations) would be incorporated in the system.

The communication and the negotiations helped the project manager and the team discover the best way to produce the required system benefits. Further, negotiations between the technicians, developers, designers, business personnel, and management helped them investigate potential benefits that would not have been found without this high level of communication. Through innovation, the team found shortcuts to implement the system faster and with greater business benefit.

The implementation steps for the credit project are shown in Figure 1.4.

This is how the credit department project implementation worked. The technical team identified a credit information handling task that could be completed within the first month. The data handling function supported the business requirement. The testing for updating of new credit information began at the end of the first month.

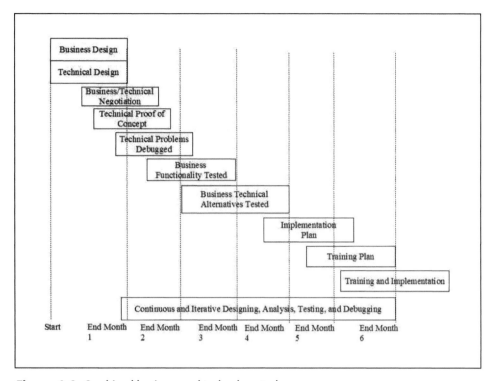

Figure 1.4 Combined business and technology tasks.

With this success, more credit business personnel became involved. The team resolved many technical problems by the end of the second month. It tested full business functionality by the end of the third month.

The team tested several business and technical alternatives by the end of the fourth month and developed the implementation plan by the end of the fifth month. Training personnel prepared the training by the middle of the sixth month, and the team implemented the project by the end of the sixth month.

The actual implementation of the credit project shows the success of the CS-PM innovation process used. Here is what happened with the training for the implementation of the project. Training and implementation were scheduled for one of the credit centrals.

This is a large organization, and there are many credit centrals. The system was intended for use at one of the credit centrals. The other credit centrals would be trained later.

The people in the credit central were trained from 7:00 a.m. until 9:00 a.m. They then returned to work. By 10:00 a.m., none of the trainees had returned to ask questions. The trainers assumed that no one was using the system.

So the trainers observed the credit central people. Not only were the trainees using the system, but credit central personnel throughout the entire country were using the system. This credit system was implemented ahead of schedule, under budget, with zero defects, and with many unrequested advantages.

Make Your Mistakes Early and Devise Alternatives

To make the CS-PM innovative project process work, you need to recognize that the project could change for the better. The tasks documented in the development methodology could change. You will learn that project control for the outcome does not come from adding paperwork to the process. You will document the advantages of business strategies and of technical strategies. You will also document the changes that occur during the project and the advantages these bring to the business.

When I looked at the waterfall development process, I could see the steps that were missing. The waterfall development process, without the innovative process, has always had a high failure rate. The spiral development process does not achieve all of the innovation and business improvements possible. Adding and controlling innovation within the process provides the tools to make both the waterfall and spiral development project control processes work.

You need to know that running successful projects requires a high degree of innovation, but innovative projects require the exploration of unknown territory. Success in an innovative project does not depend on the certainty of being right. Running innovative projects depends on experimentation, rapid learning, and fast adaptations to what has been learned.

You need to be prepared to accept the fact that innovative projects do not always occur according to plan. This is a challenge to the traditional project management methodologies. You need to be prepared to learn how to manage innovative projects differently.

For example, in one of my early innovative projects, I described the business advantages to management. Management believed that the advantages would provide new business for the company. But I was pushing the frontiers of information processing.

I found a professor who was on sabbatical from MIT for a year. We talked and solved the technical problems of a year while I completed the task. This part of the task required research. When the research was completed, the business was able to take advantage of the new system.

My past experiences indicate that innovative projects have a high success rate. I have implemented many of my CS-PM projects ahead of schedule, under budget, and with few defects. I have also been able to provide unplanned benefits to the company.

When you apply CS-PM, you will want to benchmark your development against a standard methodology. You can use a standard estimating process and a standard developmental methodology as a basis for the benchmark. Your success will be evident.

You will make mistakes. But mistakes are made early while correction costs are low. Your new concepts either work, or they are dropped at a very low overall cost.

As you learn more about CS-PM, you will find that the innovative project management process is like the entrepreneurial process, but it remains in-house and is simpler. Your innovative project requires internal sponsorship and even special funding. Your internal sponsorship is like requiring some venture capital.

Definitions

An *entrepreneur* has a new idea or product that could be brought into the market and could make a profit. The entrepreneur is willing to take the risks necessary to bring this new idea or product to market.

Entrepreneurial denotes the process and willingness to take the risks to bring an idea or a product to market.

Intrapreneurial describes the process and willingness to take the risks to bring an idea or a product to market while remaining inside a company.

An *intrapreneur* is a person who has a new idea or the idea for a product, wants to remain within the company, and wants company support to create that idea or product.

You need to understand a little about how venture capitalists view tasks. Venture capitalists say that they would rather have an A class entrepreneur with a B class idea than an A class idea with a B class entrepreneur.

You will need to pick innovative people with the passion for making an internal entrepreneurial project work. It is more important than picking the right plan for creating the innovative project. Gifford Pinchot says:

> The plan will be proven wrong in a short period of time as the team makes mistakes and learns from them. But if you have picked a good team and given them freedom and accountability, it will most likely find a way to make something worthwhile happen. Perhaps this is the reason why venture capitalists say they base 80 percent of the decision to invest on the quality of the people in a venture team and only 20 percent on what those people plan to do.

> Corporations can greatly increase their return on innovation efforts by moving the emphasis in their innovation management systems from selecting the right plan to selecting the right team to trust. This is a fundamental shift. Bureaucracy is based on the idea that people are essentially interchangeable parts. But intrapreneurs are not interchangeable and cannot easily be replaced.

Your innovative project requires the same type of innovative talent as intrapreneurship. Your innovation comes from the members of your team. You need a diverse group of people on the team for the team to succeed.

Innovative projects need:

- Business people
- Designers
- Developers
- Managers
- Customers (potentially)

Over time you will find that your innovative projects enhance existing project requirements. Your innovation will remain within the company, but the benefits can create new corporate business. The innovation occurs within your project. This does at times lead to your having created new products as well as new processes.

The innovative process applies innovation through project management, and it gains an immediate benefit for the company. This benefit is sometimes known as a *value added* because it was not part of the original project charter. These unearned increments constitute the value added through innovation, a value that would have otherwise been discarded.

What You Learned in This Chapter

In this chapter, you learned that the CS-PM process is an extension of the existing project management processes. You learned to introduce checklists for innovation, and procedures that provide for negotiation with all interested parties. You learned to identify and add value to projects. That value could be stated in terms of projects completed early, in new corporate products or processes, or the creation of a competitive edge that helps gain more business.

You learned that you should amass an innovative team including:

- Business people
- Designers
- Developers
- Managers
- Customers (potentially)

You learned to add value through a cyclic implementation process and through the team members that you gather. You will be able to create value in terms of projects completed early, the addition of new products, or the creation of a competitive edge for the business against its competitors.

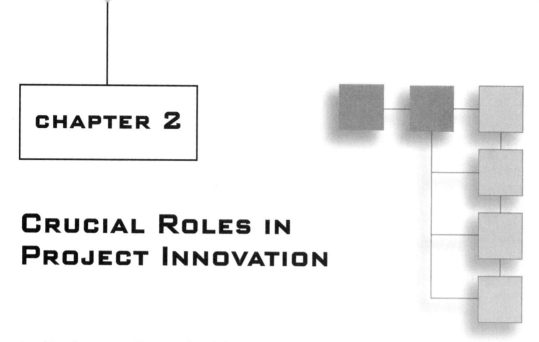

CHAPTER 2

CRUCIAL ROLES IN PROJECT INNOVATION

In this chapter, I discuss the different skill sets that Common Sense in Project Management, an innovative process, requires. You need idea generators for two different tasks: first, they create new ideas for new products, processes, or procedures; second, they help implement projects on or ahead of schedule. Idea generators also help identify and bypass work that does not provide project value. These ideas add value to the project.

You need sponsors that support the project and provide the authority and the budget for the project. For an innovative project, you also need a sponsor that supports project innovation and challenges your teams to continuously increase and immediately implement new benefits.

You need a team to create and enhance the new value objects. Your team contains many different types of people including innovators, idea people, business people, and possibly even customers. You also need technical personnel who can create the base architecture for the project.

Your innovative business personnel will challenge your technical personnel to find better business and technical solutions, and provide customer-facing ideas while also creating and enhancing business value. The business value could be new business products or procedures that make the products easier for the customer to use. The business value could also be the reduction of cost for producing the product.

Your project team also needs to provide an architecture to support and extend business concepts, and to help identify new value objects. They use technology to support the required business needs and to extend business concepts. They provide the basis for valuable future growth.

Staffing a project this way changes the project structure at its very beginning. Technicians or architects provide the technical background upon which the project is built. Buildings are built using an architect from the beginning of the project.

The Common Sense in Project Management process adds to your existing project or process structures. I have included forms and procedures as best practices to control and add knowledge to your projects, thereby adding value to them. The value could be new products, products that are simpler for customers to use, or the reduction of the time necessary to implement your projects.

Project Innovation

Project innovation proceeds best when each of the key roles is performed well (see Figure 2.1). These roles include:

- The project leader
- The idea people
- The innovative team
- The sponsor
- The climate maker
- Business personnel
- Customers

The following sections describe these roles and how they work together.

Project Manager

Note

I use the terms *Project Manager* and *Project Leader* interchangeably, and I use *PM* as an abbreviation for Project Manager.

Your Project Manager has responsibility for the entire project, and is responsible for all of the team members. The PM brings your team members together. Team members include business people, customers, idea people, and innovators.

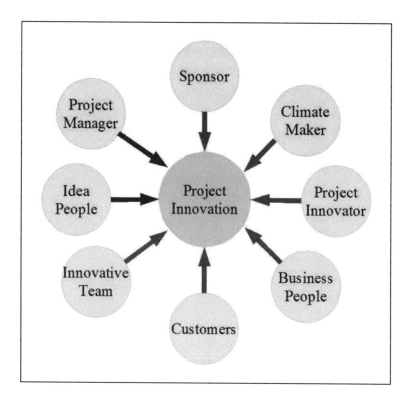

Figure 2.1
The major participants in an innovative project.

Your PM is not the sponsor of the project, and does not normally request that the project be created. The PM is not usually the climate maker.

The PM is responsible for planning the entire project and selecting the team members, although in some businesses, the team members are selected by the business for the PM. The PM establishes and controls the project schedule, keeps the project on schedule, and finally delivers the project on schedule.

For example, the project manager for a credit system created her project schedule by using a function point analysis program. Although the business selected the team members for her, she knew enough people in the business area to have them willingly join her team. The entire team altered the schedule to improve the project deliverables and still were able to implement their project ahead of schedule.

The role of the project manager begins with understanding and planning for the project. This sets a stake in the ground. Project schedules have been set with tasks using the waterfall methodology, spiral development methodology, or other project control methodologies.

In an innovative project, this gives the project manager a starting point from which innovation can begin. This brief planning exercise identifies the basic business project benefits and lists technical functions or system architecture. This is the starting point of the project.

Note

You include both the business and technical system architecture in the project starting point.

The project manager collects the team of participants to satisfy the project requirements. In some companies, the project manager chooses people to participate on the team. In other companies, the PM is given the team. In each case, the PM determines the best use of each person.

To make a project innovative, your project manager needs idea people. Some idea people discover alternatives that satisfy business requirements. Other idea people identify architectures and technologies that enhance the project implementation. Your idea people need to include business people, analysts, and architects.

In the previous credit example, the project leader chose business and technical personnel for her project. The business person presented business concepts that better fit the needs of the business. The technical person presented an architecture that simplified the project deliverables and could incorporate features from existing systems.

Some of your team members will fill more than one project role. For example, a technical person may also be an idea person. A business person may also be a good technical person. Your project manager should understand the skills of the team and use their skills to advantage. In some cases, the project manager alters and shortens the project by the use of skilled team members.

The members of your project team need to have open minds, and they need to contribute ideas that benefit the company. The benefits are for the business department, the customer, and even the supporting technology. In fact, the innovative team needs to fulfill all of these contributing factors. It is suggested that the project manager include customers and business personnel on the team.

During the planning phase, the project manager identifies risks to the project. As a risk becomes an issue, it is tracked.

The project manager reviews the risk and issue log at every project meeting when necessary. (Note that not every issue is important at every project meeting.) You will have a status for each issue and an assigned "owner"—the person responsible for handling the issue. Risks and issues are discussed with sponsors and champions throughout the project, following a communication plan.

Idea People

This is an area of major difference with most projects. Your Common Sense in Project Management project needs to have idea people; possibly, every team member is an idea person.

Note

Idea people can identify and present different alternatives for the business or for the architecture. They are able to identify new products, ways of improving existing products, or ways of shortening the project.

An innovative idea person contributes ideas that are closely aligned with project goals. The ideas could extend the business, assist the business department, or extend the technology. There is no restriction in the creation of ideas.

Ideas that are not aligned with the project will be captured for other potential uses, because ideas not related to the project may still be needed by the company and may eventually be used. Facets of the extraneous ideas could be implemented within this project as long as they do not cause a deviation from the project goal. Even extraneous ideas should relate to the project, the business, the customer, or the technology.

Note

Extraneous ideas are not directly related to the specific project. They may, however, be useful to the company.

Some of the team members will not be idea people. Many professionals, excellently schooled in their craft, typically will not contribute new ideas, and in fact, some of the professionals will be against new proposed ideas. Ideas, beneficial to the project, or even the company, must be supported by the project leader, and at times the project leader will need to fight for these ideas.

Some ideas are alternatives to the project, business, customer requirements, architecture, or technology. Alternatives to ideas are assessed for their usefulness, which includes ease of implementation, ability to be separated from other ideas, and ease of early implementation.

Early implementation of the ideas provides the project with the look and feel of a spiral development, even though this is more of a circular development. There are marked differences between a spiral development and a circular development process. I will discuss these differences in the next section.

The circular development process is shown in Figure 2.2. The concept of circular development is also sometimes called *cyclical design* because the design continues through all of the project cycles. Each cycle includes a learning and correction step.

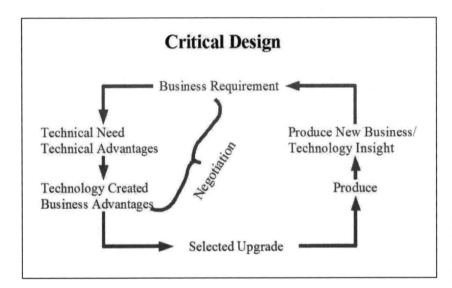

Figure 2.2
The circular development process.

Innovative Team

Your team works together to implement the project and create good new ideas. Then your team reviews and selects the specific ideas that fit the project. For each idea, there are alternatives, and your team works to find alternatives to implement the project ideas.

The team quickly studies the useful ideas for implementing the project, studying the business aspects of the project, as well as the project's technical aspects. Remember that the business aspect does not directly define the technical aspect or architecture.

For example, I created a system that predicted the cost of project overruns throughout the life cycle of a project. The predictions were made from mathematical equations, work requirements, the receipt of material, and actual accomplishments. The system used a matrix architecture. When I was finished with the system, the company discovered that they needed an entirely different set of calculations, and fortunately the matrix architecture allowed me to make this large change within a day.

Comparison between Spiral Development and Circular Development Methodologies

Spiral Development Methodology

1. You define new system requirements usually by interviewing users.
2. You create a preliminary design.
3. You create a first prototype.
4. You review the prior prototypes and improve this prototype.
5. You continue iterating prototypes until the customer accepts the system.
6. You produce the system based on the final prototype.
7. The system is thoroughly tested and implemented in production.

Circular Development Methodology

1. Management describes the initial requirements.
2. You negotiate with management and business personnel to understand the different ways in which their requirements can be met.
3. You determine the technology and architecture that will be needed to support the requirement.
4. You determine the technical advantages that can be gained from the technology and architecture.
5. You define the business advantages that can be gained from the technology and architecture.
6. You form the negotiation with all of the departments involved to identify the best of the combined business and technology functions.
7. You negotiate to select a part of the system to implement.
8. You produce the system supporting the business with the selected technology.
9. You review the process to discover new business and technology insights.
10. You modify the requirements and, if necessary, start the process again.

One primary difference is that technology and architecture are used to improve business, and business is used to improve the technology or architecture. The use of technology and architecture creates a technical competitive advantage. Another difference is that each cycle of the project provides a production-ready section. (I have observed that business personnel do not have time to look very closely at prototypes.)

It is the customer who buys your products. So when your team creates new ideas, there should be a customer focus. The customer needs to be drawn either to purchase a new product or by the simplicity of working with your product.

It is not always possible for your team to study business goals because business goals are not always conveyed to the personnel. So some of your team studies are based upon your perceived business goals, making the information that your team uses either true or not true. In Figure 2.2, I have identified the perceived business goals as the "business requirement."

The business requirements, as you understand them, will be supported through technology or architecture. In Figure 2.2, I have indicated the technology by "Technical Need" and "Technical Advantages." When you use a specific technology to satisfy a business need, it is common for the technology to support further business advantages. This is indicated in Figure 2.2 as technical advantages.

Your team will study the business and technology (or architecture) alternatives, and will select the best of the alternatives for implementation. You will select a combination of business and technical alternatives for implementation. Customer benefits are included in your study and selection.

In the previous credit example, the team identified the different ways in which they could satisfy the presentation of credit information and technical goals and alternatives. They negotiated to deliver the best business, determining the best ways that architecture could support the business and provide customer benefits for the least cost.

You will identify the technology or architecture that will support the business requirements along with the business advantages. These two items, business and technology or architecture, are identified as "Technology Created" and "Business Advantages" in Figure 2.2.

Although not shown in Figure 2.2, fallback alternatives for business processes and technology or architecture are identified. Your selection of alternatives helps to mitigate project risks.

These studies must be performed quickly by your innovative team, and should not be bogged down in corporate bureaucracy. Old-timer analysts within a large corporation would tend to over-study these alternatives. But you need to select the alternatives, place them in their proper perspective, and create an implementation schedule. I have indicated this by the title "Selected Upgrade" in Figure 2.2. In Appendix A, "Forms," I have presented some forms that identify the tasks you will perform within this process.

For example, in the credit project that I described, the initial investigation of business requirements and alternatives, and of technical requirements and alternatives, took two weeks.

Your innovation team will identify the elements that are critical to the business and the technology. You need to study these and determine how these critical elements support the business. As a part of studying the critical business and technology elements, your innovative project manager also identifies the business impact of each critical element.

Again, from the credit project, the team identified the potential of using database access functions from an existing system. The team made a few changes and had this critical element up and testable within the first month.

These studies keep your project focused on the business critical issues while ignoring specific details that are of little concern to long-term business. Your team studies the critical technical issues. Your team will ignore non-critical technical issues wherever possible.

Your team selects an upgrade for immediate implementation and produces the selected upgrade. You can use any viable project control process to control the production of this selected upgrade. You can use either the waterfall or the spiral development methodology. Once produced, your company needs to absorb the upgrade into the business.

After your innovators implement a project, they will know how they could have produced the task better. After implementation, your business and technology personnel can improve business requirements and system technology or architecture that your team has learned through the CS-PM process. I show this in Figure 2.2 as "Produce New Business/Technology Insight."

In the credit project, when the system was implemented, the business personnel found new ways of using the implemented business functions.

Innovative Project Management Applied to a Health Insurance Project

Here's an example from the health care environment. The example shows how I have applied the principles. I started project research with business department discussions involving the departmental head. We discussed and identified business requirements and their alternatives.

I studied the needs of the customers. I designed the system architecture to stand on its own, and yet the architecture supported the business functions but did not mimic them.

The head of the business department and I investigated systems of other health care insurers. We established a camaraderie through these studies and conversations. The system that our company was replacing performed better than the system being investigated.

I kept the business department involved throughout the project. Our working relationship provided me with a good understanding of the business and of what I needed to accomplish for the business. I designed the system architecture to support rapid processing, which minimized computer processing time. The design would also provide for a rapid system implementation.

At first, I proposed a system architecture that would have been easy to implement. But this architecture did not simplify the business department job, so I rejected it. Other business department personnel provided workable alternatives, and the new structure satisfied both business and technology.

I followed the concepts as they are described in Figure 2.2. My team selected the business requirements and the technical architecture. My team selected the concepts to provide an immediate system upgrade. Our technology design made the system extremely flexible and easy to maintain, and it provided the opportunity to create new business.

The business team members provided the knowledge to create technology (architecture) advantages, and they gained insights from our early implementation. Our insights involved business, as well as technology. Our insights helped define new business requirements, and new technical and architecture needs.

We had the opportunity to compare our development with the development of another team. The other team created a similar system. While we paid doctor claims, they paid hospital claims. The complexity was the same, so we have a valid level of comparison.

My results from this example are indicated in Figure 2.3.

Cyclic Implementation Advantages

- Reuse of Code was High
- Modification Costs were Low
- Implementation was Rapid
- Process was Efficient
- Implemented with Zero Defects
- Project was Under Budget

Figure 2.3
Results of innovative project management.

The results can be described as follows:

- Our team completed on schedule. The other team was behind schedule.
- Our team implemented on budget. The other team was 1/3 over budget.
- Our team had a high level of reuse. The other team did not have a high level of reuse.
- Our team implemented our process and the cyclic development process. The other team implemented their system using a standard methodology.
- Our system could process 15,000 claims in one hour. Their system could process only 1,000 claims per hour.
- Our system was implemented with zero defects. We helped the other team recover their system so that it could process.

Our project was innovative, so we created many benefits. These benefits are shown in Figure 2.3. Our project communication remained high throughout the project with all the project members, and our business and management areas remained fully involved with the project. I was the innovative project manager, and I made sure that our system was built to use the knowledge of each member of the team.

Our system architecture was implemented early. Our business functionality fit within the architecture. Our architecture provided an easy way to complete each implementation cycle.

Sponsor

In some organizations, the sponsor is the person who will gain the business benefits from the project. This type of sponsor handles the management reviews. In other organizations, the sponsor is the funder and the project champion, called the sponsor/champion. A sponsor/champion supports the project in the management reviews. A sponsor or sponsor/champion can initiate a project. In the case of the sponsor/champion, anyone could have initiated the project, but the sponsor/champion supports and gives credence to the project and supports it in management review.

Note

Sometimes the sponsor is not the project champion but is still the funder of the project. For smaller projects, the project champion may be the same as the sponsor. For larger projects, the sponsor is normally not the champion.

Either the sponsor or the champion sets the basic project goal. In an innovative project, the sponsor or champion supports the project restatement or revision. In the next paragraphs, I will call both positions the sponsor.

Your innovative projects will increase benefits to the customer, to management, and to the business department. When you use a business supporting architecture, you provide future opportunities to simplify business. Your advanced architectures create a potential to create new business.

For example, I used a new system architecture at an insurance company. The architecture relied on handling data by using a database in a way that was completely flexible. The data flexibility allowed business to capture information needed by the state, a potential client. The added data flexibility allowed the company to sell this potential client.

Your potential architecture applications can support future business benefits in this same way. As cycles of a project are implemented, both business and technical advantages can be discovered.

When management requests a project, the project requirements should be specified in a way that allows project innovation. Your basic business requirements need to be stated specifically, and your project goals need to be clear. However, how you attain the goals must be flexible and allow for innovation in both business and technical architecture.

Your sponsor needs to be open to the inquiring project participants' minds, and needs to support the ideas that will contribute to the successful, innovative project. Your sponsor is an active participant in advantageous project negotiations. Your sponsor needs to support the expression of new project ideas.

Your project innovation will provide business and technical alternatives and options. When you provide advantageous, technical architectures, that architecture provides a way to achieve business goals. You will combine business and technical alternatives to create a successful project, and your technical personnel will identify the critical technical and architecture elements needed for your project.

The project team needs members from the business community to help design the business process and ideas. The sponsor needs to support new business ideas critical to the business and may even contribute new business ideas to your project. The sponsor needs to be open to the technology and architecture ideas that will support the new goals, and may even use the new architecture ideas to support new business functions.

Your innovative project is implemented incrementally, in a phased approach, so your project goals can change with each phase as new discoveries are made. This will happen throughout the life of your project, and it is not a detriment. Your business and architecture benefits provide a solid foundation for changes as they become obvious.

According to Gifford Pinchot, "Sponsors support their people's ideas by protecting them from the corporate immune system." Sponsors or champions coach innovators and raise tough questions. Then they let the innovators find their own answers. They help the group gather needed resources.

Effective sponsors or champions do the following:

1. Assist the project manager in identifying compelling ideas. Effective sponsors coordinate efforts between several different projects. They help to make project managers more innovative. (This process is considered integration project management.)

2. Assist the project manager in finding the right people to fit the innovative project structure. Selected team members are eager to identify new ways to develop and implement a project. Their goal benefits the corporation, the business department, and the customers.

3. Take the time to coach and guide the project manager and the project team. They challenge the project manager to extract the best contributions from the team. Your project manager spearheads team innovation with the sponsor's assistance.

4. Anticipate any political obstacles and help alleviate them.

Sponsors do a lot of behind-the-scenes lobbying to ensure that your project will run smoothly. (This is the project champion's job, although in some instances it could be part of what the sponsor does. This is usually done when the champion and sponsor is the same person.)

Projects falter when either the sponsor or the champion is not present. According to Gifford Pinchot, "In every case, at least one sponsor guided the innovative team around obstacles and intervened with the hierarchy to keep the project alive."

I have seen a project fail when not properly supported. In this case, a manager wanted to capture the benefits of success, and he took over the work of the innovative project team. Unfortunately, this project quickly died because the manager did not have the support of the sponsor. Here's another example:

A sponsor worked with several different project teams within a city environment, and selected several project leaders for specific projects. Then he guided each project to form an initial project plan.

The sponsor directed the project leaders to investigate project alternatives, which helped the project leaders to fully understand the different ways to accomplish their projects. The alternatives included both business and systems architectures.

> In the city environment, many of the systems are controlled by statutes and directives from the city council. In business, most projects must work within regulations, statutes, or directives outside their control.

To be successful, your sponsor or project manager must meet with personnel from each business area. Information is gathered from each business interface, and your sponsor, project manager, and interface work together to find the best solutions to the problems or obstacles.

Your sponsor can help business to identify new functions to lighten the interface personnel load. You will discuss each described option in full with each business department.

As the implementation progresses, your sponsor will identify political situations and will properly discuss the political situations within and about each area. You may discuss the political situation with the project team. Your entire project team, including the business departments, should be informed about the progress and the problems encountered.

All of your involved personnel will discuss the resolutions to business problems, covering appropriate technical solutions with all of your personnel, including systems and business departments.

As you discover new risks and issues, they are discussed with the entire project team. Your sponsor and champion are included in these discussions because they can assist you in finding good solutions for the risks.

The Climate Maker

Senior management always want projects to be successful, which means on schedule, under budget, with few defects, and adding value to the business. Innovative projects help to accomplish this.

For years, project managers have relied on the waterfall or spiral development project methodologies. When projects fall behind, management wants to apply more control using these existing methodologies. Experience has shown that increasing reporting structures and mandating a more formal project management structure does not assure a successful project implementation. Frequently, this type of process can defeat a project before it even gets implemented.

These methodologies have not always worked well. The Standish Group International, Inc. produced the *Chaos Report*. The report indicates that few projects are implemented as required.

Progressive companies and managers are introducing the innovative project management process. The companies are experiencing an increase in on-time, and on-budget project implementations. Even if your company does not fully accept an innovative project management process, you, as a project leader, can use the features to make your projects work.

When you break a project into attainable phases, this allows your business to benefit from early phased implementation. When you design your project in phases, your business and architecture benefits from better information gathering and requirements, and when you use an innovative process like CS-PM, your business is able to change rapidly. You will assess each change as it is presented rather than dismissing it as "not possible." Your innovative architecture will help support changes and additions to your business functionality.

Business Personnel

Your business personnel need to participate in the project environment to make the project a success. When they participate, it is much simpler to provide the project innovation that makes a project successful. Your business personnel are more business savvy than either your technical department personnel or management.

For example, in a credit project, the team met with the credit business personnel, usually over lunch. The systems part of the team discussed the possibility of immediately extending credit to a customer who was over the credit limit. The business personnel participated in describing the possibility and advantages to their management. The team implemented the system.

When properly informed, your business personnel will easily determine processes that will perform better. But business personnel do not have all of the answers. Your business personnel do not fully understand data processing and potential data processing accomplishments. Your business personnel do not always know the overall goals of the corporation.

Your management can champion and fund a project but rarely knows what can be accomplished through innovation. Only by involving the business user will you get the actual, innovative, business processes.

Note

A business is innovative when it continuously tries to create new products that satisfy its customers, finds new ways of performing its current tasks, or reduces its costs for either products or processes.

Incremental business improvements build upon the current business processes or business states. To progress to an innovative business process, you first identify the current business state and then determine what your business needs to either create new products or to reduce the costs of your current processes. Innovative business people extend their innovation by working with innovative business and technology architects.

Together, through negotiation, your group determines how to best serve your customer and improve your business. You will discover or create all of the tools that you need to improve your business department, or you will discover changes that will make your current products more saleable.

You will achieve revolutionary business improvements through a combination of advanced architecture application and business foresight. You design revolutionary business improvements by using "what if" statements such as:

What if I could provide you with this tool?

What if I could provide you with this type of information?

What if we could provide our customers this…?

What if systems could perform this…?

If there is any way possible, could you provide the following business functions?

You will format some of your "what if" questions from an architectural standpoint, using your understanding of the business goals. You base these questions upon functions that a system could perform if beneficial to the business. Sometimes, you form new companies from these questions, and a technology (or architecture) solution must be presented as a business solution.

For example, companies like Boeing, Kodak, 3M, and others challenge their personnel to find new business ventures. They hold special classes where their personnel learn how to envision, start, and manage new business or new products. They either form new companies, create new departments within their companies, or extend existing departments.

Your business personnel will determine other "what if" questions based upon the extreme wishes for creating either new business or products. How your business wants (needs) the business process to work might not appear to be feasible. Alternative architectures can provide solutions to your apparently nonfeasible requirements. Here you define all of the options and alternatives, both business and technical (architectural).

Note

An *extreme wish* describes a possibility that could happen if the architecture would support it or as a new process or product that would be of high interest to your customer.

You will obtain workable results through negotiations and studies that combine business and technical architectures. Again, the innovative aspect comes in your knowing the big picture before you section it off into phases for implementation.

With incremental implementations, you will discover new options and alternatives. When the first phase is implemented and used, everyone discovers the advantages and disadvantages of your project phase. There is time for you to define new options and changes to the overall project plan based upon new understanding and negotiations. With these changes, you will increase business opportunities and simplify your system design and architecture. Here is an example from the health care environment:

I had a fulltime, experienced member from the business department on my team. This business team member helped design our business functionality and helped us understand and refine business alternatives. My technicians defined the potential architectures and alternatives, creating the technical design with the knowledge of the business functions to be supported.

I had my team combine the business and technical alternatives and select the best combinations of business and technology for implementation. They performed the implementation of the combinations using the waterfall development methodology.

My team understood the different alternatives that would satisfy the business requirements. The team defined the alternatives that were critical for the business and technology and that were easy for the team to combine.

This large system needed a structured testing system to prove its correctness. My business team member assisted in creating the regression testing environment and helped with the regression testing process. My team performed regression testing daily, keeping the project bug-free throughout the cyclic creation process.

My team needed to test the architectural concepts. The team created the architectural structure and the initial business requirements that were to be implemented using this new architecture.

Note

Regression testing is a continuous testing process, where changes to a system are continuously checked to make sure they have not destroyed another part of the system or that the entire system continues to function correctly.

Customers

Your customers are the driving force of the business because they know specifically what they want. They are very specific about why they choose one product over another product.

Sometimes, however, new product features will confuse customers, causing them to buy a different product. Customers tend to reject overly complicated products that are difficult to use. Having an actual customer (buyer) available helps the team understand the decision to buy. You will use the customer to better understand how the project needs to be structured to support the customer's decision to buy.

Handling of Risk by All Participants

Projects are intended to add value to the corporation, so your project needs to add value. Innovative projects help the project leader add value to the project, requiring both business and technical competitive advantages. When you change something that is critical, you create a competitive advantage while you take a risk.

You will mitigate many risks by using the Common Sense in Project Management, innovative, project management process. You mitigate some of the risks by keeping all of the required participants continuously involved in the project.

> For example, the budget process of any large organization is excruciating. Once the budget is in place, some specific unplanned event or disaster can drastically alter the budget needs. There is never a good way to handle the budget requirements for a disaster or a specific unplanned event. Personnel creating their specific budgets play many "what if" games deciding specifically what to budget.

> I had a team involved in the budget process that included all the involved parties. We planned the budgeting process to handle unplanned events. My team found sufficient technology to handle and simplify this process.

> Our budget personnel need to approach this system using all of their budget information and using all of their "what if" games. The budget team aggregated all the separate budgets to form an entire budget that

covered the potential disaster. Our budget team played "what if" games at a high level and then applied the budget knowledge to each lower budget level.

Our budget team used this system to quickly recover when the unplanned event occurred. The "what if" games helped to reapportion the budget, and provide new budget figures for use across the company.

Our budget example required budget supported architectures. All the business people needed to be involved. The application of the technology was an integration of business and technology.

You implement phases of the overall goal rapidly and in cycles. You negotiate continuously, seeking the best way to rapidly create the deliverables that your selected processes create.

However, it is possible that the selected implementation that you choose will not work. When you are faced with this problem, you have alternatives to use to fulfill the requirements. During the study, you find the alternatives for the project, and although the alternatives are not as good as the primary solution, the alternatives mitigate the risk of not being able to complete the project.

You assess risks within the negotiation process. Innovation requires discovery. Discovery is used again when a portion of the project is implemented, so you handle discovery as a special process within the project.

Many companies use a client acceptance process prior to implementation. You need to use a client acceptance process when your system is put into a trial run. The clients use the system as they would during their business day, and they provide feedback about what needs to be changed so that those things can be changed rapidly. You will take more complex changes under advisement for follow-on phases.

You will use alternatives to avoid a specific task failure. You investigate risks as a part of the negotiation and discovery process, continuously making decisions to provide the best possible set of tasks. You use these tasks to create the desired competitive advantages.

When you complete a cycle of the project, you will review the added business and technical value. Did your project achieve the benefits you believed? Did your project provide benefits that you had not considered?

When you have implemented the system, achieved the benefits, and reviewed the benefits, then the project cycle is complete. At that point, you have mitigated all of the risks and issues. You have achieved the goal of the cycle.

Your review at the end of the project cycle, your end-discovery process, will highlight new projects or project changes. Your found changes will add value to the corporation. This end-discovery process is a recap of what went well and what didn't; think of it as lessons learned.

Your project recap includes proposed next steps, including both business and technology. Your lessons learned include separate sessions of your technical team and your business clients/sponsor/champion. Your sessions should also be combined to include all these groups.

Specifically, your risks are identified and studied, and alternatives are provided. Sometimes, the alternatives are used to implement the project. The risks are directly assessed, risk control is planned, and risks are mitigated.

Your risks will have been mitigated using several different techniques. You can accept the risk and plan to mitigate it, or you can choose not to accept the risk. You can determine how the risk affects the project directly, and you can determine how your alternatives affect the risk. You may pass the risk to another party. You may address the risk. You may reduce or eliminate the task that produced the risk by using alternatives.

You handle risks as identified as "what could happen." Your risk mitigation studies include "what if" scenarios. When a risk becomes an issue, you will implement the scenario found in the study of critical issues and alternatives. Your new issues get their own plan for maintaining or handling the risk.

Some companies use risk logs containing:

1. Title
2. Potential Impact
3. Status
4. Probability of occurrence (1–5 rating)
5. Impact of risk (1–5 rating)
6. Risk level (obtained by multiplying 4 and 5)
7. Assigned to (the person who owns it)
8. Discussion/Response
9. Date logged (when risk was identified)
10. Date closed (no longer a risk)

When risks become issues, then an issues log is used. An issues log can contain the following information:

1. Title
2. Priority
3. Status
4. Target Date (close it out)
5. Assigned to (owner to complete)
6. Discussion/Resolution
7. Date Created (issue identified)
8. Date closed

Conclusion

In this chapter, I showed the different skill sets used to deliver competitive value. I showed the importance of idea generators, and how your project team members enhance the new value objects of innovative people.

I described the sponsors of the innovation, how business people challenge architects, and how architects challenge business people. The challenge helps create new value-based ideas. The value could be products, products that are simpler for customers to use, or the reduction of costs to implement the projects.

You need these skill sets to create competitive project value.

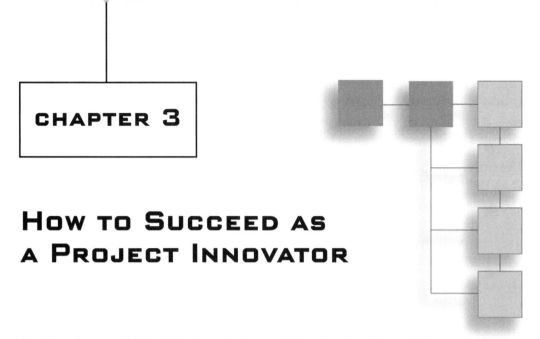

CHAPTER 3

How to Succeed as a Project Innovator

In this chapter, I identify the mission and levels of each participant, including senior management, business personnel, technicians, and architects. This associates the position and the expected tasks needed to create the competitive value.

Your senior management sets the initial project goals and monitors the project as it progresses. You add value through your project when the project adds new products, makes products easier for customers to use, or reduces the cost of the project. Senior management approves these value-added contributions from your project and team members.

Business personnel have a major stake in the project, because they identify your project requirements to satisfy senior management, business needs, and customer needs. Business personnel participate and extend business and technical ideas that add value to the project.

Technicians supply an architecture to support the stated business requirements. If your architecture is flexible, it will extend the stated requirements and increase the business potential. A flexible architecture supports adding competitive value to the project. Competitive value makes it easier to win sales over your competition.

Succeeding as a Project Innovator

Your corporation has goals. Your project is expected to achieve some part of the corporate goals, and you, the innovative project leader, are expected to meet that portion of the goal.

You, the project leader, may not know the goal, senior management may not apprise you of the goal, and so you may need to make assumptions about the goal. It would even be helpful if you understood the conditions for setting the goal, because this knowledge will help provide you with specific project approaches.

The project manager doesn't need to delve too deeply into the financial or business goals that are privy to senior management only, but he needs to know something about the general goals of the company and where his project fits into them. So the information that I present in this chapter outlines the basis for the knowledge that a senior manager has when he makes these decisions.

How Senior Management Sets Goals

You build your projects one piece at a time, just as your corporation meets its goals one step at a time. A senior manager determines that a particular function would be helpful and makes that item part of their goal. What factors did your senior management study in order to understand and set this goal, and what is the knowledge behind this goal?

There are three problems that senior managers confront; the first is that they do not always understand customer needs. Sometimes, senior management understands the customer, but just as often, they do not. Your senior manager may not fully understand what the customers really need.

Senior managers do not go out and observe customers to understand what makes them buy one particular product rather than another. Even if senior managers do observe customers firsthand, you need to know what they understood. It is unlikely that the true reasons customers buy specific products are obvious.

Conclusions based on observations would not fully reveal the goals that your senior management should set. So senior management is lacking some knowledge that would help them set their goals. In the following paragraphs, I will describe some of the information that is lacking when senior managers set a particular goal.

Senior managers do not usually have the time to visit customers. So senior managers seldom go where customers buy the company's products. They do not observe what the customers are doing or what the competition is doing, because they take care of their own corporate business. Senior managers are removed from day-to-day operations. Their concentration is on plan setting, profit analysis, and reporting to the board or an owner.

Senior managers also don't have time to see what is happening around them. It is usually sales personnel who keep track of customers and their interests. Sales personnel, however, are interested in creating the biggest bonuses possible for themselves; consequently, they pay very close attention to those customer needs that add to their own personal bottom line.

Senior managers do not have the time to fully understand everything that happens within a business department, so they do not grasp the detailed activities within the business departments. For many functions, senior managers do not know the specifics or the utilitarian value of each business process.

Senior managers are either promoted from specific departments or have been brought in from the outside. If they come from a specific department, they will have been absent from that department for a long time, so a senior manager's concepts of business might refer to the way that business operated in the past. Many things have changed since the senior managers were in the business departments, and they will have forgotten a lot of the specifics.

If they come from outside the company, they will not have all of the background that might help them to make their decisions. In either case, senior management usually does not have a clear picture of what can now be accomplished.

Senior management needs to turn a profit for the shareholders. They are not so much looking at what will be beneficial to the customer as they are set on creating immediate profits.

Senior managers only see what they know, and they have a vision that is not focused on the detail. Senior managers do not understand the things that could actually be done if the opportunity were made available, and they have trouble seeing what could be beneficial to the customer. But they have made their decision, and that decision is presented to the organization to be placed in a project and accomplished.

The third problem that senior managers confront is technology. Seldom do senior managers have a good perspective of technology. They don't see the goals that can be achieved through the optimum use of technology.

So senior management goals may lack some potential benefits inspired through technology. They don't take into account the potential of technology driven accomplishments. Even managers savvy in data processing have trouble setting project goals; this results in projects that are not on schedule or within budget, and that do not fulfill business needs. So senior management may either under- or over-request data processing.

Figure 3.1 shows what happens with the different levels of miscommunication. Your project is not likely to produce the desired results. Communications between the different levels of personnel are problematic.

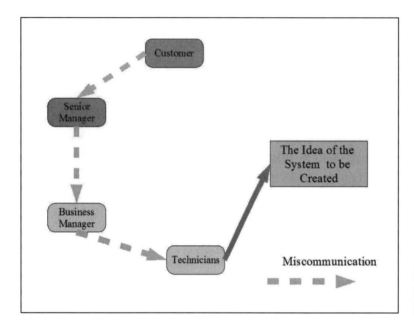

Figure 3.1
Miscommunication in creating a system.

I have shown you the information that senior management is likely to have. So how do projects get started when senior management participates in an innovative project?

The following example from a health insurance company provides an example of how senior management was engaged in a project.

> I had the opportunity to have my senior management, business departments, and innovative project team participate in business discussions at the start of a new project. I started the discussion with the intention of extending existing business processes, and I stated the question as follows: Would it be possible for the business to benefit from the following business procedures?
>
> I did not use a technical description; rather, I used a business description aimed directly at business personnel. I also described the customer usage.
>
> The company needed to add a new type of health care coverage to our insurance payment processes. I could simply have added yet another

object, one similar to the existing objects, to perform this task. But if I made a change to the architecture, I could continue to add new types of health care processing without incurring the cost of creating another new object each time. By changing the architecture, I could also reduce the cost of maintaining the current system, and I could use the altered system to handle a completely different type of insurance.

I needed to make the proposition to senior management in terms of the potential benefit to the business. I estimated the cost and presented this to senior management. I used an existing business request for changes to the system as a basis for my request.

In this case, senior management and the business departments were interested in this extension. I showed that by making small changes to the existing project and the existing system, I could provide new product for the company to sell to customers who were interested in buying.

When you, the innovative project manager, make proposals to senior management, the proposals will not necessarily benefit the business. In some cases, your recommendations could require a considerable change to the business. It could be extremely difficult for the business to use.

In the example above, I made a recommendation to senior management that resulted in the creation of new business. You will involve your entire innovative team to create new business for your corporation. Your team will consist of the project team, business management, and senior management.

The Business Department's Altered Understanding

Your business department also has three problems, and the first concerns communication with senior management. The business departments play a role in the initiation of standard projects. Business departments usually are given directives from senior management, and those directives usually involve improving the business or the procedures within the business.

The business department can interpret a directive as something other than what senior management wanted. This is an initial miscommunication between the departments in a company. This is similar to what happens in the game of whispering messages from one person to another through a series of people. The end message is nowhere close in content to the original message because of the differing backgrounds of the people involved.

The second problem of the business department concerns understanding the current and future needs of the business and its customers. A business department is supposed to run the business, so it concentrates on running the business. Running the business leaves little time to look into the future, so the business department can't see what is ahead.

If you can't look ahead, you can't determine how best to satisfy your customers, and you can't determine how a system should assist in making business easier to perform. Peter Senge refers to the process as seeing the forest and the trees at the same time. The business department can't see the forest and the trees at the same time (i.e., they can't see the overall picture of the business and the detailed picture at the same time).

As a business person, I am in a department, and I can see only what my department needs. Senior management gives the business department a directive to foresee business needs in a way that requires an understanding of the entire business. So the focus is central to the business department. It does not satisfy the overall customer or the customer's needs.

The business department needs time to review the customer needs, and yet the business department does not have the time or does not take the opportunity to understand the customer needs. Your business department is too busy running the business to be able to go out and observe customer needs.

The third problem of the business department deals with understanding the technology that can be used to make business better. The business department does not understand the technology. Thus, the business department can't specify the technical systems functions and architectures for their needs.

The business department can't see very far ahead, so they can only specify functions they believe will accomplish simple business tasks. And the task that they specify will be really small. The business department is business focused and does not understand the customer or the technology.

Most business departments have trouble looking into the future. They will not take business concepts into the future, and they won't obtain the best features from the project being developed.

The following is an example from a government project where a business department participated in the development of the innovative project. We started by discussing the business processes, which were to create the city budget.

The city needed a flexible computer system to create a city budget for over 4,000 employees. The budget required many different processes. The budget process was complex and difficult to integrate.

The budget process could be simplified significantly if alternative budgets could be prepared by each specific department. The budget controller would then coordinate the separate departmental budgets into one city budget. Doing this by hand required the city to begin the process starting in March to be completed in December for passage in the middle of January.

With the flexible budget system, the budget director easily balanced the budget using the system with alternative budgets. The budget contained all of the city requirements incorporating political significance. The flexible budget simplified the process of budgeting significantly. This was accomplished only through the participation of both systems and the budget department.

Note

> The budget of the city incorporates special projects for each of the separate wards. These are funds that are used at the discretion of each alderman. These special funds are of *political significance*. If the alderman pleases his constituents, he is likely to be re-elected.

The Technician's Altered Understanding

You need three parts to create a new system or to adapt an existing system:

1. Senior management needs to request useful business functionality of benefit to the customer.
2. The business department needs to simplify their business process.
3. Technicians need to create the new business functionality.

In the next few paragraphs, I will discuss the part that technicians play in providing this system. Technicians usually have no idea what the customer needs, and the business department does not have the perception about what your project could accomplish and how you need to set your project goals.

Technicians do not know the business goals, and they only have a partial understanding of what the business department tells them. So this communication is also flawed. This means that your entire set of communications (from senior management, through the business department, to your technical area) is flawed at least twice.

Technicians only see what is valuable for a part of the technology, and they don't see what is valuable for the overall system or business. They see the screen designs, perceived business processes, and misunderstood requests. Technicians think they see the steps of the business process, so they could develop a system that looks like the series of business steps.

In fact, technicians usually follow the structure of the business procedure as the basic design of their system. If this is what your systems personnel do, they will not have selected a valid system architecture. If you follow this architecture, you will make an inflexible system that is extremely hard to maintain.

Your technology team needs to create an architecture that stands completely on its own. It must have its own architecture that supports the business, but does not follow the design of the business. Your system and architecture must be flexible and easy to maintain.

Following is an example of an architecture that I used for the City of Chicago:

> I created a transaction-handling architecture. The system architecture was designed to support the processing of several different bureaus.

> The different bureaus, or departments, included heating, ventilation, elevator, electrical, structure inspection, and other bureaus. Each bureau satisfied its business requirements differently, yet one simple architecture supported each of the business structures.

> Because I created a transaction-handling architecture, the processing for each bureau could be added without major system modification. Each inspection had an inspection type. My transaction-handling architecture used the inspection type to select system control rules for that type of inspection. The rules directed the system to perform the tasks required for each bureau in the way required by that bureau.

> The system architecture did not change from bureau to bureau. The system remained constant, while bureau processing was different. This allowed the system to be implemented in cycles, one cycle for each of the bureaus.

The Task of the Innovative Project Manager

My prior discussion shows one of the main tasks of the innovative project manager. Your company, and almost every other company, has communication problems. You may be talking and working together, but your backgrounds and differing job exposure lead to miscommunications.

Figure 3.1 showed you the different types of miscommunication that you will encounter. Figure 3.2 shows the innovative project manager tasks of assisting in proper communication between all the different people. You, as a project manager, need to clear up communications between the different areas.

You need to restore communication clarity. The project manager gathers and clarifies information from multiple sources. Part of your opportunity to clarify the communication comes with installing parts of the system often. When you install parts of a system, all the participants can see exactly what has been installed, and they can form better ideas of the near future. The installed parts can also be repaired to perform the specific tasks that are needed.

The innovative project manager fills the miscommunication gaps between the senior manager, the business department, and technicians. You, as the innovative project manager, will, unfortunately, also be part of the miscommunication, and you will need to be alert for and ready to remove miscommunications throughout the entire project and all of its cycles.

By experience, I have observed that business departments don't communicate all of their needs. Your business departments will not provide complete request needs because projects are always late, and you do not need yet another request. Your business departments put these requests on hold because they don't want to slow down their existing projects, and they want systems to work on the projects that they feel are most important.

I have successfully investigated specific, hidden business requests that would fit directly with the requested project. So you, as a project manager, need to uncover hidden requests that reside in the business department. Some of these requirements could make the system easier to implement or could add significant competitive advantage to your existing projects.

For example, for the credit system, one of the credit managers worked with us to identify the entire list of credit requirements. Through discussions with this manager, the team determined which requests could easily be included with this project. We added these project requirements to the current project. Even with the added requests, we implemented this project ahead of schedule.

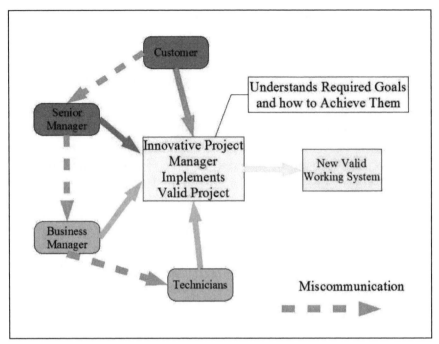

Figure 3.2
Handling miscommunications and creating a working system.

You, the innovative project manager, also need to satisfy the customer, the ultimate buyer of your product. You may determine other customer needs if you are customer savvy. When you add customer savvy tasks, you add benefits that are of value to the customers and, when added to the flexible architecture, do not extend the length of the project.

The Department of Defense says that only two percent of projects are used as delivered. So why would you, the innovative project manager, want a larger responsibility than initially requested? When you add business and customer oriented tasks, you could simplify the overall process and shorten the implementation time.

For example, the addition of new tasks to the credit project simplified the delivery of the system, and removed almost two full man months of system programming:

The initial project requested a specific screen to display credit information. The team discovered that more useful information would be available through the new system, and the team described the upgrade and the reduction in project costs to the business department. It was easier to provide the added data than the initial proposed data.

Discussions with their business department showed that the altered process served the business department better. The business department was unaware that this specific process could be performed and that it would simplify the project. They needed this recommendation from systems.

You, the innovative project manager, will find system parts to be delivered in an early cycle of the overall project. Like the spiral development methodology, cyclic projects provide for early task delivery. Your early project and product delivery exposes communication and thought process flaws that keep projects from being successful.

You will expose both business and technical flaws. Your early implementation helps you observe new usable processes, reduce communication problems, and see business needs further into the future. Senior management and business management can use the implemented system parts to begin to determine new beneficial needs.

Innovative Project Manager Tasks

You will identify extremely important business issues, which I call critical issues. You will identify and describe why specific issues are important to the business. You will describe what happens when the need is solved and what happens when it is not solved. You will implement these critical tasks early.

Note

A *business issue* is critical when *not* implementing the issue would cause the company to lose business.

A *technical issue* is critical if it supports a critical business issue. A technical issue is also critical if it supports the architecture that simplifies the project and the future needs of the project.

You will use specific technology and architecture to implement the important business benefits. Your technology is produced early to reduce and mitigate risks. This means important business benefits and needs are implemented early.

You will use technology and architecture to simplify and help accomplish your implementation goals. Your special technology and architecture elements need to be implemented early.

In the city, I created a transaction-handling process, which was an architecture that simplified the creation of the building inspection system. The transaction-handling process divided the processing into each of the common inspection processes. Reusable processes were selected and used as required for each inspection bureau.

At a health care insurance company, my team created a multitasking system controller to handle the processing of health insurance claims. This application handled the 50 different types of health care rapidly, without errors, was extremely flexible, and extended the ability of the business. The team implemented the critical technology functions early. We built much of the system, taking advantage of our solid architectural foundation.

You will see that almost nothing goes as planned, and so you, the innovative project manager, need to find business and technology alternatives. You will find that sometimes your primary alternative will not work according to plan, causing you to use one of the alternatives to implement the task. With CS-PM you have a fallback mechanism that helps mitigate the risks in the project.

When you have a fallback process, you reduce the need for risk management processes because you have internalized the risk management within your project. I have saved many projects by using alternatives. Your selection of alternatives is part of the implementation process, and alternatives are the best possible compromise between the customer, business, and technology, or architecture.

You will search for and find functions that have already been produced in other projects. Your found function will help you to accomplish a specific task. This is reuse, where your reuse of found functions will supply the required benefit. In your study, you will define reusable functions, as well as find reusable functions.

For example, in the large retail environment, my team found database handling functions that simplified the system implementation. By reusing these database handling processes, my team implemented the data handling requirements by the end of the first month of the project.

You will determine the new tools and reusable tools that will be developed by implementing this task. Near the end of an implementation cycle, you will create the new reusable tools. Some of the tools that you create will be used by other project leaders, and some of your tools will be used within other cycles of this project.

For example, I created a tool that shows the benefits of reusable tool creation. That specific tool was used by other project leaders even before it was used within my own project. This tool was used over 25 times before it was used in my project. I produced good documentation that allowed other projects to reuse this task. So with CS-PM you will provide good documentation.

You will shorten your project implementation time this way. Here are the advantages that I have obtained from CS-PM:

A high level of reuse

Speed of system processing

Less time to implement

Zero defects

Lower implementation costs

Continued lower maintenance costs

Conclusion

In this chapter, I presented the different missions of each of the participants. Senior management sets the initial project goals. Business personnel and technicians extend the initial ideas of senior management.

Your project is built around a flexible architecture. Your goal is to support not only your project, but also other projects and future projects. You will gain advantages for your projects and for the business.

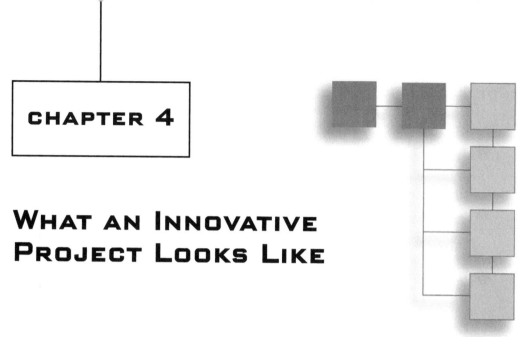

CHAPTER 4

WHAT AN INNOVATIVE PROJECT LOOKS LIKE

In this chapter, you will learn how to use innovative project management to gain both business and technical competitive advantages and how to minimize project risks.

Note

When business finds the ideas that cause a customer to buy their product rather than that of a competitor, they have identified a *business competitive advantage.*

I will show you how to identify business requirements and create a business competitive advantage, and how to find alternatives that reduce or mitigate risk and add a technical competitive advantage.

Note

A *technical competitive advantage* is created when a business uses technology or architecture to form a competitive advantage. The technical competitive advantage is difficult for a competitor to create or match.

You will learn how to find technical architectures that support business advantages and technical alternatives that reduce or mitigate the risk involved in implementing the technical advantages. You will learn how cyclic implementation helps to gain immediate business and technical advantages.

Creating an Innovative Organization

You will learn how the innovative project leader creates an innovative organization and how to introduce innovation within the project.

1. You, the innovative project leader, direct business and technical team members to share and to learn from their combined strategies. You help to simultaneously create business and technical innovations.

2. You align business and technical strategies, provide ways to implement the combined business and technical strategies, and use a circular development methodology. This circular development methodology provides an opportunity to create better outcomes, better business processes and requirements, and better architectures and architectural requirements.

3. You support project implementations that are beneficial to the business and to the project.

4. You provide new business/technology insights.

These four concepts are shown in Figure 4.1.

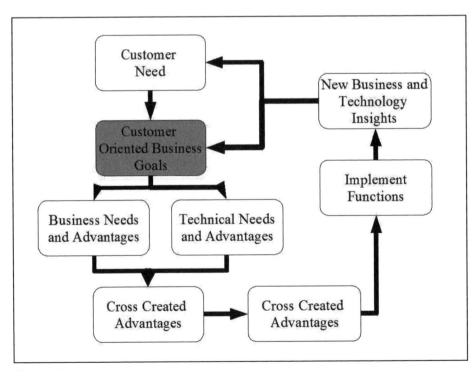

Figure 4.1
The cyclic implementation cycle.

I have prepared a short review of the cyclic process. It will be easier to see if you refer to Figure 4.1 as you read this review. Your business sets its goals based upon customer and business needs. Your project requirements are passed to the business and technology areas.

Note

In an innovative project, both business and technical areas receive their project information at the same time, providing time for technical personnel to create the proper technical architecture for the project.

Business departments and business analysts set the initial business goals and identify business critical functions. The technology area, and architects, set the technology goals and identify technical critical functions and architectures to support the project. A project creates technical goals that are based on business requirements. The project extends business goals based on the technology or architecture being used.

You set business and technology goals, and select specific functions for rapid implementation. You implement these functions. Once implemented, you review the results and form new insights based on knowledge gained from the early implementations. You begin the next cycle using the knowledge gained from the previous cycle. At each cycle of the project, you make changes based upon the insights formed from the prior implementation.

Sharing the Strategy

Use innovative controls for your project, controls that provide the team with an understanding of business goals and strategies. The internal controls also provide the team with an understanding of the technical goals and strategies that you have determined for this project.

Your technical strategy may also work for other projects. For your first innovative project, you may create a technical strategy and then use that initial technical strategy, as established, for future projects. You merge business and technical strategies for project implementation. Since you learn the business and technical functions that work from your early implementations, you need to complete your first implementation cycle as early as possible.

For your innovative project, the business and technical strategies have equal importance. For this discussion, I will concentrate on business first and then on technology. Finally, I will bring the two separate parts together to form the basis for your early implementation.

Defining the Business Requirement

Your cyclic implementation process and innovative project begins with understanding the ideas in the mind of the customer. The customer's actions describe how they need to use your product. This shows how they intend to capitalize on their ideas and your product.

Business capitalizes on the reasons that make a customer buy your product rather than a competitor's. This is how you know what to create for the business competitive advantage. The competitive advantage begins with your tactic, which is the competitive mental angle, or the idea that is in the mind of the customer.

Note

You can tailor the product and special features to take advantage of the wants and needs of the customer. This creates your business competitive advantage. If you can add a technical competitive advantage, you will lock your competitors out of this part of the business for a long period of time.

Your overall business and system strategies should support this customer-focused idea and should become the business requirement.

Following is an example that shows this customer focus.

> An Illinois health insurance company was composed of several different companies. The customer thought of health care as one item, health care, and the customer needed to have all of her health care needs satisfied as if by one company.

> Unfortunately, each separate company worked like a separate company. Health care payment notices were sent separately. A customer receiving payment notices received three, four, or even five payment notices. The customer was immediately confused. "What really got paid?" Customers couldn't make any sense out of this mess.

> Since the customers were confused, it was harder to sell this insurance than the insurance of a competitor. Each competitor was a single company, and they acted like a single company. Their interactions with the customer were that of a single company, which eliminated the customer's confusion.

> My specific goal was to make the separate companies appear as one, and this was my business strategy. Business and systems personnel recognized the problem and negotiated ways to make the company appear as one (instead of separate companies).

> The payment checks were not a part of the problem because the insurance company sent the checks directly to the provider of service (i.e., the hospital or the doctor). We needed to make the notice of payment from the various organizations appear as one to make the company appear as one company.
>
> We accumulated the payments for a week from the various organizations before automatically preparing the notice of payment for the subscriber. This took care of the biggest part of the problem. All of the bills submitted within a week, for the same health care service, would be accumulated and reported to the subscriber.

Your business and systems personnel negotiate to identify the business requirements, as happened in the above example. Your negotiations provide documentation and definition of functions for system implementation. You will have identified the best possible business requirements, and, through negotiation, your requirements create the best possible competitive advantage with the least possible cost.

Common Sense in Project Management, an innovative project management process, has several phases. Phase I of the Innovative Project is divided into a number of tasks that fall into specific work categories. The work categories define the business content for the project.

You investigate the needs and identify the critical business issues. In the health care example, the goal was to make the separate companies appear as one company. After you have defined the critical business issues, you need to identify the different ways in which you can satisfy the business need and identify plausible business alternatives.

In the health care example, we had different possible ways to make the company look like one company. The company could have created an interface department to coordinate all messages sent to the customer. The company could have created a coordination system, which would accumulate customer messaging before sending the information to the customer. Or the company could have automated the system processes within each separate processing system.

Most companies have existing systems that were created to satisfy business needs and perform specific functions. You can use some of these functions in your implementation. You, the innovative project manager, will check to determine the advantages of existing processes.

You will study the summary description of tools that have been created from prior projects. In Appendix A, "Forms," you will find forms that can be used to create and use reusable tools. When you start your first innovative project, you probably will not find the type of information that will help you reuse prior tools, so you may need to search for tools and identify them where you find them. The tools that you will find are probably procedures or interfaces to existing systems.

For every process and alternative that you define or find, there are advantages and disadvantages. In the health care example, business alternatives for integrating customer messaging were defined.

The team described the advantages and disadvantages of the alternatives of each defined process. These described advantages and disadvantages were the best guess by the business and technology systems personnel. The process and technology advantages and disadvantages were described when the project was created.

Only after process installation and use can the real advantages and disadvantages be determined. A study at the end of the project determines the benefits. After a period of time, while the processes are in use, the advantages and disadvantages can be stated. You should make an early study just after installation and make a late study after the process has been in use for a period of time. These studies provide new insights.

Your business departments and your systems departments capture and share knowledge. With the captured knowledge, you discover the critical nature of the business. You will also discover ways in which to simplify the business and technical processes.

As you investigate, you will find solutions and alternatives. Your team reviews and prepares reports on the results of the project with its advantages and disadvantages and for the alternatives selected. The reports help create knowledge for future projects and cycles.

The information that you have gathered includes knowledge about the business, how the business runs, how technology is used to support the business, the way that the business processes are used, and how systems use the technology that you have created.

Your gathered knowledge also exists throughout the business. After collecting this knowledge, you use it to identify the tactic of the corporation and build your project. Your knowledge will be used to set business goals and requirements. It also supports setting the technology goals and capabilities. As business requirements and technology requirements are combined, further knowledge is accumulated.

In Phase I of Common Sense in Project Management, you will determine the business tasks and the technology or architecture that satisfy these business requirements.

Through your knowledge, you can extend your corporate business goals and define alternative goals. Your goals will be stated as new business requirements.

Defining the Technical Need and Technical Advantages

You, the innovative project manager, meet the business needs, technical needs and system architectures. With these, you will enhance the project, the business, and possibly other projects. Your technical advantages need to stand on their own, and yet they need to support specific business requirements and possibly many different business requirements.

You will satisfy many business and technical requirements through reuse of process or code, and you will create or enhance business competitive advantages or create appropriate technical processes. Your creation of Common Sense in Project Management projects should be at the highest level of a *Capability Maturity Model Integration*.

Capability Maturity Model Integration

The Software Engineering Institute (SEI) created the Capability Maturity Model (CMM) and its replacement Capability Maturity Model Integration (CMMI). This is sponsored by the Department of Defense and produced by Carnegie Mellon University.

CMMI is a process designed to help corporations determine how capable they are of designing, producing, and implementing new projects. If your corporations fully follow these directions, they are considered to be at the highest level of CMMI.

The processes include:

1. Adherence to processes that are repeatable and help the corporation meet its project goals.
2. Ability to determine costs and to meet those costs within their projects.
3. Projects are scheduled and the schedule is met within the project.
4. The level of productivity is increased and is the highest possible throughout the company and each project.
5. Quality goals of the end products are met.
6. Customers are satisfied with the products.

Follow these instructions to meet technical goals for your project:

- Clearly describe the critical business issue that this technical issue satisfied.
- Summarize the technical critical issue.
- Describe why this technical critical issue is technically critical.
- Describe the technical alternatives.
- Present the technical recommendation.
- Participate in the integration of the business and technical integration that satisfies the business requirements.

Following is an example to illustrate the importance of the technology.

> Our company needed to look like one company instead of many companies. Technology capabilities made the process possible.
>
> The company decided to make payment notification from one department. This notification department became the sole source of patient notification. The innovative project team created a system to make payments as if they had come from one company. The technical system architecture supported the business requirement, and yet the technical architecture did not look quite like the business environment.
>
> The technical system structure used database storage features. The notification department coordinated database information from several different systems gathering payment information.
>
> The company had other technical alternatives, so the innovative project team studied all of the alternatives. The team used the business and technical alternatives to understand how the technology satisfied the business requirements. The team also described how the business requirements were satisfied by the technology.
>
> In another health care example, the company needed to pay a new type of health care claim. The innovative project team altered the system architecture to drastically reduce cost and add a high level of flexibility. The business and systems people negotiated to allow the use of the new architecture, while the new architecture supported additional business benefits.
>
> The innovative project manager described all of these benefits. The business department agreed with the additional business functionality and agreed to provide the extra required funding. These changes were implemented as planned.

You will learn to use technology to advance business capabilities and to create a competitive business advantage based on competitive technical advantages. You will build a barrier to entry from both the business and technical competitive advantages. Your technical barrier to entry makes it very difficult for a competitor to duplicate this advantage, making it more difficult for the competition to enter the market.

You use CS-PM to identify the technical need. Cyclic implementation creates an early technical advantage and satisfies a specific technical need. Business and technical personnel create the business and technical competitive advantage.

Business personnel determine the business advantages and processes. Technical personnel determine the technical advantages and technical processes and functions. The technical structure does not look like the business process.

If the technical structure mirrors the business process, you have not satisfied the business needs in an optimal manner. Technical architecture should be reusable and not limited by the current business process.

Implementation in Small Phases

In the prior two sections, I discussed the business and technical issues. I defined what is critical to business and technology. I showed you how to select and combine critical business and technology for implementation. You learned to identify business and technology alternatives.

Your alternatives reduce the project risk. You now select functions for an immediate implementation. You design, program, and implement the combined critical business and technical selections as early as possible.

Once your selection is implemented, you review the critical issues. This review provides a better understanding of the business and technical issues, and it helps you discover discrepancies between what business wanted and what is actually needed. You will also discover discrepancies between what you planned technically and what worked correctly, comparing what you said you wanted with what is needed.

This procedure is shown in Figure 4.2.

Here is a checklist to follow as you progress with your project.

1. You determine what is critical to both business and technology.
2. You find alternatives to reduce the risk.
3. You make sure that the customer benefits from the project.

4. You select items for immediate implementation.

5. The items that you forwarded make sense for an immediate implementation.

Managing Innovation Through Projects

Determine Project Requirements	Select Best Alternatives	Requirements Analysis	Design and Implement
• Determine Identify Business/Technology Alternatives • Determine Project Participants • Determine Business Department Personnel • Determine Senior Management Involved • Determine Customer Benefits • Select Immediate Implementation • Determine Reuse • Determine Critical to Business/Technology	• Determine Benefits to the Business • Determine Benefits of Technology (Architecture) • Determine Benefits of Each Alternative • Integration of Business and Technology Issues • Determine and Describe Benefits of the Combined Business and Technology	• Determine Specification Needs from Phase II Alternatives • Describe Requirements for Combined Business and Technology (Architecture) • Begin Description of System Parts • Write Use Cases for the Selected Items • Determine Possible Reuse	• Write the Specifications • Determine the Potential Problems • Determine How to Test • Write User Documentation • Test the System (All Levels) • Implement the System • Operate the System • Discover Problems and Reuse

Figure 4.2
Review the critical issues.

You do not forward all items for immediate implementation. Some items will require continuous study or will be held for future implementation, and others will be implemented only after you have learned how best to perform the implementation.

Study these items to determine the best of the alternatives. Combine the business and technology issues. Describe the benefits of the combined business and technology issues, and send the best of the combinations to Phase III for a requirements analysis.

You and your team will describe the requirements for system implementation and you will send the requirements to Phase IV to be designed and implemented.

During the design process, you write specifications and codes and implement the system. After you have implemented the system, you review it and determine whether there are new benefits and alternatives.

In an innovative project, you do not completely design the project and then implement it as designed. One reason that you do not do that is because no one has perfect communications between senior management, the business departments, and systems. It is also impossible for you to see into the future.

When you implement early and often, you have a better vision of the real needs. You will see that some things would be better done differently, so once you have completed an implementation cycle, you can find better solutions.

It is difficult for you to see and understand all the ramifications of your solutions. Implementing early helps you to uncover problems because your solutions may have unanticipated side effects. When you review the results, you will have a better opportunity to understand the goals.

The steps that you take to satisfy the goal become clearer. You can more easily identify critical business and technology issues while you can determine different tasks that should be implemented early.

Note

When you review the selection that you implemented in earlier cycles, you get a better view and understanding. This view is a *vantage point*. The early cycles contain critical elements, so your early vantage points are about the critical implemented parts.

You gain a vantage point of the critical implemented piece, so you will better understand the project ramifications. You are also able to modify the design to eliminate unforeseen problems and discover benefits that you did not see before. You can alter the design to take advantage of these benefits continuing further implementation along the same cyclic pattern as I described before.

The following is an example from the City of Chicago:

> The payroll system at the City of Chicago is a perfect example of this cyclic process in action. The City was replacing a large legacy payroll system. The innovative team selected a new system to replace the old system.
>
> The team selected tasks that were critical to the business and system implementation, needing to make a smooth transition from the existing system to the new system. The team wanted to implement this system in phases.
>
> The team discovered that a critical element was the creation of a distributive processing data distribution system. The distributed system would collect and forward data to either the new system or the old system.

The distributed payroll entry system needed to be implemented early. This was the first step in our implementation process.

This concept was easy to sell to the comptroller's office. It simplified their existing data entry problem, making it easy for payroll personnel to collect payroll information. This system could forward payroll information to the new or old system as needed, which simplified the conversion process.

When first implemented, all of the data was sent to the old payroll system. Then, department by department, data was forwarded to the new system. This provided a smooth transition from the old system to the new system. It also provided a cyclic implementation by department.

Created Business Advantages

You may see possible new business advantages in the first phase of a project. You could create these business advantages from specific technology, as technology-created business advantages.

Your study of technology-supported business helps to determine how you can create new business advantages. Your team of business personnel, management, and technical personnel share useful information. This information helps you to determine the best approach to define, design, create, and implement your system.

In this way, technology helps create new business and new business advantages. Your steps are as follows:

1. Your team describes how the combined business and technology approach meets the *business* requirements.
2. Your team describes how the combined business and technology approach meets the *technical* requirements.
3. Your team describes the trade-off analysis of the combined business and technical approach.
4. Your team selects the best business and technical approaches and their backups.
5. You use the results of the study to write the appropriate project plans.
6. You and your team analyze the risk, based on the best approach and a backup approach.
7. You and your team define the business goals as a set of deliverables.
8. You also define the technical goals as a set of deliverables.

Each of your deliverables has one or more tasks to be delivered. The combination is the combination of a unique business task with a unique technical task. You and your team will pair business and technical tasks that are compatible.

Each unique task that you have defined either already exists or needs to be created. If the combined business and technical tasks already exist, then you only need to add reuse knowledge. Otherwise, you will produce the design for the creation of a reusable item. Knowledge is added.

Note

Reuse knowledge is the set of instructions that describes how to reuse the specific task that has already been created and that has been identified.

Following is an example from a large retail credit department:

In a large retail credit environment, the innovative project manager and management had many business and technical goals. Each goal was a separate task. The project manager assembled the team, which consisted of business analysts and technical or architectural personnel.

When the innovative project manager called a meeting, several business personnel attended. The team discussed the advantages and disadvantages of each proposed task and solution. The team studied the advantages and disadvantages of business critical requirements, along with the advantages and disadvantages of the technical proposals.

The team found that some of the business requirements matched some of the technology requirements. That meant that the team could pair the business and technical solutions and produce this combination of solutions early.

The team matched business processes to the technical proposed solutions, studied each combination, and developed recommendations. The team recognized that database functions fit with the types of information needed for business.

After a short study, the team found that a usable database function already existed, allowing for a rapid implementation. The team implemented this database-oriented business solution early.

Before this project, the business personnel had no confidence in the systems personnel. The rapid implementation changed their minds and made working with systems personnel more attractive to the business department. The business personnel saw results early. This initial implementation took one month.

Create Implementation Channels

Just how should your team implement a specific project? You, the innovative project manager, need to understand the innovation steps and project control processes, identify the business needs, and figure out how the system will satisfy those needs.

You are now ready to plan the path to upgrade the business process. You have already chosen the implementation tasks and your technical support functions and architectures. You still need to select the business and technical alternatives. You will perform this task using the following types of documentation, which have been advanced from your prior study:

1. Your team studies and documents the combined business and technical issues.

2. Your team studies and documents the backup combined business and technical issues.

3. You describe the costs to support the alternative study.

4. You create a timeline for the study of alternatives.

5. Your team performs a preliminary business and system design.

6. You create estimates for producing system modules.

7. You or your team create preliminary test plans.

Your project team reviews the business, technical, and combined requirements. When the team has completed the Phase I study, they could pass it to Phase II. If the Phase I study included sufficient information to bypass the combining of business and technical tasks, then the Phase I study could be passed directly to Phase III. If the Phase I study also included sufficient requirements information, it could then be passed to Phase IV.

In Phase II, you study the alternatives. You have primary and secondary (or backup) solutions. It is usual for your prime solutions to have excellent benefits for the company. But it is usually more difficult to implement your primary alternatives because they have a higher risk of failure. Your secondary alternatives are usually less beneficial, but they are easier to implement and have less risk. But when you have implemented early, you reduce the risk for your follow-on phases.

Once you have completed your reviews, you produce a timeline and cost estimates. Your timeline and costs are used in deciding whether to pursue the project or to cancel the project. If the project is accepted, your study materials and plans are passed to Phase III or possibly Phase IV.

In Phase III, you create some preliminary business and system design elements. You make initial estimates for producing the system modules. Your systems need to be thoroughly tested so you construct preliminary test plans.

When you have completed the analysis of alternatives, the best of your alternatives is selected along with your secondary or fallback alternatives. Your secondary or fallback alternatives provide for a recovery and risk mitigation in case your primary alternatives do not work.

So here is a summary of what you have accomplished:

- You studied the business approach and the technical approaches for your project.
- You studied how to combine business and technical approaches, and you performed a comprehensive comparative analysis of the approaches.
- You studied the conclusions from your studies and made recommendations based upon this knowledge.
- You selected or rejected approaches and then you presented your findings. Management either selects or rejects the approaches studied.

Here is an example from the credit department of a large retail store.

The team analysts studied the best business options. The team selected the best of the business alternatives for further discussion, and, at the same time, the technical personnel studied the technical alternatives for implementing the system. They selected the best of the technical alternatives for further discussion.

The business analysts and technical personnel studied the combined business and technical alternatives. They drew comparisons of the combined alternatives. They drew conclusions about the viability of the alternatives. They made specific recommendations about implementing the system.

They made recommendations from all the project data, and costs and time estimates that they had prepared. Here are some of the recommendations that were made:

- The team could modify an existing database accessing process.
- The team proposed different ways for handling credit screening information (how credit information is shown on the computer screen).
- The team proposed different screen scrolling information for ease of use (i.e., how a business person views large quantities of information).

- The team proposed ways of rapidly reporting specific credit information (placing the most important information within easy view of a credit business person).

The team studied different combinations of alternatives. Some of the team's alternatives were rejected. Other alternatives were selected as the best of alternatives presented by the team. Some of the team's alternatives were put on the back burner as potential backup processes. Among the alternatives were specification changes to make the system extremely easy for business personnel.

Some business alternatives can be implemented directly through the use of knowledge, while other alternatives will need the development of an architecture or standard system. For any business, your implementation of a standard system involves creating or using reusable items and knowledge.

Your innovation process begins with one or many business requirements. Some of these requirements are critical. Study the different architectures or technical processes to develop a system. Some architectures are critical to producing a flexible business system.

Study the critical business and critical architectural requirements, where specific technical architectures support and satisfy your business requirements. Architectural support is critical for proper business support.

Combine and study critical business issues and critical technical issues. Your study demonstrates many different ways to use critical business and critical technical issues in an implementation plan. The most promising alternatives should be selected for further study.

In Figure 4.2, I show how technical alternatives can make a positive contribution to satisfying the business. You should apply these alternatives and negotiate these issues. Your negotiation involves your project team, project manager, middle management, and sometimes senior management.

The conclusion of your negotiation provides both a business advantage and a technical or architecture advantage. The alternatives that you selected are from the best available alternatives. You select a primary alternative and (at least one) back-up alternative, and then you begin the design for implementation. So your study preceded the creation of design specifications.

Your study and creation of specifications continues while your study of the selected alternatives is completed. This alternative study completion is necessary before your team can prepare design specifications.

You will have finished your study of the combined business and technical issues, and next you will have finished the study of the backup combined business and technical issues. You then design this specific project part for its combined business and technical issues and the integrated system using this specific alternative.

Finally, you will create the system design. When your design is finished, you produce the quality assurance test plans, and finally, you identify new tools and functions that can be reused to reduce the cost of future system implementations.

Support the Project Launches

Most of your remaining steps are similar to existing project management processes. For these steps, you can use the waterfall, spiral development methodology, or any other development methodology. To complete the implementation of your project, you will perform standard methodology tasks.

You can find these items in any standard development methodology. The steps include the writing of specifications, coding the programs or making the design, and possibly creating new tools and functions. After you have completed these tasks, you will debug the system or process, install the end result of the project, and finally operate the project.

You add to the standard process the procedure of creating reusable segments. Early in the project, you will have identified reusable functions, which you will produce here. At this stage of the project, you may have discovered other processes that could be reused, and you will also produce these here.

Provide New Business/Technology Insights

You will implement the business processes and technology or supporting architecture. Once you have implemented the system, you will measure and determine the benefits and liabilities. You will find that some processes will not provide the usefulness as initially thought, and on the other hand, your processes might be more useful than originally thought.

Often you will hear phrases such as:

> "I thought that this information would be sufficient to perform these tasks, but I found that this information was not sufficient."

> "After using the system/procedure I discovered that the system/procedure was also usable to perform... ."

Here is an example from the installation of the retail credit system:.

> At the end of the credit process, credit personnel made some very interesting discoveries. First, because the innovative process included personnel from the credit departments when the system was implemented, the credit personnel easily understood and used the system.

> The implementation could be described as follows: The training was performed from 7:30 a.m. to 10 a.m. Then the credit personnel performed their tasks. They thought that this process was simple and usable. The trained personnel called credit personnel in other parts of the country and trained the rest of credit personnel (from other parts of the country), who were then also able to use the system.

So if you design the system with user personnel involved, the system could be extremely easy to use. Little training was needed for the personnel to perform their jobs using this new system.

You can learn from the information and knowledge that has been gathered. Your use of the business/technical functions is also knowledge that you gathered after the implementation, so you need to hypothesize about the implementation process as it might now be performed using your new implementation knowledge.

As you are implementing the process/technical function, you may find that your solution is complicated. You may have provided an alternate path or a different implementation that would have worked better. You gather and document this specific knowledge. This specific knowledge consists of facts that your management needs to hear, rather than what management wants to hear.

Your implementation needs to be completely open and participatory. The full participation of your project needs to include management, business, and technology. This participation is what you have needed for the duration of the project. Often this is called "lessons learned." Frequently, this part of the process is skipped. Yet "lessons learned" is extremely useful in a phased or cyclic approach.

Conclusion

In this chapter, you learned how to obtain both business and technical competitive advantages and how to minimize risks. I described the identification of business requirements. I showed how to use alternatives to add value to the project and to mitigate risks. Architecture and technical alternatives enhanced the potential project value. I showed how to use a cyclic implementation to immediately provide value from the project.

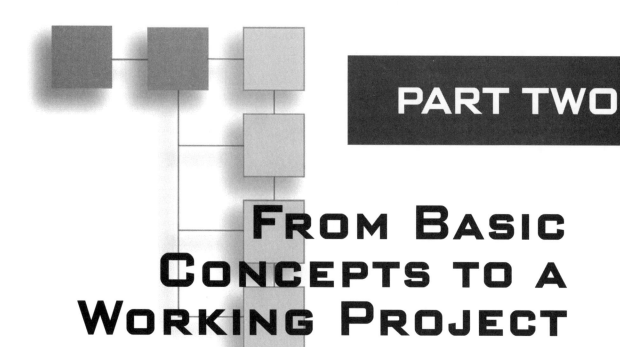

PART TWO

FROM BASIC CONCEPTS TO A WORKING PROJECT

CHAPTER 5

GETTING STARTED

In this chapter, I show you how to move from basic project concepts to a working project. You will learn how a project moves from the introductory concepts to obtaining corporate support. You will learn the process from the beginning.

I address the complete construction process from business through technology. You will guide and obtain the consensus of the entire project team and identify innovative ideas that will add both technical and business competitive advantages.

Your company gains a competitive advantage by providing products that make it desirable for the customer to buy your product rather than that of a competitor. The technical competitive advantage also makes it more difficult for the competition to mimic your differences. You network and negotiate your ideas throughout the participating divisions of the company. Once you have finished networking your ideas, you put the accepted ideas into a project plan, and you design the project plan for a cyclic delivery of the many parts of the project and parts of the ideas.

You will identify and apply innovation where applicable throughout the project. Not everything that you plan will work the way you would like, so surprises are caught early. Surprises are sources for new knowledge, and you use the new knowledge to create competitive value.

Note

The differences that help a corporation gain the sale over a competitor comprise the *competitive value*.

You usually take the first step in a Common Sense in Project Management project before the formal steps that you recognize within a project. I include task lists that describe these steps. I have placed the task lists in popular formats so that managers can add them to their plans and schedules.

You start an innovative project in a different way than you start other projects. People outside of your project will have trouble seeing the difference because you have designers in your project and they have designers in their projects. They tend not to notice that some of your people are architects and technologists, while they only have designers. Many of your fellow project leaders will tell you that your project is no different from what they are doing. You need to remember that an innovative project is quite different and will lead you to very positive results. Your architects, technologists, and designers are challenging each other to find the best solutions to business, technology, and architecture needs. When you don't concentrate on this interaction, you won't notice it.

Building Consensus

Your project team does not need to fully understand how you, the project leader, have structured your project because they will be helping to structure the output of your project. You will use all of the team's talents. You add technical personnel and architects to your staff at the same time that you add business analysts or designers.

Note

You create a major *project differentiation* when you start your technical personnel and architects at the same time that you start your business personnel. Business personnel, technologists, and architects will challenge each other to find advances to the stated requirements and to product therein creating the *product differentiation.*

Your entire staff defines project team goals and contributes ideas from the beginning of the project. Their ideas are presented, considered, and modified to be incorporated in the project. You include some of their ideas in the project, but not all.

The participation of your team creates a positive team atmosphere. Through continued participation, your team learns innovative skills and techniques.

Not everyone on your team will understand the innovative concept from the beginning. The designers in a retail environment had trouble understanding early inclusion of technology. However, the technicians and consultants immediately understood and contributed to the innovative structure of the project. As the project progressed, the designers began to understand the process, and they were able to make positive contributions to the project.

In the health care environment, which I will discuss later in this chapter, my entire team was new. I formed a team of technicians, designers, and user department personnel. The entire team negotiated with business personnel and senior management. Together, this team created the project environment.

My technicians provided the technical and architectural structure on which we built the system. My team selected the best technical architecture of the technical alternatives studied and designed. Designers set the business requirements to be supported by the architecture.

My designers quickly learned the benefits of innovation, and they tried to make other project leaders understand and use the innovative project process. Other project leaders and teams could not see the difference between their projects and our innovative project. However, senior and business management saw the benefits of the innovative project early in the project development, and they approved of the innovative process. Some major differences included implementing the project with zero defects, being on schedule, having a system that did not *abend* (stop running in the middle of the night so that the coders needed to burn midnight oil recovering their system).

Begin Explaining Your Idea Modestly

Your innovative project process will include many people, and the business departments will help plan the process by contributing their ideas. If possible, your customers will be involved and will help create the project requirements. Technicians will contribute the architectural design for your system. Participants set the goals of the project, while they slowly learn the power of their participation.

The following is a health care insurance example:

> I was the project leader in a large health insurance company where I used a very technical project architecture. Senior management understood that the technical architecture I used had worked, and I requested their permission to reuse the architecture.

> My team used business-oriented objects (in our case macros) to simplify the creation of the system code. We placed these objects into a multithreaded (multitasking) architectural structure with a high level of reuse.

I negotiated with business and senior management to create a precise set of project goals. In the first project cycle, I proved again that the architecture would support the business process. Then, once senior management understood that I could meet my project goals, they supported the process. After the initial project cycle was completed, senior management used the process to enhance their business and sold the state an insurance contract based upon the database portion of our system.

Network Internally

Your innovative ideas are very delicate and need to be nurtured, discussed, described, thought through again, and altered before you give them wide review. So you begin to describe your ideas where they will have the best acceptance, within your own network. After you fine-tune your ideas, you need to expand them to include more people, and more departments. Figure 5.1 pictures an idea as beginning inside a small group and growing as it is expanded across many groups.

Sometimes, it is necessary for your team to work with outside people to understand their needs. Once their needs are understood, they can be used by your group to form the initial ideas for your project and for the architecture of your project. Then the initial idea can be nurtured within your own immediate project group.

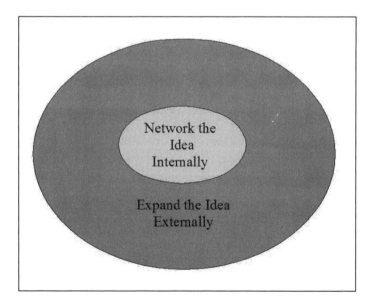

Figure 5.1
Expand the audience for your idea.

The following is a large retail organization example:

> All of the team members visited and worked with credit central personnel. This began an internal networking that strengthened the ties within the group.

> Through networking, the credit central personnel asked their customers project-related questions. Credit central personnel and the systems group formed an excellent communication setup that included customer input. IT management also participated in the project decisions and ran problem interference for the political and business management aspects of the system. This helped to keep project integrity.

Here is an example from the budget department of the city:

> Handling budget information in the city is very complicated. I used the innovative processes on the city budget. We discussed specific long-term budget needs between the systems department and the budget department. I described specific business benefits that technical software could provide for the budget department.

> Together the budget department and my budget team identified critical budget processes. Some technical processes would not satisfy their business requirements, and the budget department rejected our initial technical proposals. Through negotiations, we established the goals of the project, and these goals, helped us identify the next IT tasks.

Explore Externally

You will find that much of the information that you need to complete your projects exists outside your work environment. You and your team may obtain useful information over the Internet or from other companies. Internet-based information is easily used by both technicians and business people.

You also need to network outside your corporation. Networking provides you with a good way to meet people with similar interests. When you network, you are on a two-way street because you will assist some people and others will assist you.

When you have outside contacts or knowledge, you are better able to find specific information that can make it easier to complete your project. For example, in one project, through my networking, I found a printing company that made it easy to automate the printing of our government budget.

Entrepreneurial networks help people start new companies. But entrepreneurial networks can also help intrapreneurs.

Note

Intrapreneurs are innovators who do not intend to leave their companies. They provide innovative ideas that could create new business for their corporation. Their ideas could help the corporation form new departments.

When you network, you need to describe who you are and what you do. So as either an entrepreneur or intrapreneur (innovator), you need to be ready with your own elevator pitch to quickly describe what you want to accomplish. You will also need to remember the elevator pitches that others use.

Note

In an elevator pitch, you have only a few seconds of time to describe who you are and what you have to offer. The time is limited by the amount of time it takes the elevator to move from one floor to another.

Elevators are also appropriate places to extract much needed information from others.

You use the elevator pitches of others to determine whom you should approach for assistance. You will either use your elevator pitch or the highlights of the other person's elevator pitch to introduce yourself, and you will keep in contact with the people whom you meet at these networking meetings. In a short period of time, you will have hundreds of people who can help you with your projects.

Many technical organizations have speakers for different events. These people are also resources for both your information and contacts for assistance.

Build Your Project Plan Early

Start your innovative project plans from your understanding of the initial requirement. You will hypothesize about the advantages that you can gain from your architecture, and you will determine the steps that you need in your project plan that relate to your use of an architecture. If your architecture works really well, you will need far less time for your project, but the needed steps will change.

Start from your standard project plan with the architecture. Build your project plan the same way that you would normally build a project plan, except that you identify the use of your architecture. You do not need to be afraid to do this because projects never work according to plan. Project planners never know everything that must be contained within their plan, and your planning is either made more difficult or simplified by an architecture.

If you have created innovative project plans before, you already know the effects of using a good, supporting architecture, and you will make a close estimate of your steps. If you are sure of the innovative savings, then make the estimate as close as possible, including the savings.

Here are the steps that you will use when you create your new project plan. Figure 5.2 gives a high level picture of the steps that are defined in the following list.

1. Determine the requirements for your project.

2. Identify the architecture that will best satisfy the requirements.

3. Define tasks that need to be contained within your project plan, given the architecture that you plan to use.

4. Define time estimates for each tasks.

5. Identify the background of required personnel and identify the personnel with whom to work and network.

6. Check for interdependencies between the different tasks. If one task needs to be completed before another can be started, make sure that this dependency is shown within your project plan.

7. Note the assumptions that you make while constructing the plan.

8. Investigate the assumptions as you record them.

9. Mark tasks critical if you do not understand them or if they are critical either to the business or to implementing the architecture. You will need to prove that the critical tasks work. You should demonstrate this as early in the project as possible.

10. Make sure that critical tasks identified are completed early in the project.

11. Check the completed project plan for overall consistency.

12. Continue checking the critical tasks and assumptions.

13. Gradually replace guesses with current information when you obtain that information. Note that some of your tasks will become shorter, while other tasks become longer.

14. As you continue implementing your plan, you will find new dependencies. Insert the new dependencies in the plan.

15. Continue to take action and measure your results. When you have results, change the plan based upon your new knowledge. Your project plan is a working document.

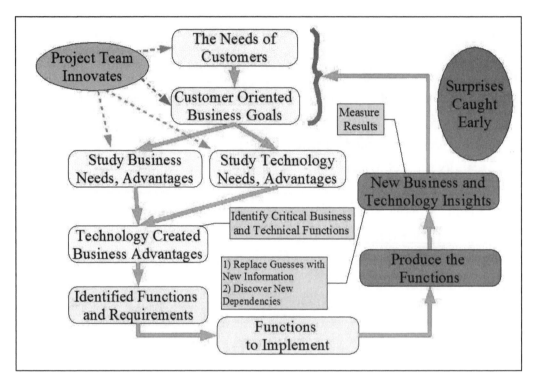

Figure 5.2
Handling the innovative project plan.

You can see how to represent your innovative handling of a project cycle in Figure 5.2. Note that you identify critical business functions or processes and that your critical technical or architectural functions are identified at the same time as your critical business functions.

After you complete an implementation cycle, you have more knowledge, and you will use this knowledge for your future project implementation cycles. You use the knowledge to change the overall project because your business now knows that there are functions that will create a much better competitive advantage.

Here I give an example from the building inspection bureau of the city:

> The building inspection system of a large city used research tasks. The research tasks represented one cycle, which, when successfully completed, provided the basis for the remainder of the project. In creating the business plan with this critical research, the project plan showed this research dependency, and the business alternatives followed either the research step or an alternative. If standard processes had been followed, the technical project tasks would have required more time, but with successful research, the remaining technical tasks took less time. The research steps were the basis for the system architecture and significantly reduced the cost of implementing the system.

In your initial project plan, you will identify and highlight the most critical project steps. In the example of the large city, I had control of the research that was critical to my project. I completed this critical project step before I started the remainder of the project.

There are some project steps that you believe are not critical. However, as you gain more information throughout your project, you may find these supposedly non-critical items to be critical. Make sure that you leave enough time in your project plan so that you can recover from these unknown critical items.

The following are steps to include in your innovative project plan:

- Time estimates for business and technical functions
- Types of people to design and implement tasks
- Task interdependencies
- Note the assumptions about each business function
- Note the assumptions about each technical function
- Investigate the business and technical functions
- Identify critical business functions
- Identify critical technical functions
- Handle critical business and technical functions early

These are some of the steps that you will include in your innovative project plan. In your technical estimates, you will include the amount of time that it takes to identify an architecture to correctly support the business. But before you can estimate your time, you need technical and business team members who can negotiate to help find a valid architecture for the system.

Here is an example from creating an accounting system for a large chemical company:

> How important is the architecture? I needed to create a new accounting system for a large chemical company. The department performed many different types of accounting, so a standard accounting system would have many different functions and would have required a rather large system. This is what the company originally planned.
>
> But the accounting departments of large corporations have books that they call "Chart of Accounts," which in this book I call a chart. The chart describes the actions that need to be taken by an accountant to post the transaction to the accounting system. But my team created a system that used the chart of accounts to control the system. Using the chart as the system control completely altered the list of tasks to be performed to create the system. We drastically reduced the amount of time that it took to create this system.

Conclusion

In this chapter I showed you how to create a project from the basic CS-PM concepts. You move your project forward from the introductory concepts to obtain corporate support. You address both the needs of your business and your supporting technology or architecture.

I showed you the benefits of team participation. Your team identifies your business and technical innovative ideas. The ideas of your team are networked throughout the participating company divisions.

You built a project plan for cyclic implementation. You provide for an early implementation of your key value needs. Your early implementation contributes to early project value and return on investment for your company. Your early implementation also makes new knowledge available, and I showed how your new knowledge adds to your company's new competitive value.

CHAPTER 6

FINDING GOOD IDEAS WITHIN THE PROJECT

In this chapter, you will learn how to incorporate innovative ideas into your projects. These innovative ideas will help your corporation to be more competitive, and your company will be able to make products that fit the needs of the customers better, to create new products of interest to the customer, or to implement your projects with less cost.

You will learn to identify those processes or procedures that make it hard for your corporation to change for the better, and you will learn how to help your corporation change for the better through initiating innovative ideas. You will learn how to provide a flexible business structure through your innovative ideas. You will learn how to easily support change and reduce the resistance to change.

I will show you how to take advantage of architectures that support the project or business. I will help you find an architecture that is a good business support.

Note

An *architecture* is a structure that is the foundation upon which a part of the business is built.

I will help you identify the different types of participants needed to create or enhance the competitive position in your business, and I will describe the roles of each type of project participant. I will show you how to use each participant to create new insights that add value to the initial project charter, and how to find and use alternatives to reduce your project risk while adding flexibility.

The process that follows adds to your existing project processes and tools. The tasks included shorten the length of projects.

Adapting Your Project to Satisfy Customer Needs

You need to change your business constantly to keep up with the needs of the customer. Change is forced by your competition or by a change in customer tastes or needs. The change may reflect a change in your customers' desires or needs, and it may require a change to gain or keep your current corporate market position. In order to keep up with your customer, you adapt your business to new ideas, which forces the business to change.

Your corporation has inhibitors that make it difficult to change, and these inhibitors are built into your business processes. Your system structures and departmental structures make it difficult to change, because your departments use formalized and standardized processes that are unchangeable systems.

You need to remove some of the fixed structures that keep your businesses from adapting to changes required by the business. You will apply new ideas that bring change for the advantage of your corporation, where your changes are driven by your innovation. Your innovation is supported by your projects and ideas that help the business stay competitive by helping it satisfy the needs of your customers.

Your ideas, through negotiation with all of the participants, will add value to the business. You will use architectures and system structures to support your new ideas and to ensure that the ideas are flexible and capable of being changed. However, there are some architectures and system structures that will not support your new and flexible ideas. These architectures and system structures need to be avoided.

If your existing business architecture or structure is not flexible, it should be removed. Architectures and system structures that are based on the existing business process are not able to change, and they should be avoided or, if possible, removed.

Unfortunately, most projects are designed in a straightforward manner and use the business structure as the architecture. Both the fixed business structure and the system structure need to be made flexible.

The following is an example of changing the way a house is built.

The project plan calls for the house to be constructed in the following order:

1. Build the foundation first.
2. Build the outside walls.

3. Add the plumbing and the wiring.

4. Add the intercommunications systems.

5. Build the inside walls.

6. Add the kitchen and its fixtures.

7. Add the bedroom appointments.

8. Finally, add the other rooms.

All of these things are planned in a top down manner. Little thought is given to different orders of construction.

Parallel activities would shorten construction time and result in fewer cost overruns. House prefabrication is a case in point. The house walls are prefabricated, including electrical wiring, communication ports, water (where appropriate), heating ducts, air conditioning ducts, and air return ducts.

The walls for the house are built at the same time that the foundation is being laid. When the foundation is ready, the prefabricated walls are erected and fastened into place, and the required interconnections are made.

This example shows the shortening of implementation time by performing tasks in parallel. Both architecture and project planning are required to reduce the implementation time.

The following is an example of changing the way a house is enhanced:

The same parallel construction process can be used to extend a house. This time, rather than using prefabrication, we will use a simultaneous fabrication process. The tasks that need to be done are: laying the foundation, building the outer walls with wiring, windows, outer doorway to a porch, building an inner wall with electricity, doorway, plumbing for a sink and small restroom.

This is an extension to an old house, and the owners want the addition to appear much like the old house with nine-inch mopboards. Because this is an extension to an old house, there are only three outside walls and these walls are unique to this building. There is enough room in the garage at the back of the house to build the walls there.

There is a lot of work that can be performed in parallel:

- Pouring the cement foundation
- Constructing the three outside walls for the first floor (one at a time)
- Constructing the inside wall
- Building the floor assembly for the first floor
- Providing the plumbing connections for the bathroom floor
- Constructing the ceilings

The second group of parallel construction includes:

- Mounting the first floor assembly on the foundation
- Building the second floor assembly
- Running the electricity for the outer walls
- Running the electricity for the ceilings
- Running the electricity, electronics, and plumbing for the inside wall
- Providing the plumbing connections for the bathroom walls
- Constructing the three outside walls for the second floor (one at a time)
- Constructing the inside wall

The third group of parallel construction includes:

- Mounting the outside walls to the foundation
- Mounting the floor assembly for the second floor and interconnecting electrical and electronic hookups
- Mounting the inside walls and interconnecting electricity, electronics, and plumbing
- Mounting the ceiling to the wall structures and interconnecting the electricity from the walls to the ceiling
- Building the roof structure

The fourth group of parallel construction included:

- Mounting the outside walls to the first floor outside walls and interconnecting electrical and electronic hookups

- Mounting the inside walls and interconnecting electricity, electronics, and plumbing

- Mounting the ceiling to the wall structures and interconnecting the electricity from the walls to the ceiling

- Mounting the roof structures

The items of interest include the parallel construction points, and the work that is performed on the ground instead of up in the air. These items spread the production of the house extension. Also note that if there are problems in constructing the first floor, they can be corrected first and then subsequently corrected for the second floor.

Generating Ideas for the Project

I will define some fundamental computer concepts that will help you define your systems so that they are flexible and potentially reusable. In general, computer systems are used to perform a few monotonous tasks over and over. A single computer system is seldom used for doing many different things for business.

Sometimes, several computer systems are used to do the same things with slightly different data. Sometimes, the data represents completely diverse business functions, where again several different computer systems are used. We make use of computer functions by hypothesizing that the computers are a part of the business process, so a particular computer system has a particular meaning and performs specific business functions.

But the computer does not know, does not care, and does not need to know the meaning of the process it is performing. The computer only needs to perform some specific task (as a series of steps) with some specific data. So a computer system could be used to provide similar steps for totally disparate business needs, and a computer system that does this is completely flexible.

Computer systems and business processes provide and support separate functions, so when you plan for a computer system, you usually divide the functions and processes into their most basic components. You then build the components in such a way that they are usable by only one business function. Instead, you need to design and build your business or computer functions so that they are capable of performing more than one function or business process.

Systems last for a long time, which means that you need to build a robust system architecture to support a system for a long time. But system architectures that are based solely on the business structure are not robust, and they do not last long. System architectures based only on the business structure are inflexible and restrict future business, and ultimately make it difficult to retain or add customers.

Your systems need to support the business and to provide a usable and flexible architectural structure, so that you can continue to grow your business to support your customers. Your solution needs to support (and possibly simplify) the business processes that are critical to the business, while your solutions may be able to support more than one business function. Your solutions also need to provide for the critical technical or architectural issues.

Your system's technical architecture needs to be capable of supporting business now and as it changes. When I talk about architecture, I mean a system structure that supports parallel activities, reuse, single purpose objects, and several business functions. Your system architecture needs to be an extremely flexible system that supports many of your business requirements over long periods of time.

A Retail Example

At a large retail company, an entire project team worked together to create ideas. The team structure is shown in Figure 6.1. The team consisted of a technical consultant, several designers, an architect, a credit business adviser, and a project manager. I served as an advisor to the project manager and filled several other functions as well.

Note

Normally, projects are started with the project team believing that they understand the solution. In this example, the team did not assume that they knew the answer. They searched for solutions that would solve the stated goal and could possibly satisfy other needs at the same time.

I helped the team create new ideas and made sure that both the business critical and technical critical ideas were identified and were coordinated to provide a good business solution. I provided the tools for the group to perform these critical studies.

The team had a business adviser from the credit department who provided both business knowledge and a description of the long-term business requirements. The list of long-term requirements was very large and would have required many years of separate projects, but he guided the understanding of long-term credit needs and critical business functions to incorporate into this project.

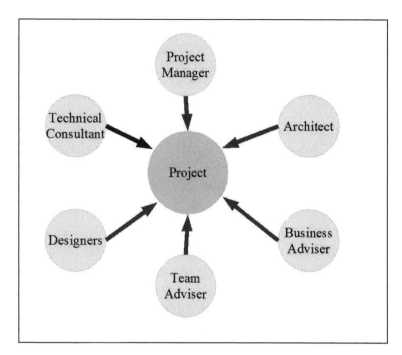

Figure 6.1
Project team members.

Because of all the participants, the group's starting knowledge included the requested project and the long-term credit requirements. The team decided that adding each specific long-term requirement would increase project value without increasing project cost. These valued and low-cost requirements were included in the project.

The technical consultant provided the technical architecture (and alternatives), and he described each of the potential technical advantages to the group. The description included the advantages and disadvantages of each of the alternatives. The presence of the architecture provided the opportunity to include the new business advantages that were being defined through the business advisor.

The designers understood the existing credit systems, the business, and they described the different business alternatives that satisfied the business requirements. They described the advantages and disadvantages of each of these business alternatives. They also described new business advantages that could be incorporated in the project.

The designers came to understand the technical requirements for creating the system, and they helped to describe the different alternatives that could be used to program the system, along with the advantages and disadvantages of each of the processes. They worked with the entire team in negotiating the features, business processes, and technology that would support the system.

Note

The team did not assume that their best alternatives would actually work. So if problems were encountered with their primary alternatives, they had backup alternatives that could be used to implement a part of the project.

The entire group studied the needs of the customer, business requirements, and system architecture alternatives. They provided alternatives for each of the specific program parts, and studied the fit of each business or technical requirement with current and future requirements.

The entire team studied the business and technical requirements and formed combinations between the different types of technology most likely to support a business function. They studied each of the combined alternatives and identified the best alternatives, and the studies revealed that large parts of the system could be implemented rapidly. They identified existing systems functions and used them to satisfy some of the requirements. Their early implementations simplified the overall system implementation.

Users and customers were included in discussions of the alternatives. They asked questions like, "How will the customers be assisted through the business department?" They determined that customers expect specific help from the credit personnel.

The team involved in this example created insights. Figure 6.2 shows how the new insights were created. It also shows the intercommunications between the business functions and the technical functions. The customer is the target for setting business goals because customers buy product. The team created business advantages and business needs to satisfy the customer. The team created different business opportunities through the technical architecture. It also formed new business, technical, and working insights using the new ideas.

An Insurance Company Example

Customer contracts provide some level of coverage at a large health care insurance company. The insurance company may need to make a payment when the customer visits the doctor, and the contracts determine if a doctor's service was covered.

A process determines if the insurance company should pay for a health care service. If the payment should be made, then either the customer or the doctor will be paid. The process is quite repetitive and can be performed by a computer. If the service was covered, the system determines the payment amount and makes the payment.

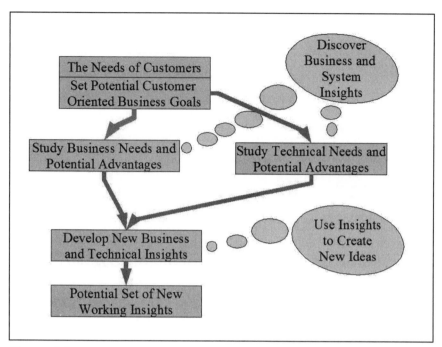

Figure 6.2
Creating new insights.

A system team could use several different system architectures to make these payments. The systems could mimic the business structure, but this would make the system inflexible and hard to maintain.

The team found new constraints and determined that a new architecture was needed. The team determined that computer availability was a problem, and the team could use a multithreading technical architecture to satisfy the constraints. Multithreading allowed the system to handle up to 100 claims simultaneously and up to 15,000 claims within an hour.

System architects designed the multithreading process and fail-safe automatic recovery. The fail-safe process allows processing to continue even if a major system problem occurs. The system reports major problems by following these steps:

1. Report the problem.
2. Provide a method of paying the claim.
3. Continue processing.

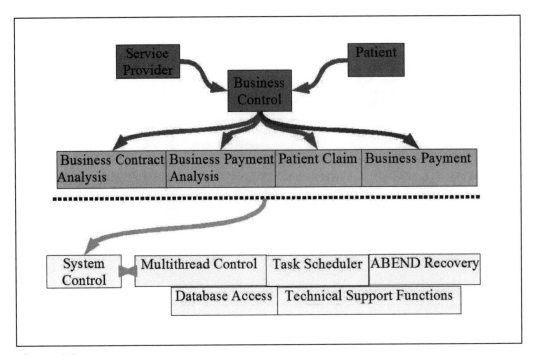

Figure 6.3
Business layer and architecture layer separation.

The team discussed the advantages and disadvantages of each different technical architecture, and enhanced and formalized the architectures. The team used the architecture shown in Figure 6.3 as the architecture for the system.

The team identified common business, technical, and architectural processes and also identified business and technically critical items. They described and discussed alternatives and the advantages and disadvantages of each alternative, and finally the designers described each system part.

The business designers followed the business structure in describing the business and system needs. The developers and architects, however, designed an architecture that would support the business, but did not follow the structure of the business.

This system proved its business flexibility over many years. The system was designed to pay doctor claims. In one instance, a business manager used the system to pay hospital claims, because the system flexibility made it easier, faster, and cheaper to pay hospital claims using the doctor payment system. So the system adaptability and flexibility proved itself over a long period of time.

Ways to Find Good Ideas

Gifford Pinchot and Ron Pellman show ways of creating ideas in their book *Intrepreneuring in Action.* In the same way, you need to find good ideas within Common Sense in Project Management. However, you direct your ideas toward the specific end goal of the project. As a specific end goal, you will produce a system that satisfies specific business goals.

Your system needs to be flexible and allow your business to change. When you have a flexible system, you can easily upgrade it to support new business functions. Flexible systems help the business strive to remain competitive and to create new competitive ideas.

Pinchot and Pellman discussed some interesting ideas. You need to know how and when you are most creative and use that creative time to create new ideas. You will create many new ideas at the beginning, and later you will determine which of the ideas are valuable.

You brainstorm for ideas, trying to find anything that might be different or might apply to the basic project requirements. You ask yourself questions, trying to find yet another angle that would be good for the project or possibly something entirely different that could help the project. You scan many different fields of interest to find something that might be useful to your project or to the business, because you do not know when or how you could have a good idea. So you should carry around a note-taking medium to immediately capture your ideas.

Note

Note-taking devices include a notebook and pen or pencil, Palm Pilot, BlackBerry, recorder, text messaging, phone messaging, laptop computer, phone recorder, and even napkins.

You need to be ready to take notes at any time, even when waking from a sleep. Your mind solves many problems during sleep. You may even want to build a little visual model of what you are considering because the visual concept may enhance your thoughts on the subject.

Once you have your ideas, you begin to sort them out by asking some very specific questions. First, does your particular idea work for the customer? Even if your idea works for the customer, is it an idea that could work for the company or is it an idea that would never be implemented by the company? Finally, does the idea work with you and does it fit within the project?

I have placed forms in Appendix A to support capturing your ideas. My processes provide a mechanism for changing these ideas into the reality required for systems.

Conclusion

In this chapter, you learned how to incorporate innovative ideas into your projects to create competitive value. You learned about the inhibitors that you encounter to your changes. You learned how to incorporate flexible business and technical structures into your project and systems to make changes easy. You learned how architectures can support the needed flexibility.

You learned about the different types of participants in projects. These participants help create new competitive value. You learned how the participants create new insights that add value to the project. Finally, you learned how alternatives are used to reduce risk and add project flexibility.

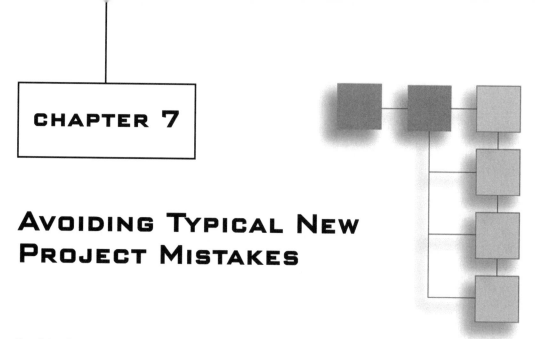

CHAPTER 7

AVOIDING TYPICAL NEW PROJECT MISTAKES

In this chapter, I will show you how to initiate and control a project to avoid the usual mistakes. You will learn to establish a foundation that helps you bypass the causes of problems. I will also show you how to set the foundation to create innovative enhancements to the project charter for your corporate benefit.

You will learn how to enhance communications between all participants, and your project team will learn more because team communication will have been improved. Team learning adds to your ability to add project enhancements with better value.

I will show you how to use the cyclic implementation of Common Sense in Project Management to provide value from the project as early as possible and to identify and provide new business advantages. At each cycle, you have the opportunity to enhance the original project charter and gain benefits for your corporation, and at each step you will use the innovation of all your participants to find the best corporate value.

You will use alternatives to reduce project risk and to improve the business value of your project. You will find items that add little or no value to the project or to the corporation and eliminate them. You will then identify and implement the most important tasks first.

You will be able to take advantage of your new knowledge at each step and each cycle of your project. On the companion Web site for this book, you will find a task list in many popular formats for your business and technical managers to use as planning tools for the Common Sense in Project Management process.

Avoiding Mistakes

You can make a few things work extremely well for you with an innovative project management process because you will determine the parts of your project that are most critical to the success of your project and your business itself. You will complete these critical parts as soon as possible.

You will find that your critical project parts can cause you problems because they are usually difficult to implement, and they are usually implemented last. These parts are critical and tricky, and when you try to implement them early you may fail, which may cause you to use one of the simpler alternatives. It is easy for you to implement these critical parts early when you use small project cycles to implement your project.

When you make mistakes early in a project, the mistakes are easily corrected and with less expense than if you fail at implementing these critical elements late in the project. I have supplied forms and processes in Appendix A, "Forms," to help you control these critical elements. The forms and processes will help you, the project manager, to identify and implement critical elements early.

It is wise for you to complete the most critical elements as early as possible. You should complete these items and place them in production as early as possible. You will learn many things about both business and technical benefits when you implement the critical elements early.

Project Initiation Often Causes Problems

You will encounter most of your problems at the time of project initiation because your data processing projects are initiated with several communication disconnects that cause problems. You will find these disconnects between senior management and your customer, between business departments and senior management, and between the systems department and the business departments.

Figure 7.1 demonstrates the decreasing level of communication that starts with the customer and ends at the information technology department. You will note how the level of correctness in the communication drops as it proceeds. I have shown the way that you can repair this communication by increasing the communications between all the involved parties.

Figure 7.1 shows the major communication disconnects that cause your completed projects to lack needed customer benefits. Because of these disconnects, you will miss company requirements and ignore business department processes. You will also fail to provide a proper information services architecture because you do not understand the true business needs.

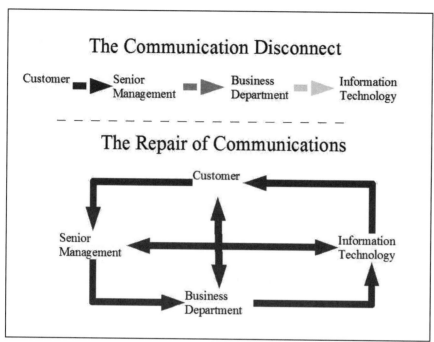

Figure 7.1
Repairing the communication disconnect.

Figure 7.1 shows you both the communication connections and disconnections. The top part of the diagram shows you the message passing game. The true needs are first understood at the customer level. Senior management gathers a different understanding than the needs of the customer and applies this understanding to the business.

When senior management communicates the message to departmental management, the message is understood in terms of the department manager and not always as senior management intended. Finally, you receive the message from your business department management, and your understanding of the message is different still. You have a discrepancy in information.

You reduce this discrepancy by increasing the information flow between all of the parties; you should not exclude any participant. You change the form of your communication and enter into a negotiating process where you clarify the basic differences in the requirements or needs. You will discuss and negotiate different alternatives about the needs of each of the parties, allowing the best of the alternatives to be selected.

You will discuss the business elements that are critical to the business and some of their alternatives for satisfying critical business issues. You will determine the technical or architectural elements and alternatives that are critical to the business and the architecture. Installing critical elements early creates different levels of discovery, which will help identify and satisfy problems caused by the communications disconnects.

> For example, in the health care insurance environment, I worked closely with the department head of the doctor payment department. This manager was a "detail person" (quite comfortable with a high level of detail). We were able to identify basic system requirements and the type of business requirements that we would satisfy.
>
> The business manager and I were able to identify the functions that were critical to providing the processing that would be required by the department. From the technical side, I was able to define basic architectures that could satisfy these requirements. With the team, we identified parts of the system that we could create early to prove that our theories would satisfy the business requirements. We created the architecture and two types of health care payments. These proved that our theories were correct and that we could meet our production schedule.
>
> The system needed to handle a total of 50 different types of health care. We implemented about 6 types at a time. We used 8 cycles to implement the entire project. We also prepared a testing system to ensure that the new functions that we added to the system did not destroy any of the existing functions.
>
> Our testing functions were adopted and used by other projects, including hospital payments and history capture.

You will satisfy the needs of the consumer, business department, and information services when you resolve the communication disconnects. When you implement your project early, it helps the participating parties to understand and communicate better because they can see what needs to be stated to complete the discussion of their needs. Your business departments discover how well the implemented system supports the described benefits, and your architects discover how well the implemented architecture supports the technical needs.

With early implementation, your company satisfies customer needs early and easily. Early implementation resolves any information disconnect that might exist. Your customer and business department needs will be satisfied, and further, your technical system architecture is exposed by the early implementation, and its success is measurable.

In the retail environment, the accessing of credit information was implemented by the end of the first month of the project. This got the attention of the credit business department. They increased their participation with the credit systems group and provided much better information. This early implementation demonstrated that the system architecture was correct. The next functions that were implemented included the architecture and the initial screen handling processes. Later, the screen handling processes were enhanced to include the full knowledge necessary for a credit central person to provide immediate customer credit information to a clerk at the cash register.

An innovative project implements system parts early and often (because it is cyclic). Early implementation provides an opportunity to review the project parts that you have delivered. You can assist in correcting communication and implementation problems that have arisen because of miscommunication between any of the parties. With early implementation, your problem correction costs are minimal. Further, if your proposed solution does not work, your recovery process is low cost and swift.

When you have a shortfall in the implementation, you can easily correct it without a high cost, and you learn from the implementation. Your learning process includes understanding new meanings of customer benefits, senior management goals, business requirements, and systems technology and architecture.

You will understand how the project worked for each of these areas, and you need to correct any benefit shortfall for each area. You need to apply any new project understanding needs to the remainder of the project and its cycles.

In the building inspection project, an early implementation for handling court requirements provided knowledge about requirements for building inspection. The building department personnel were excited about the system and quickly identified problems. These problems were quickly handled and helped these two departments to work more closely together.

You will see new valuable processes and benefits from each project implementation cycle, and you will add these new benefits to the project, beginning with the next cycle. The business departments will understand your new system benefits for senior management and for their business department. Senior management will see enhanced business benefits, customer advantages, and their own needs, and the systems department better understands technology features and their application to business, senior management, and the customer. You will have closed the communication and information gap.

The business department needs to take special care to satisfy customer needs. Your innovative project management team should use either customer information or customers themselves in determining the needs of the customers. If you can have customers involved in determining the requirements, you will have reduced the risk of not satisfying customer benefits and needs.

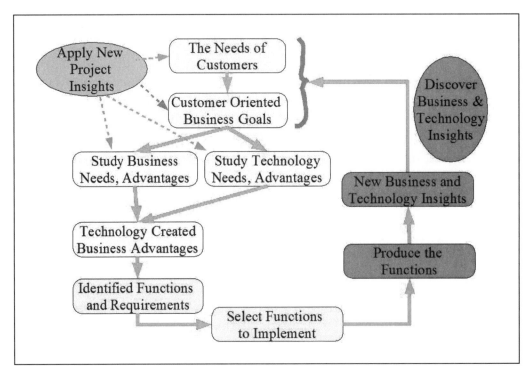

Figure 7.2
Discover and apply insights.

Your innovative project is implemented in phases or cycles, so you have the opportunity to discover new benefits from one cycle to the next. Implementing early is like prototyping in production, except that you have many production implementation phases.

Many systems departments normally create prototypes. A prototype is a demonstration, a model, or a simulation of the features to be implemented. Unfortunately, prototypes are not always taken seriously, and they often miss required features because they are not used in production, consequently you will use your actual production system for your innovative demonstration model.

Your production system provides the opportunity to understand the true needs of the customer, management, business, and systems. Misunderstandings between the customer, senior management, the business department, and information services are seen early and can be eliminated easily.

Your early (and often) implementations make benefits available immediately, where your production environment provides the best hands-on evaluation possible. For an innovative project, the simulation stage is really a project cycle that is rapidly moved to production.

Your early production prototype reduces the number of unpleasant surprises. You will not encounter problems late in the project because you will have implemented your most critical elements early, and you will have removed your miscommunications through better communications. You will not need to make special changes late in the development of the project. Late changes are extremely high cost and cause loss of time.

In the credit project, the surprises after the project was implemented, were pleasant. The credit personnel found more uses for the system than were originally envisioned. They created a newspaper to communicate the new uses. These uses made it easier to implement new functions for the credit departments.

One of the subsequent credit cycles included the use of artificial intelligence to automatically extend the credit limit to support a purchase. Credit was extended only to a creditworthy person.

Some Common Mistakes

When you innovate within a project, it never proceeds according to your plan, so it is easy for you to fall back into your bureaucratic ways of managing projects. You will cause your projects to fail if you fall back into your old ways.

Even research environments have the same problems. They often back into projects as usual and follow project processes that are like the bureaucratic ways of managing projects. This will cause them to fail.

A Complex Engineering Example

I worked on an extremely complex electrical engineering system project in which I created a new system architecture to implement the system. Prior systems of this type had all failed.

I headed an innovative team that consisted of engineers and systems personnel. I studied and proposed several alternatives to create the system, and I consulted with several corporate divisions to determine the soundness of the innovative ideas. Once the divisions pronounced the idea as sound, I was able to begin system construction.

This system placed electronic switching equipment onto a telephone company floor plan. This is similar to using a computer to design better computers. Our early project cycles provided the system architecture. The architecture described the importance of placing specific telephone switching equipment onto a specific place on the floor.

The first cycle determined how to place the most critical equipment on the floor. This equipment would be similar to the central processing chip in a computer. We drew this output to x-inch scale.

Subsequent cycles added specific pieces of equipment to the implementation. The system made many decisions to design these floor plans. We completed the project by using the process 20 different times to produce 20 different floor plans. The system architecture provided the flexibility required for the system to perform many groups of decisions to create 20 different floor plans.

Management and telephone company personnel would select the floor plan that they liked best. That floor plan would then be recorded as the floor plan design.

Early in the project, I discovered a better way of implementing it. The new process invalidated portions of the project plan, and yet our senior management had already approved the project plan. Because our corporate environment was not innovative, I decided that senior management would not understand the changes, so I reported progress according to the initial project plan. It was a mistake not to share the project changes with senior management. However, I constructed the system according to the new plan, and senior management should have known exactly how I was implementing this project.

It would have been far easier for me to have clearly presented all of the facts to senior management so that they would understand the changes. I should have changed the plan, but I did not. I should have prepared senior management reports according to the new plan.

In a supportive, innovative climate, I would have communicated the project changes. I had no trouble working according to the changes because my design team was able to implement the needed system. At and within each project cycle, my team made new discoveries and recognized new advantages, and I incorporated the changes into the project.

Senior management was informed about the project progress from the end results. The project determined how to place large equipment onto the telephone company floor plan. We were able to show our project results with computer-created drawings to ¼-inch scale. This was the key result for senior management. The innovative process was successful.

Common Problems in Projects

Some of the discoveries that you will encounter and recognize include things like:

- Your primary business alternative will not work or is more difficult than you had planned.
- Your primary technical alternative will not work or is more difficult than you had planned.
- Your combined business and technical alternatives will not work together as you had planned.
- One of your other business alternatives appears better than your primary business alternative.
- One of your other technical alternatives appears better than your primary technical alternative.
- After you have implemented a cycle, there are unanticipated benefits and different ways that your company can use the system or that you can use the technology or the architecture.
- Your new business benefits could easily be made available if....
- Your new technical (architectural) benefits could make the system easier or easy to implement if....

You cannot know everything about a project before you start the project, so you will learn from early-stage discoveries, and you will make mistakes. You will have overlooked or misunderstood some facts, causing required changes and making discoveries necessary. Many things can go wrong within your project.

The standard project management procedures have not worked in 40 years, so you cannot expect them to work well now. You will make your projects work by adding CS-PM processes that can make your projects successful. With Common Sense in Project Management, you will use many of the existing project management functions, so that you have only a few processes and procedures to learn.

I will describe some of the missing project management items that cause problems, and I will identify the concepts and procedures that Common Sense in Project Management adds to the process to correct the problems. You and your company do not always understand the needs of the customer. Using CS-PM, you will gather as much customer-oriented information as you can to add an understanding of the customer.

Your company may not have innovative project leaders, so you may not have role models to follow. Most project leaders just study the basic requirements, set a list of tasks that appear to implement those requirements, and from that they try to control their projects. You will extend your projects by finding innovative business and technical or architectural solutions. You will expand the competitive advantages of your business and simplify and extend your technology to support your current and future projects.

Here is what we want you to move away from. Many projects have a lengthy implementation and execution cycle, which means it takes a long time to complete a project. Without CS-PM, project managers and designers tend to design the entire project first, then take the steps to implement when they have designed the entire project). Instead, your team will design cycles of the project according to the CS-PM method. You will implement your project in cycles, each cycle being rather small, and each cycle implementing something that is critical to the project. You will discover new business and technical benefits through the knowledge that you gain at each cycle of implementation.

For example, in the health care insurance project, we implemented the basic architecture and two types of health care early. These tasks proved that the project theories were correct. They also provided knowledge about what the doctor payment project would perform for these two types of health care. These functions were critical to the correct handling of health care claims.

We subsequently added more health care functions to the system. We also tested each health care function to ensure that we did not destroy any processing with our new functions.

In most current projects, there is not a task that one uses to help find the critical project elements. Project managers tend not to confront these critical elements early in the project, leaving them for later, and yet it is usually these critical elements that cause the project to fail and to have high costs and time overruns. You will investigate the project to identify the critical elements within it, and you will find primary and alternative solutions to these critical elements., By making this critical investigation, you will mitigate many of the risks that you face as a project leader.

Most project leaders do not search for new ideas and, consequently, do not have the opportunity to sell their new ideas and create new business opportunities. You and your entire team will create innovative ideas that cover the entire work space of the project: customer needs, senior management needs, business department needs, and technology architectures and uses, and you will sell these ideas at all of these levels and to all people involved.

In most projects, there is not a process where the project participants negotiate to identify the best alternatives to satisfy known needs. JAD sessions usually identify only the needs and requirements that are known at the beginning of a project. You will initiate and participate in many different negotiations that will continue throughout your project and will make your project better. Part of your communications will consist of negotiating and selling your ideas and the ideas of your entire team.

Note

JAD, or *Joint Application Development*, brings together business personnel and information technology personnel. They enter into a negotiation to determine what the users really need in their system. The information technology personnel then establish a way to implement the defined needs.

In the next section, I will consider each of these points in more detail and give examples so that you can create your own CS-PM environment. When you begin by taking the first CS-PM steps, you are entering into a continuous improvement and innovation process, so enjoy and have fun.

Misunderstanding the Customer

A fatal project omission is the failure to fully understand the customer benefits. Instead, many projects supply product features that are of no interest to the customer.

Look for the root cause of any customer problem, or customer need, and you will begin to understand the underlying effects of making specific changes. When you make a specific change that solves one problem, you might create another problem as a consequence of the change, so you need to know the full effects of each change in order to provide the customer benefit without causing other problems that have a negative effect on your customer or on your project.

You will work to understand the business benefits and alternatives available to satisfy a specific business need. Not all of your business alternatives will work. Some of them will cause other business problems, and a few will fit within the business environment.

In the health care insurance environment, our plan for creating a hierarchical code to describe the procedure would have caused the claim coding to have been quite complex. This design would not fit within the business environment.

One of your business goals is to deliver customer benefits at a profit. You, as a project leader, must understand the customer, solve a real customer need, and do it at a profit. You want to solve the problem so that it is beneficial to your project and your department.

You need to handle your internal business processes easily. You, the project leader, will negotiate to satisfy your company's internal business needs, and at the same time you will not sacrifice your business and customer goals.

Your system, when implemented, will not have extraneous features that add to your production cost. Your system should also be easy to change, so that as your corporate business needs change or your customer needs change, your system will be easy to adapt and change. You will implement your systems with a flexible system architecture that provides a good *return on investment* (ROI) over a long period of time.

A Large Chemical Company

The company, Amoco Chemicals' North Eastern Polystyrene Division, had an equipment-driven process that met the customer needs. The manufacturing process was a bit different than the process at other company divisions.

The chemicals were created and immediately placed into a hopper car for shipment, and they were shipped immediately. The chemical company kept a small portion of each shipment to measure the quality and color of the chemicals being shipped. The quality and the color were used to set the exact product code on the product, and it was also used to determine the product price because the price depended upon the color and the quality of the material.

The material was already in a hopper car, and the railroad would move the material before the exact nature of the product had been determined. The plant set a hypothetical color and quality for the chemicals being shipped and posted the inventory as shipped, but they did not post the actual inventory. This created a negative inventory for the hypothetical product of that color and quality. After they determined the actual chemical and color, a process that took about one week, they added the quantity to the inventory for the material. If the plant needed to, they removed the hypothetical negative inventory and added the real product to inventory and then to material shipped.

This was a very convoluted process for identifying and controlling inventory, and it caused a few system problems. This process was different from the processes at other divisions, and yet we did not review this complex process. I had designed a system to handle the processing at all of the other chemical divisions.

The system recorded the chemical and its hypothetical quality. Inventory was reduced by the amount of inventory shipped. Most often this division was correct in its assessment of product quality, but the inventory would be recorded as a negative inventory until the exact nature of the product was known. Once it was known, the production of that amount of chemical material was recorded, raising the negative quantity to zero.

The recorded negative inventories caused a problem for accounting. An eager accountant noticed the negative inventories and, assuming that there was no such thing as a negative inventory, zeroed the negative inventory.

When the division recorded the inventory, that caused the total inventory to appear greater that it was. Sales personnel noticing the positive inventory would then sell the product (which did not exist). This caused both inventory and customer problems.

The actual problem was a misunderstanding between all of the parties involved, including the customer, the manufacturing department (business department), and systems. This example shows just how important it is to understand the full detail of what is being systematized.

Lack of an Intrapreneur

Note

> An *intrapreneur* is an innovator or entrepreneur who creates new business but remains within the company. An entrepreneur creates a new business and forms a new company around the new business.

Your project needs an innovator, or an intrapreneur. Not every project leader is an innovator. In many companies, management procedures prohibit the project innovators from benefiting the company. Without an innovative project manager, a project is restricted from discovering competitive business and technical alternatives.

Rigid Management Structures Prohibit Innovative Benefits

Systems management often enforces rigid control structures on business systems development. For example, I trained an innovative project manager for a large telephone company to complete his projects successfully. The sidebar called "The Steps Used by a CS-PM Project Manager" are the steps that I taught this project manager. His projects were successful and were implemented on schedule and within budget, and they added value to his company and satisfied the needs of his customer. See the sidebar for the steps used by a CS-PM project manager.

The Steps Used by a CS-PM Project Manager

The following is the set of steps followed by a CS-PM project manager:

This is the beginning of Phase I. Review the stated requirements and do not assume that you know how this set of requirements could be solved.

Prepare an introductory project plan.

Add architect, technician, and business designer.

Determine how the requirements will affect the customer and ask the customer how this affects him.

Use the team to determine what might be done to satisfy the business requirements and look for alternatives.

Use the team to determine the different types of architectures that could support the business requirements.

Identify what is critical to the business (i.e., to create the business competitive advantage).

Identify what is critical to the technology and architecture (i.e., to create a technical competitive advantage).

Identify any existing business or technology that simplifies implementing the business or technology elements of the requirements.

Update the project plan to make it more realistic, based upon the collected information.

Identify any new business processes, technology, or architecture components that should become reusable.

The Steps Used by a CS-PM Project Manager *(continued)*

Identify business, technology, or architecture elements that are of little or no value so that they could be dropped.

Determine the most likely combinations of critical business and critical technology elements that could be paired for implementation. (These are selected from the described business and technical alternatives.)

Determine the critical (and later non-critical) paired business and technical requirements that should be implemented rapidly. These are passed to Phase II.

This begins Phase II. Study the critical business and critical technology elements to determine their likelihood of being successfully implemented. Compare these to the other combined alternatives.

Select the best and backup alternatives for implementation. Pass these forward to Phase III for a requirements analysis.

Perform the requirements analysis for the combined business and technical requirements.

Describe the parts (business and architectural).

Make a better determination of reuse.

Write the specifications for the parts being implemented.

Identify potential problems with either the business or architectural portions of the system.

Provide testing plans.

Write usage and user documentation.

Test the system.

Implement the system.

Create the reuse.

Operate the system.

Discover problems with the architecture and business implementation.

The first 16 steps are not performed within standard development methodologies. These steps provide the project manager with a superior level of knowledge from which to make decisions. Through practice, the project leaders discover how to apply these steps rapidly and how to use them to recover projects that are having problems.

There are several ways of performing cyclic implementation with this process. Using one method, you can take the first critical elements all the way to implementation before releasing any other elements for investigation and implementation. In another method, you can release critical elements to Phase II for implementation and then release other elements to be worked in Phase I. These releases of work depend on the number and quality of personnel.

His management was impressed with his abilities and assigned him to help recover the projects of other project managers. He helped other project managers to develop their projects so that they were on schedule and within budget. He determined the missing information specific to each project. By asking each project manager and team for specific information, he forced the project managers to obtain the missing information. He then required specific plans for the use of the knowledge that each project manager had just gained.

Management was very impressed with his capabilities. Other project managers did not have the same skills. In short, this person used the talents from his innovative training.

This telephone company was purchased by a larger telephone company. The purchasing company had a very structured project management methodology. Bureaucratic procedures have kept him from applying his knowledge and understanding in assisting other project managers to recover their projects. As a result, projects were again late, over budget, and did not meet customer requirements.

In another case, a bureaucratic manager took over a project from an innovative project manager. The bureaucratic project manager was not innovative and did not have the confidence, or the ear, of the entire team. He did not understand all of the politics that had been set in place, did not know how to handle each of the different participating departments, and consequently, he failed. The CS-PM knowledge about a project is significant and provides information about how to coordinate the implementation process. Lacking this information makes it very difficult for a non–CS-PM project leader to take over a project without all of this significant information. These two instances show the intense focus required of the innovative project manager.

I have shown, through these experiences, that the bureaucratic process, when used for project management, does not work because the project manager lacks the knowledge gained by the first 16 steps of CS-PM. Innovative project managers help to meet the requirements of the customer, management, the business department, and systems. Through their innovation, they make a project work. When you apply the innovative principles, you will also make projects work.

Where to Find Innovators

Not everyone within a corporation has the ability to be an innovative project manager. But in every corporation there are many people who have the ability to be innovators and even project innovators. Innovators have a curiosity, and when they fail to implement a project, they want to know why and how to make it succeed. When the innovator fails, the innovator wants to know what could have averted the failure.

I can tell you that it is fun watching project leaders blossom as they become innovative. They learn the principles of innovative project managing, and the more the innovative project leader understands and learns, the better their projects become.

Here I describe some of the processes you as an innovative project manager will use in your projects. Your initial corporate and project goals are clearly defined and are open to be changed for the better. You alter these goals by determining the elements that are critical to the business and technology. You find all of the alternatives for satisfying these goals. You negotiate to find the best combined solutions to satisfy these goals.

After you determine the alternatives to satisfy these goals, you will prepare your sales presentations for senior management, business management, and technical management. Your management needs to be willing to listen to your sales pitches and to negotiate to enhance your ideas for their benefit.

In the health care insurance environment, we found a way to simplify the addition of new business functions within the doctor payment system. The changes were based upon alternatives that provided a much better knowledge of the type of processing required from an extension of contract data. In negotiating with senior management, we discovered that there was a business need that could fund changing the system to use this alternative. The alternative would simplify maintenance and reduce the cost of adding any new health care functions.

Your specific customer benefits are clearly understood and are open to negotiation to better satisfy their needs. The specific goals of your business department are clearly understood, but they are open to expansion to increase or alter their deliverables or to enhance or simplify their business.

All of your participants in the innovative project are willing to negotiate to enhance their benefits and the benefits of the other participants. Your participants include the customer, business personnel, systems, and senior management. Your entire team participates in creating, restating, and selling project goals.

Your team works to find the project tasks that are critical to the project and to define the critical tasks from and with all of the parties, including senior management, business, systems, and the customer. Your team also participates in finding ways to implement and deliver the critical tasks early. Your early delivery is done in cycles, so your entire team participates in deciding what and how to deliver in each cycle.

Your business and systems managers together make the innovative process successful, and they require all of your participants to perform the innovation necessary to make the project work. They are open to your recommendations and enhancements to the project. They challenge your team to create the innovative ideas that will enhance the business.

In the credit project, the entire team participated in defining the tasks that were critical in rapidly showing credit information. The team defined a number of business functions as being critical, including obtaining data, displaying customer credit information, and moving between one screen and another. They found ways to accomplish these tasks rapidly.

Your project requirements and plans are screened by management to provide high value benefits. Your company will be looking for both short-term ROI and long-term ROI, and they will be willing to yield some short-term profits for higher long-term profits. You will be expected to deliver on the long-term profits. Your projects need to be flexible to accommodate beneficial changes for your customers, business, and systems. You will use this flexibility to create the best business advantages possible from what you know and where you believe that your corporation is going. Your management will accept and help create new ideas.

Your new ideas are accepted, studied, and become solution alternatives that could be implemented in this project cycle or could be scheduled for a later cycle for implementation. Your best benefits and alternatives are selected and used for the project. The corporation will nurture your team of innovators, and it will accept mistakes. The team barriers that you face are removed by business and systems management.

In Figure 7.3 you can see the basic steps within an innovative project and the negotiation used to arrive at the best alternatives. You then identify and produce the critical project tasks. Your implementation is performed cyclically so that you achieve benefits as soon as possible. The project then meets its requirements and is successful.

Not Meeting Customer Needs

Your projects may not always meet customer needs. In fact, some of your business requirements could conflict with customer needs, which could cause a negative effect on your business. Your customers may no longer buy your products.

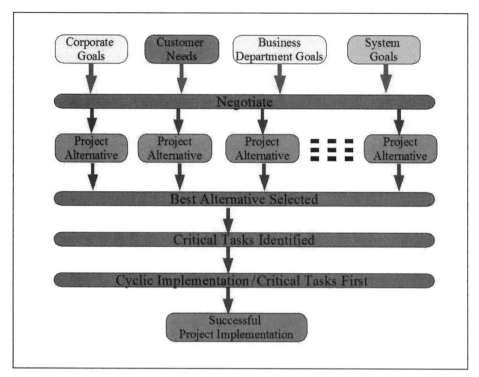

Figure 7.3
Getting to a successful innovative project.

You need to entice your customers through your business and technical benefits. Sometimes, you need to reorganize the internal business departments to gain either a business or technical strategic value sufficient to support the project. In some cases, your customer will help establish a project.

Your innovative ideas should enhance the strategic intent of the business for the benefit of your customers. You will sell your discovered customer benefits to senior management, thereby obtaining internal support for the innovation within your project and within your company. You need to identify supportive decision-makers to help sell the customer benefits within your company, and you need to court the customer and your internal support people to obtain your project benefits. The astute, innovative project manager will understand these tasks and benefits.

In some cases, your innovative ideas will be the formation of a new company. In the field of Customer Relationship Management (CRM), customers have difficulty in getting assistance solving their product problems. They call the Customer Support Representative (CSR) and often need several calls and a lot of wasted time before their problem is solved.

There were companies that captured information that was prepared by the CSRs. They believed that they could make the information available to the CSRs. But the information became voluminous. They tried search techniques, but the information collected became so large that the search techniques proved useless.

As an entrepreneur, I determined that the use of artificial intelligence could be used to pick the correct solution from the problem description. I formed a new company to supply this information. This new use of artificial intelligence provided the knowledge that CSRs needed to provide to their customers on the first call.

Note

When you make a call to a company to receive assistance, your call is handled by a *customer support representative (CSR)*. The functional area in the company in which CSRs work is called *Customer Relationship Management (CRM)*.

A Large Health Care Insurance Company

For example, I worked for a health insurance company that looked like it was many single health insurance companies instead of one. Looking like many companies was a competitive disadvantage because it was confusing to the customer. I needed to help the company to look like one company, even though it was several different companies.

Our competition was one company and operated as one company, and we operated as several different companies, so our customers were confused. Our customers did not understand how the company was handling their insurance claims, because one of our companies would reject the claim and send a rejection letter, and another of our companies would pay the same claim and describe the covered benefits.

This contradictory payment information would happen when the basic insurance coverage would not pay for the specific procedure, but it would be covered under the major medical coverage (two separate companies). The claim would be forwarded to the major medical company from the basic insurance company. In some cases, the confused person would submit a second claim, which would be seen as a duplicate claim and rejected.

I understood the problem and proposed both a business and technical solution to our business management. My solutions were complex, but they needed to be implemented to keep from losing customers. Our business management agreed to support the project.

I crossed many bureaucratic hurdles, but together with management, we determined how to traverse these hurdles. In the bureaucracy, we used a request and problem description form. The form could be routed to one of several different systems departments. There were many different departments that could have received the request, including hospital payments, doctor payments, claim validation processes, and membership processes.

We needed to describe the requirement in such a way that the paperwork would be properly routed to the doctor payment system and not the hospital payment system. I would often spend several days making sure that the request was written so that I would receive it. I requested the required system changes through the bureaucratic channels, and the correct bureaucratic paperwork arrived at my office. I was then able to have the system implemented.

Who Wants to Own Your Project—City of Chicago

I have another example from a government organization. Government organizations have trouble creating and balancing budgets because budget requirements continuously change. The budget processes are fixed in time and yet need to be extremely flexible. Budgets are at the center of large voting thrusts, requiring approvals from the city council. This makes budgeting extremely complex.

Government budgeting systems are rather rare, and so budgeting departments could use budget processes to simplify their budget preparation. I worked and negotiated with the budget department to simplify their budget preparation process. At the city, the budget cycle begins in March and continues through the end of January. I proposed using a flexible budgeting process to derive the budget and to handle disasters when they occurred.

Most budgeting processes require each department to prepare their basic budget from a given starting point. The managers of each department would make changes to the department budgets and then accumulate their budgets. This was a multilevel process.

In the city, the mayor and council members determine the maximum amount of the budget, and they negotiate for the specific budget contents and budget funding. The budgets are then changed again and sent back down through the departments. Each manager makes changes again, and the budget process proceeds upward.

Budget negotiation continues for several cycles. It is altered by changes in taxes, special circumstances, and special projects from aldermen.

The flexible budget allows each department to prepare several budgets, where each budget is based upon some basic assumptions of potential city council funding, like the number of employees or the amount of funds to be allocated for snow removal. Then several budgets are forwarded to the managers. The managers have the ability to alter any of these budgets to form yet more potential funding scenarios. They can, for instance, alter the number of workers allocated to a specific department to fulfill a specific requirement.

Finally, when the budget goes to the city council, the council members can determine which functions are more important and again alter the budgets for a higher or lower funding level for snow removal, building inspection, or licensing fees. The budgets can easily be varied, tested, and negotiated based upon incoming funds compared to planned expenses.

I negotiated with the budget department and sold them on the idea of a flexible budget. During the negotiation, I made progress at each of our meetings, and I made the concepts clear so that the budget department understood them, agreed with them, and supported them.

Each department within the city prepares its own budget. My proposal gave more control of budget changes to each department. With the new system, the budget department was able to balance the budget faster and could try many budget alternatives rapidly.

The flexible budget process shortened the budget cycle and helped the budget department reduce the numerous budget mistakes. This made the process easier for all of the departments. My innovation improved the budget process.

Rapid Execution and Implementation

Information service departments usually do not deliver their products on schedule and do not satisfy the needs of business personnel. Business departments expect system delivery as it is originally scheduled, and business departments also expect the systems to perform the functions required.

Business departments plan for and train their people to use new systems when the systems are scheduled for delivery. The missed schedules undermine confidence in the systems department, while systems that do not perform according to requirements lower business department confidence. Unfortunately, information service departments have performed this way for years.

What happens when systems departments deliver on schedule and with zero defects? Then the business departments raise their expectations and confidence.

With Common Sense in Project Management, you will involve and negotiate with business departments to produce the needed systems and make the business department a part of the project.

You create good will by understanding the requirements of the business department and negotiating with them to achieve the best system for the company. You help create good will, making the company more mindful and participative in the project progress. You make the business more willing to assist in achieving the project goals by satisfying their needs.

A Retail Credit Example

In general, business departments do not have confidence in systems departments. The retail credit business department was very skeptical of systems. The project leader used CS-PM and delivered parts of the project early, creating excitement within the business department, so that from that point, the project leader received a high level of cooperation from the business department. The business department actively contributed to rapidly advancing the project.

The project leader developed the project and delivered it on schedule. The business department found new ways to use the product. The business department created a newsletter about the new project and their newly discovered uses. Many users contributed new ideas about the technology usage. There was excitement all around.

The business department produced a newsletter with pictures of all the project participants including both business and systems together, in the same room. Each participant wore a T-shirt that represented the project (a big credit card). The participants included both systems and business. The business department celebrated the event and continued by fully participating in the negotiations for the follow-on projects.

Accept Some Risk

Here are some milestones that typically occur within an innovative project. The project team had studied the alternatives and understood the business benefits for each of the business alternatives. The team also understood the technology benefits for each of the technical alternatives and the system architecture.

The team, including the customer departments, participated in the study. They determined the level of risk of each alternative. Some business alternatives are riskier than others, and the higher risk projects usually have a better payoff.

In the same way, high risk architectures usually have a better payoff. Some architecture alternatives are riskier than others. However, for the risk there is a better payoff.

In a CS-PM project, you combine business and technology alternatives. The team determines the level of risk that it is willing to take, and you will implement your project risks early. The team took its risks up front and kept its recovery cost at a minimum, while minimizing the risks by using alternatives.

Project managers have repeated the CS-PM process many times, and it seems to work well. You understand risks and tolerate mistakes. When you find mistakes, they are corrected.

You can make mistakes on or about critical tasks, so it is important to have alternatives. Because you handle critical tasks first, critical mistakes are usually found at the beginning of the project where your mistakes cost less to correct. Mistakes made early cost less to correct, thereby minimizing overall costs.

Your team looks for critical business functions and critical technical functions and investigates the combined alternatives for implementing the critical functions and the project. The team then implements the combined critical business and technical functions.

You produce your systems using many implementation cycles. Your last cycles will have few critical functions because critical functions are usually implemented early.

Contrast this innovative development process to the standard development process. Criticality is not normally a part of the requirements study of a project. Often, at the end of the project time, major logic flaws are found, and many parts of the project need to be redesigned.

The standard project usually goes into restructure mode at somewhere around 80% to 90% complete. When you restructure projects, new problems seem to appear continuously. Standard project implementations seem to remain at 80% to 90% complete for very long periods of time. Usually major project problems are found at 80% to 90% complete.

In a standard project, the project personnel try to patch the symptoms rather than correcting the problem. Patching the symptoms (of the system) does not usually work and requires more time than doing a valid redesign.

Conclusion

In this chapter, you learned how to avoid the usual mistakes while creating innovative projects and innovative enhancements to project charters. I incorporated flexible business and technical structures to make change easy and showed how architectures supported the needed flexibility. I also showed how cyclic or phased implementation provides early project value.

I showed how innovation is discovered within each project cycle and indicated how needless tasks are eliminated. I gave examples of alternatives that are used to reduce project risk and improve project value.

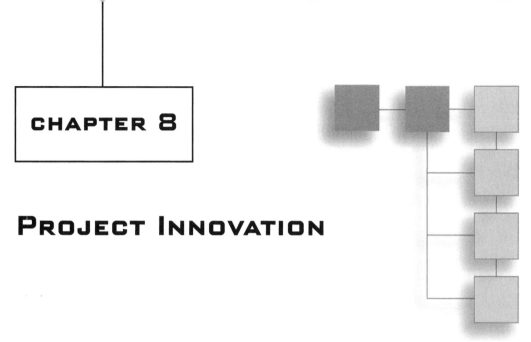

CHAPTER 8

PROJECT INNOVATION

In this chapter, I describe the key attributes that make a project and a team successful. You will use business and technical alternatives to increase a project's value. You will study how to combine business and technical alternatives to mitigate any risk that you could face in handling critical business and critical technical functions.

I will show you the key steps you must take to create and successfully complete a project. You should perform review processes during and at the end of each project cycle to help you identify unforeseen project benefits. You must continuously communicate, investigate, and negotiate with all participants to find new project benefits. You will also investigate ways of lowering the costs of this project and future projects while you mitigate risks.

Changes in Standard Project Management Processes

You want to implement projects on schedule, within budget, and without defects, and you want each project to add value to the corporation. Your added value may provide a business competitive advantage from new products, enhanced projects, or from lowering the cost of your project.

Note

You add value to a corporation by reducing the cost of projects, extending the benefits of your current products, or by creating new and profitable products.

The Standish Group International, Inc. in its *Chaos Report* indicates that few projects are implemented as required, and these projects are rarely successful. Most projects were not delivered on time, were over budget, or had many defects.

Corporations have tried to solve this problem by *routinizing* project management. They have employed many different strategies, and they have tried to standardize the processes.

They have used forms to guide the analysis, but the forms contributed to a glut of information, making it difficult to control projects. Forms alone did not control the process. You use forms to document information, but the mere documentation of information does not help you deliver a project on schedule.

Corporations added improved project scheduling tools, and they had their project managers divide projects into tasks and subtasks. They captured tasks and times to produce each task. They captured the amount of time and the personnel assigned to the tasks. They combined time and tasks to determine the project length to produce project schedules, but they found that this scheduling did not work either.

Next, managers passed the responsibility for task completion to the project members. Each member was responsible for completing his or her tasks on schedule, but this did not work and only managed to frustrate the personnel.

Several companies tried to automate project management functions. Unfortunately, the functions that they chose to automate did not work. When you automate functions that do not work, you end up with automated functions that do not work because the functions were flawed to begin with.

Innovative Project Management Processes

So why do these routinized functions not work? Standardizing processes works very well for routine activities, but project management is not a routine activity.

Project management can be performed without innovation. You need to use innovation to create competitive business and technical advantages. You will couple innovation with project management to provide a workable project structure. Your innovation will help to complete projects on schedule and within budget, adding value and providing competitive advantages.

You, the innovative project manager, need many valuable attributes, including ingenuity, courage, integrity, perseverance, creativity, respect, and trust. You will have problems implementing projects without these personal attributes. You also need to be a salesperson because you need to sell your project ideas.

With your ideas and concepts, you create business and technical competitive advantages, and you need to sell these advantages in order to properly convey your project concepts. You will identify concepts that relate to the advantages for customers, management, business personnel, and information technologists.

Your innovation and creativity will help you find the benefits for implementing new projects, and you will follow your instincts to gain project advantages. You will investigate alternatives to attain advantages or to mitigate risks for critical business or technical functions. You will find and implement customer benefits, senior management vision, business department functions, and the technology or architecture advantages.

The innovation within projects and in Common Sense in Project Management is a new concept. As a CS-PM practitioner, you need to learn what works and what does not work. You will support and control project management using specific procedures, while you and your team members identify tasks that are critical to the business and technology. You will perform a series of investigative tasks to drive your innovation.

Tasks That Drive Innovation

Your team uses processes to help identify the critical business and technical elements, including the architecture that will support the system. You hunt for innovative ways to satisfy business and technical requirements, combining both your business and technical ideas and searching for the best of the supported solutions.

You need sponsors to support you while you perform the investigations required for your innovative project. Sponsors support the processes of the innovative project manager and team, while the innovative project manager guides the assembled team to create the innovation. The innovation identifies and simplifies critical business functions while identifying the technical support functions needed to handle the critical business functions.

Sponsors support and guide you and your team to innovate and to handle critical components of the project. They guide your innovations to satisfy project needs and benefits, and they guide your project to satisfy customer, senior management, and business department needs.

Projects and project innovations always have surprises, and some of them are negative. You need to catch your negative surprises early, so you can make your project work. Other surprises are positive, so you need to take advantage of these positive surprises.

In the health care insurance project, when the company changed operating systems, our project would cause the computer to stop functioning altogether. Our project worked on other computers, just not on our company's computer. We created a workaround to bypass the cause of the problem.

In the credit project, the user departments found the system to be extremely easy to use. The users identified new applications in handling customer credit that were not part of the initial design of the system. The users created the initial added benefits. We were all able to take advantage of this feature in the subsequent cycles of our project.

You will use alternatives to critical business and technical functions to help control the project and to mitigate your project risks. Your alternatives make it easier to handle the project surprises, and your alternatives help you reach your project end goals.

You can use the forms contained in Appendix A, "Forms," to guide your team to innovate and to keep the project working properly. You and your team of innovators can use the forms for identifying and dealing with the critical elements of the project as best fits your project needs.

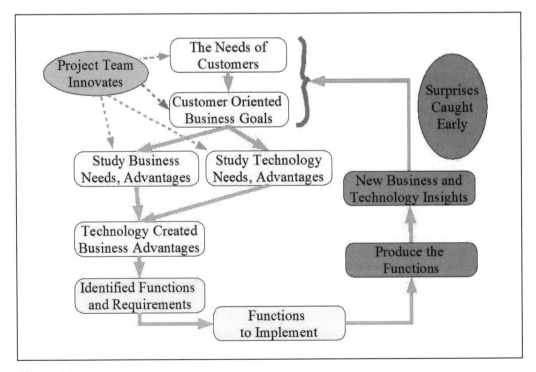

Figure 8.1
Innovating and catching early surprises.

In Figure 8.1 you can see the path your project team should take for your innovative project. You begin the process with a knowledge of customer-oriented business goals. Your team innovates and identifies business and technology advantages. You base your systems technology on your architecture. Your architecture needs to be flexible and able to handle more business processes than originally required. You do this to create new business advantages.

Figure 8.1 shows that you choose specific functions (both technical and business) for implementation. You and your team then implement these functions, and finally, at the end of the project, you perform a review, which provides new insights for both your business and technology.

These basic CS-PM processes guide your innovation process. The forms and procedures in Appendix A are a starting point for project innovation.

Your process is customer-focused (guided by what causes the customer to buy your specific product rather than the product of a competitor).

Negotiations

You will negotiate with many different people and departments within your project. In many cases, you will negotiate with senior management to include the corporate goals as senior management sees them, and you will negotiate to extend the corporate goals to include goals that your project can support. You will also negotiate with the business departments that you are serving to determine and support their critical business issues.

You will negotiate with customer representatives, and in some cases, even with the customers, to supply the benefits that the customer needs. You also need to deal with the architects of your system so that you supply the technology that is critical for the system to support your new innovations.

Your architecture and technology satisfy your technical project requirements, extend your business capabilities, add to the customer benefits, help to meet the long range management goals, and make it easier for the business departments to satisfy the needs of the customer. In Figure 8.2, you can see the critical steps to performing an innovative project.

You will complete and install tasks that you have selected for immediate implementation, and yet you have other tasks for which your requirements have yet to be determined. Note that you will emphasize and implement critical business and technology issues first. Your integration of business and technology is also key to your innovative process.

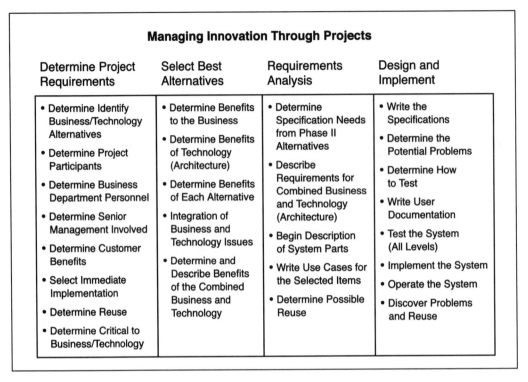

Figure 8.2
Managing innovation through projects.

A Health Care Insurance Company Example

In a large health care insurance company, my project followed the innovative process described in Figures 8.1 and 8.2. My project team created a doctor claim payment system, which replaced a system that automatically administered 50 percent of the claims presented. Management wanted to automatically administer over 80 percent of the claims.

A business expert provided a business alternative, and she provided the required business processes in a decision table format. I used her assistance to create a starting point for the technical architecture. Her alternative satisfied both my critical business and technical requirements, and yet I still needed further technical alternatives, as an architecture, for the project.

She based her business alternative upon existing, standardized health care codes and requirements. The doctors' claims could be reviewed by the system using the standard health care codes. I chose a critical architecture structure that would be used for the application by negotiating with the technicians and the business analysts. The solution was the best one for both business and technology. The architecture consisted of common reusable business objects integrated into a multitasking, multithreaded structure.

I also considered senior management needs. I used standard reporting processes to meet corporate goals. By using standard codes, I satisfied a critical business issue.

I satisfied the critical technology requirements by using a multithreaded architecture and business-oriented objects. The architecture met flexible business functions and requirements, satisfied customer needs, and met long-range management goals.

The Structured Innovative Project Management Process

An innovative project management process requires the coordination of many disciplines. This coordination is created through negotiation with all of the interested parties. Negotiations satisfy customer needs, company long-range strategies, business department functions, and critical technological and architecture requirements.

In your project, you investigate many alternatives, including your selection of the best of all your alternatives, by using the negotiation process. Your negotiation process helps you satisfy the needs of all the various areas and allocate your personnel appropriately.

You implement the CS-PM project in cycles. Each cycle takes a part of the project completely to a production implementation. Each cycle is short, and you will make a review at the end of every cycle.

You review each part of the implementation, making sure that all the members are satisfied, from senior management, business, systems, and customers. Your review is a major part of the implementation because it tells you if you need to make some immediate changes and if you have satisfied your member needs. You need to make a follow-up review later after people have had time to use your product, because the users will have found things that annoy them or advantages that they did not initially see.

You gather review and documentation materials from the negotiation process. Separate reviews are made by senior management, the business department, and systems. Each area determines what was successful and what failed, and further determines new advantages that were heretofore unseen.

You and your team will make simple corrections immediately, and you will schedule more complex corrections for the follow-on cycles. Your new potential benefits may be immediately used, or if they require work, you will schedule them for follow-on cycles.

You have innovative and talented people throughout your corporation. Your innovative people help set the cyclic and overall goals of a project. Your team, including senior management, business personnel, and systems personnel, contributes new ideas that improve business and technology, and help find alternatives. Your use of their ideas is negotiated.

Senior management, business management, and technology personnel will assimilate the provided changes, understand the changes, and describe new requirements. You will schedule some ideas and requirements for implementation in a follow-on cycle, and you will renegotiate the goals at each cycle for the follow-on cycles.

Not all projects should be completed as initially planned. Early project cycles could indicate that there is no value in completing the project as planned, and consequently, the project should either be cancelled or changed for a different form of implementation.

Note

You have many decision points within CS-PM. At each decision point, you must decide to continue or abandon all or part of a cycle. These are called *proceed or terminate points*.

You will reject many alternatives as the project continues. Senior management, business personnel, and technical support team members can reject any of the alternatives.

I have made the cyclic structure to support short duration deliverables as a rapid implementation. You should assess, price, and control each studied alternative or combined alternative. You must use the price to determine the return on investment. Finally, you might decide to terminate a project or an alternative with a low return on investment.

How Corporations Deal with the Project Innovation Process

Management will periodically review and adjust projects in its portfolio. Your innovative project provides many summary documents for senior management review. Corporate goals, the financial situation, future project benefits, and potential benefits are factors in the review. Your review information is supplied at different stages of the project.

Here is an example with a positive return on investment:

> Personnel in the credit department of a large retail organization joined together with personnel from the systems department, to study the list of future projects. The business department graded the importance of potential requests and identified the most important request.

> The company asked systems to implement a very specific function. Together, the two departments studied the list of open projects and identified several requirements that could easily be incorporated in the current project. The team added the additional requirements to the list of project requirements. The addition lowered the cost of the overall list of projects and thus had a positive return on investment.

When senior management and sponsors begin to support the innovative project concept, many projects will progress simultaneously. Multiple projects need to interface with each other. You will create benefits for one project, and those benefits will apply to another project, and vice versa. Thus, you cross-pollinate projects.

What Works and What Doesn't Work

In the following sections I give a review of some of the different process that work for innovative projects and some that don't.

Processes That Work

You may want to choose your project sponsor, and if you understand your company, you may be able to appropriately select a sponsor who will support your project and help you bring it to a successful conclusion.

You may want to have some control over the content of your project, so you will work with this group to optimize the project, the resources, and portfolio allocation. This is much like being an intrapreneur, and you may be able to choose projects that will add significant return on investment (ROI) to your corporation.

You have many opportunities within your company to network with people from various departments. Networking could provide you with valuable and usable knowledge.

In your innovative project, you will continuously encounter tasks that are critical.

You may find a way to understand and find critical knowledge and critical background knowledge. When you accumulate critical knowledge, you will add significantly to your ability to find and deal with critical information.

Processes That Probably Will Not Work

In many corporations, senior managers want complete control. Your senior management may want to control each step that you take as a project leader. You will find yourself continuously reporting and using the time that you need to make critical decisions. You may even lose the ability to make critical decisions.

You may find yourself in a company that allows almost no innovation. Your restriction and inability to innovate will make it very difficult for you to make long-term contributions to the company. You would have little time to innovate. The process may work for a short period of time, but it would be counterproductive in the long run.

You may find yourself working in a company that expects one and only one solution to a problem. They may even expect your solution to mimic the business process. When you do not have backup alternatives, you will have difficulty when something does not work the way you expected.

You may find yourself working in a company that tries to prevent project failures, and possibly doesn't accept many mistakes. You may find that, in this company, the prevention of project failures is related to producing voluminous documents backing up each of your decisions. This process will take much of your time.

A Few Notes

From the outside, it is very difficult to tell the difference between the innovative project and a standard project. The differences are subtle but very important. Project leaders using only standard processes will not be able to tell the difference. Management just observing from the outside will not be able to tell the difference. The differences are hard to see, but the results are significant.

For example, my team in the health care project was very impressed with what we were accomplishing. They tried to entice another project leader into following our lead. The other project leader said that she did not see any differences between what we were doing and what she was doing. Unfortunately, several months later, she was replaced by a different project leader.

DePaul University Networking

Many universities have the ability to give doctoral degrees, i.e., Ph.D. DePaul University is one of those universities. They offer a degree in computer science, which is the degree in this example.

There are several ways that a doctoral candidate can select the topic for her Ph.D. thesis. DePaul University provides a beneficial networking opportunity for its doctoral candidates and assists with finding the best candidates and the best topics for those candidates. Even though the school provides networking for their candidates, some candidates supply outside networking possibilities and different goals for the thesis than those of the professor.

In this case, the adviser and student picked the thesis topic. The adviser and the school provided a grid-computing system for use in formulating the test environment for the topic. The grid-computing system was being implemented within the Chicago area using the computers of several universities and government agencies. The student added new functions and system requirements to the proposed topic.

The grid-computing system consists of many different types of servers from laptops to supercomputers. The new functions provided by the student included an artificial intelligence system capable of controlling the process and all of the various computers.

Together, the adviser and student listed the functions and the benefits required to fulfill the doctoral thesis and to provide benefits for the grid computing system. They listed the alternatives with advantages and disadvantages of each. They chose cyclic procedures to provide a rapid implementation with specific functions and benefits within each cycle.

Satisfying Corporate Goals

Your corporation is faced with integrating many elements that are important to the business. Senior management, business personnel, and systems personnel can visualize the environment, but in the end this benefits the customer.

Your system must satisfy the goal of the corporation with business and technical functions that are critical. When you are implementing a critical part of the system early, it helps to understand and achieve the corporate goal.

You should implement parts of the project early when they are critical to business, the technology, or architecture. Your benefits are derived at each implementation cycle, and your project needs to provide valid customer benefits.

When you implement a project cycle, it helps the corporation. You describe the business advantages and disadvantages for each critical element. Critical business and technology functions provide the backbone of the system, as well as a benefit to the corporation.

I have included forms in Appendix A, "Forms," to assist with this process. Using these forms, you will describe the technical advantages and disadvantages for each technical element, and you will describe how you bring business and technical critical elements together.

You will combine the business and technical elements and study the advantages and disadvantages of each combination. You will create a rough cost and time estimate.

You reuse everything that you can as one of the ways of keeping project costs at a minimum. You plan to reuse through the steps of the innovative project management process, including studying existing functions for potential reuse. You will describe tasks that can be easily reused. You will avoid some reuse when alternatives clearly provide a better return on investment.

Beyond the "Home Run Syndrome"

The cyclic development process works well for innovative projects. You should take single small steps toward eventual project implementation. At each step, your implementation cycle brings some benefits into production early. Early implementation exposes weaknesses and benefits of initial ideas.

An artificial intelligence example from my own experience:

> I created a heuristic form of artificial intelligence (AI), and it is an excellent example. I performed extensive research before I applied AI to the project.

> I divided the research into three distinct parts. I used a very high level language, LISP, for the first part, and I created a technical architecture to support my use of AI. I proved that the architectural structure was correct through this research. When the theories are not correct, the process can be stopped before the cost escalates.

> In the first research project, I proved the concepts were correct, but my new structure was not production ready. I then continued the research using a second project. My second research project embedded the AI concept within a database and business structure.

My second research project demonstrated that the concept would support many different types of business processing and would form a robust support structure for business systems. My prototype was used in production and acted as a proactive monitor for a billing system at a large telephone company.

In the third step, I used two separate research prototypes to create a production ready AI system. The production ready AI system is currently being used by Cognitor, Inc. It provides problem resolution within the Customer Relationship Management (CRM) field.

In short, I met the end goal using several implementation cycles. This is similar to hitting several singles rather than trying for a home run. In each cycle, I contributed specific areas of research. Each step was necessary to prove the concepts. When implemented, my AI system provided a business system with competitive business advantages.

The Role of Checkpoints

With the innovative project management process, you divide your project into critical elements, and you study those critical elements. You use the four phases within the CS-PM process because when you take a project to production, it usually passes through all four phases, and you use checkpoints in each of the four phases.

In the first phase, you identify alternatives, describe the benefits of each alternative, and identify elements of the business and technology that are critical. In the second phase, you study the selected sets of alternatives, combining critical business and technology. In the third phase, you complete the study and begin the requirements definition. In the fourth phase, you finish the design, coding, implementation, and operation, and you create new tools that you can use in the following parts of this project or in other projects.

The checkpoints provide you with business and technical judgments. You select and implement business and technical critical requirements in cycles to satisfy your project requirements. Your checkpoints provide sufficient information for all participants to decide whether to complete or abandon the current project cycle, or follow-on project cycles.

I have placed forms in Appendix A to cover the study of business alternatives, technical alternatives, and the combination of the business and technical alternatives.

You can document the advantages and disadvantages of each of the alternatives and provide the costs and time of implementation. Your checkpoints provide the mechanism to determine just when an alternative should replace the primary potential solution.

Conclusion

In this chapter, I described the key attributes that make a project team successful, and I showed that the project team uses business and technical alternatives to create project value. I also showed that communications and review processes are continuously performed. Each project participant continuously investigates to find new project benefits. I also described the process of continuously looking for ways of lowering project costs.

PART THREE

THE TRICKS
OF THE TRADE:
ADD SIGNIFICANT
VALUE TO YOUR
DELIVERABLES

CHAPTER 9

ADVICE FOR HANDS-ON PROJECT INNOVATORS

In this chapter, I address the moderate risks that you must take to create value-added competitive advantages for your business, and I identify the problems that keep projects from being successful.

Note

Value comes from new products, extension of an existing product, or the reduction of the cost of implementing the project. Value added to projects involves the creation of a new product that causes customers to buy your products rather that the products of a competitor. A competitive advantage is the factor that causes a customer to buy your product. The reduction of cost in producing a project is a value.

I describe the salesmanship needed throughout the project to keep all participants involved. Good salesmanship helps you select the best combination of value-based project benefits. Salesmanship is at the heart of negotiating to create new benefits.

You create an architecture as the technical basis for constructing your system. The architecture provides the basis and the flexibility that allows a system to support and extend the needed business capabilities.

You should continuously upgrade the project with new value benefits, and you can add benefits to a project at each project cycle. Use a continuous learning process to find new benefits for the project or to shorten the project schedule.

CS-PM enhances the existing project steps while creating valuable benefits.

Basic Principles

Over the years, I have discovered that innovative project managers use a few basic principles. As an innovative project manager, you will be involved in establishing the project, you will gather an exuberant team that is willing and capable of proposing alternatives, you will make sure that the project goals add the best possible value to the project, and that user personnel are included in the project.

You will find and use support personnel from both inside your company and outside your company. You will also include customers if at all possible, and you will include them as early in the process as you can.

You will find critical business functions as soon as possible, and you will use a cyclic developmental process. You will also use an architecture to help make all of the implemented functions as flexible as possible, and you will work to understand and simplify the business process through the use of a systems architecture. As you create the system, you will promise less than you can deliver.

Be a Moderate but Courageous Risk Taker

You, as an innovative project manager, will take some risks, but you will make sure that the risks are well defined and controlled. Some risks (taken immediately or early in the project) will reduce the overall project risk.

One risk you will take is to use an architecture. You can achieve some large advances in competitive advantage by using a well designed architecture.

For example, I implemented a rule-based knowledge learning system using a solid technical architecture. This project was entirely at risk. However, this risk helped create a new corporation with technical competitive advantages. The new company forged ahead of other competing corporations for specific business functions because of that initial risk.

You, as an innovative project manager, will create alternatives both for the original project and for added business functions and architectures. You will select the best combinations of alternatives and select (or invent) tools to implement these combinations. You will select these alternatives because they add value to projects.

Appendix A, "Forms," contains forms to help you enhance your creativity. You will obtain and maintain senior management support for your project, and you will describe and create business and technology benefits continuously throughout your project. You will also take the time to present these benefits as a salesperson.

You will identify and review the elements of potential failure within your project. The potential failures include your not understanding customer needs and not seeing the features that are of benefit to the customer.

Your business may require a breakthrough process to change from a commodity market to a competitive advantage. Yet you need to make small and incremental changes to implement the business functions.

For example, an entrepreneurial corporation was entering into a commodity market, creating diets for people who needed to diet. This company used AI, predictive diet selection, and defined their market to be large organizations instead of individuals. The large organizations represented those business entities most in need of specific diets: hospitals and medical organizations. The diets could be specifically tailored by the large medical organizations that monitored their patients, the diet usage, and a healthy exercise regimen.

Applying diets over the Internet fit within a commodity market. The use of AI allowed each patient to select diets that satisfied the medical basis and also satisfied their own tastes. The AI process learned the likes and dislikes of the particular patient and made menu recommendations using this patient knowledge.

This definition of customer, architecture, and business process allowed them to skirt the commodity market and enter into a lucrative market. The profit in the tailored diets came from the monitoring process, which provided information to the medical practitioners, as well as the menus for the patients, for a small fee.

Note

An entrepreneurial corporation is usually the creation of a few people, it exploits a market not usually approached by other corporations, and it creates a product for sale within this market.

There are markets in which there are many corporations competing. Their products are usually similar to one another. They compete on price and have difficulty surviving. Such markets have recently included the production of floppy disk drives for the early personal computers. They also include such markets as the soft drink markets, where grocery stores have price wars every week.

You can also fail by not finding and using a good and solid architecture. Your chosen technology or architecture needs to be forward thinking, needs to fit into the overall growth architecture of the business, and may even need to include or involve a breakthrough architecture or business.

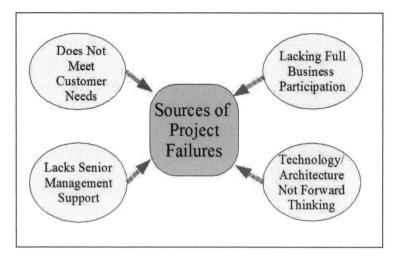

Figure 9.1
Sources of project failures.

I will discuss each of the sources of project failure as I seek to understand the elements most likely to cause project failures. In Figure 9.1, I show the four major sources for project failures. I will discuss these failures in their order of importance.

1. If you do not understand the customer's needs, you could make your project fail. When your projects ignore customer needs, you could have terrific technical successes but resounding business failures. If you do not meet the needs of the customer, you do not meet the needs of the business. You must start projects by obtaining a full and complete understanding of the features that benefit the customer.

2. If you do not obtain the sponsorship of senior management for your project, then it could fail. Senior management must want the project's output, and they must want both business and customer benefits. Senior management does not need to fully understand the project technology, but they may have certain ideas about what the customer should receive. You need to sell senior management on the features of the new project to gain their support.

3. If you do not get the participation of the business department, your project could fail. It is not unusual for the business department to not understand the business benefits perceived by senior management. Your business department performs daily tasks and does not have the opportunity to fully understand business and customer needs. The business department does not speak the same language as senior management, nor do they speak the same language as the customer.

4. Business departments see changes to systems as small and incremental. Their proposed changes may reduce or improve some internal workflow. Breakthroughs seldom come solely from the business department. Most business departments do not understand information technology capabilities, so many new systems fail to produce the system functions that could really help business departments perform better.

5. If your project lacks a solid system architecture (or valid technology), it could fail. System architectures should be used to efficiently support the business. The architecture is not the same as the business process. Proper architectures (technology) help the company to grow properly, and they provide technical competitive advantages.

Your technology needs to be forward thinking and to extend past current business usage. But if the architecture needs to go beyond the technology of today, then it is critical to the development of the business systems, and it may require special research for future development. If you need new and critical architectural elements, these elements need to be integrated with the critical business elements.

For example, you may want to bank using your cell phone. Your bank could install technologies supporting the use of cell phones for personal banking, and it needs to take special security measures to identify you. This could require the bank to use new types of cell phones that identify you. The bank would support specific transactions for which you use your cell phones.

When your systems architecture mimics the business process, your architecture will limit system and business expansion. Your valid architectures will support components that are reusable. When your business is built upon valid architectural structures, they help create the competitive business and technical advantages.

For example, in a health care field we identified and satisfied the principles of CS-PM. The customer's needs were understood, senior management sponsored the processes, the business department participated in the solution, and an advanced architecture supported the requirements.

The government required controls on increases of billing by the doctors and hospitals that were paid by the health care organization. Providers of service were restricted to the amount and number of increases over a specific time period. My database contained sufficient information for the control process.

My team produced reports for the business department to use to track changes in the doctor charges. We also provided reports and studies that required only one request item from the business department. My team accepted the unique requests for the special studies and provided the needed reports. The system automatically determined the information needed from the request and produced the reports for delivery the very next morning.

Identify Tricky Elements in the Business Process

For your projects to succeed, you need support for your critical business and technology improvements. You will present and sell the value of your critical business and technology work product to all your team members. Your team members need to clearly understand and accept the new work products as a reality.

IT personnel assume that the identified project tasks are clearly understood by all of the players, but this is not always the case. You need a constant dialog on project subjects, importance, and value to keep everybody thinking the same way.

Your innovative projects upgrade the business and architecture simultaneously and continuously, providing usable business and technology support as early and as often as possible. Your end project products are continuously upgraded, and you identify and implement new potential benefits.

Failure to approach both critical business and technology often causes projects to reach an 80% completion and then fail. Your iterative implementation allows problems to be discovered and fixed early. Early implementation also provides the opportunity to find new benefits that your corporation did not perceive before. When you deal with critical business and architecture issues, you help fix problems at the root cause.

Here is another example from the health care environment:

> In this scenario, all of the principles of Common Sense in Project Management were not followed, and the implementation was not iterative. The development team did not consider either the needs of the customer or the benefits to the business departments. In the feasibility study, the team focused only on the understanding of senior management.
>
> The team then presented the concepts to the business departments. The team did not design the system with a valid architecture but instead used the business process as the system design. The team did not divide the system into easy to implement parts.

The team did not discover problems with the design very early. Segments of the project that should have been easy to implement became failures. After several years, management selected a small portion of the project requirements and called the project a success even though the entire project was a failure.

Identifying Alternatives to Satisfy Business Needs

You install systems to satisfy the needs of customers, senior management, business management, systems, and systems management. In the following discussion, I will focus on the needs of senior management and business management.

You usually begin the process of designing systems with the definition of a specific business need. Many times you determine specifics along with the identification of the need. You have many ways to satisfy a business need.

Your innovative, information technology development can uncover new solutions to a specific business need. You will use a negotiation process to discover the best way to satisfy the need. This way you are truly building a better work product.

A credit department example follows:

> The innovative business department dealt directly with the customers. The innovative systems team met often with the business department part of the team. In fact, the group had many beneficial and fruitful lunches together, solving problems and discussing business alternatives.
>
> Both groups fully understood the features that they needed for the system. The entire group discussed business and technical alternatives to satisfy the requirements. They discussed advantages and disadvantages of each of the alternatives.
>
> The team combined the business and technical alternatives along with the best fallback alternatives. The combination satisfied the critical business and technical functions. The team recognized that if the primary alternatives did not work, then the fallback alternatives would work. Either way, the team could rapidly complete the most critical parts of the system. Because the team had fallback alternatives, they reduced the risks involved in project implementation.
>
> Primary alternatives are usually innovative and have a higher risk and payoff than secondary alternatives. Secondary alternatives are usually easier to accomplish and, when used, provide a way to remain on schedule.

In this iterative implementation, systems personnel found better business functions. The business department found more system uses and better features for the system. When the team completed the system, it provided a higher return on investment than was originally anticipated.

Be Creative about the Pathway

Your cyclic development process provides one way to consider alternatives, and your review follows your implementation cycle. Your review provides an opportunity to better understand and satisfy the needs of all team members, including customer needs, management goals, business department functions, and system architectures and functions.

Managing Innovation Through Projects

Determine Project Requirements	Select Best Alternatives	Requirements Analysis	Design and Implement
• Determine Identify Business/Technology Alternatives • Determine Project Participants • Determine Business Department Personnel • Determine Senior Management Involved • Determine Customer Benefits • Select Immediate Implementation • Determine Reuse • Determine Critical to Business/Technology	• Determine Benefits to the Business • Determine Benefits of Technology (Architecture) • Determine Benefits of Each Alternative • Integration of Business and Technology Issues • Determine and Describe Benefits of the Combined Business and Technology	• Determine Specification Needs from Phase II Alternatives • Describe Requirements for Combined Business and Technology (Architecture) • Begin Description of System Parts • Write Use Cases for the Selected Items • Determine Possible Reuse	• Write the Specifications • Determine the Potential Problems • Determine How to Test • Write User Documentation • Test the System (All Levels) • Implement the System • Operate the System • Discover Problems and Reuse

Figure 9.2
Managing innovation through projects.

In Figure 9.2 (a duplicate of Figure 1.1), I show the complete process for Common Sense in Project Management. You can add the additional steps found in the figure to the innovative process in your Work Breakdown Structure. Most of the steps that you add to your Work Breakdown Structure (WBS) are at the beginning and end of each project cycle.

Your team will have early morning team meetings, where you will assess issues. You only need to have these meetings to provide for an extremely quick implementation and when decisions need to be coordinated rapidly between all of your involved participants. On the other hand, some of your research issues would be severely hampered if team members were required to have meetings each morning.

Your morning meetings will address issues related to joint requirements and will provide a rapid joint requirements definition, wherein you will use the opportunity to study the critical business and technical issues, define the alternatives, and determine how to merge the alternatives. Your team will also assess which alternatives will add immediate value and should be implemented immediately, and which ones should be deferred for a subsequent cycle of the project.

Your team will determine how to finish the design requirements, develop, deliver, and test the processes that you are developing. Members of your team will also determine how the newly developed processes will be operated. You will find, however, that the developed processes may not be used as initially planned, although it is possible that your new processes can be used to enhance business in ways other than you planned.

When you have completed a cycle of your innovative project, you need to take the time to study and learn from the processes that have been completed. You may find that your business is not satisfied as was originally determined. You may lack some of the functionality that you anticipated, or you may find that the functionality satisfies added business features that you did not anticipate.

Your review of the architecture and the technology may determine that the technology is not satisfied as was originally determined. You may either lack some of the functionality that you anticipated, or you may find that the functionality satisfies added architecture features that you did not anticipate.

Detailed Breakdown of the Steps

In this section, I present a breakdown of the steps in the Common Sense in Project Management process. The process has four phases. I will give you a brief introduction to the phases, and I will divide each of those phases into their parts.

In short CS-PM works as follows:

1. In the first phase, you determine the project requirements and identify alternatives that could be used to implement your project.

2. In the second phase, you review the alternatives and select those that are most likely to satisfy the project requirements.

3. In the third phase, you write the requirements for your project.

4. In the fourth phase, you implement, operate, and create reusable functions for your project, and you review the results of your project.

Determine Project Requirements

You begin with a flexible set of requirements for the business followed by determining what features of these requirements are critical to the business (i.e., the functions that will add the most value to the business). You also identify the basic architectures or technologies that can support the business requirements. You identify alternatives for each business or technology function.

You need to put your team together. A team consists of business department personnel, senior management, systems management, architects, designers, coders, testers, and trainers. Your team will help you determine the customer benefits that your project needs to support.

As you study the primary functions and their alternatives, you determine which functions should be implemented early and which of the functions can be implemented later. You will have alternatives for all of the functions. The functions that are critical to the business or critical to the technology should be implemented early. That way you have good control over your project schedule.

At this early stage, you can also identify the functions that could be created so that they can be reused. If you are able to determine potential reuse at this early stage of the program, then you will be able to shorten your overall project implementation time. For example, at a telephone company I recognized and created a function that was easily reusable. That function was used 25 times before I had installed it in my own project.

Selecting the Best Alternatives

Selecting alternatives is the second phase of the Common Sense in Project Management Process. You will receive documentation that your team has prepared in Phase I of your project. You will not receive documentation for the entire project at one time, but rather you will receive documentation for the most critical functions first. Your received documentation covers both business and technology or architecture.

You will receive and review documentation that relates to the business with all of its alternatives. The documentation consists of a description of the different ways in which the business requirements can be met. You study and identify the business advantages and disadvantages of each of the functions and their alternatives. After this study, you can identify the best of the business alternatives.

You will also receive and review documentation that relates to the architecture, the technology, and all of their alternatives. The documentation consists of the different ways in which the needs of the architecture or technology can be met. You will study and identify the technical and architecture advantages and disadvantages. After this study, you can identify the best of the technical and architectural alternatives.

You need to combine the business and technical functions so that they can be implemented. In the beginning of the project, the functions that you will study are critical to the business, critical to the architecture or technology, or critical to the combination of business and technology. You can also find that the combination of business and architecture changes the advantages of the business or architecture of your project.

Requirements Analysis

You will receive information, from a prior phase, that contains the description of the combined business and technology that have already been studied and selected for implementation. You have in hand a study of the best business and architecture for implementing your project. The architecture that you received is not the same as the steps of the business process, but rather it stands on its own and will support the business processes. You know the advantages and disadvantages of each of the alternatives, and you have a combined business and technology approach. You also have primary and fallback alternatives that you can use for your project.

Here you make a requirements document for the combined business and technology requirement. Because you have these documents, your requirements definition is easy to perform and describes the best ways in which to implement your project. You further define the different parts of the system based upon the specific primary or secondary alternatives that you are describing. You mitigate the risks of your project with the secondary alternatives.

You have enough information to provide use cases to describe what you believe is the way that business will be satisfied. You also have sufficient information to make a technical use case description. Your use cases make clear the decisions that your entire team has created.

In Phase I, your team will have identified potential reuse that would simplify the construction of your system. In Phase II, you have again clarified the described reuses and possibly have identified new reusable functions. You create requirements documents for the reuse functions that have already been identified. Here in Phase III, you may again find new ways of reusing functions to make the remainder of the system simpler to implement.

Design and Implement

This is the last phase of Common Sense in Project Management. Most of the material in this phase is covered in other project management texts. I describe these so that you know and understand how CS-PM fits with your corporation's project management process.

You have the requirements definition that you completed in Phase III. You use this requirement definition to guide you in writing the specifications for the combined business and technical functions. Your business function specifications are written separately from your architecture specifications.

You determine the potential problems that you will have with implementing and operating the system. You need to write the specifications and functions so that these problems are not encountered. In this way, you make your project robust with little possibility of failure, again taking advantage of your knowledge of alternatives.

Your team needs to perform many levels of testing—testing each of the functions, either business or technical, testing the combination of business and technology or architecture together. As you add functions to the overall system, you need to perform regression tests to make sure that you have not destroyed any of the existing functions. Your testing needs to be extremely thorough and does not only test the business functionality, but also tests the robustness of your system.

Your business department and your customers will be users of your system. You need to document just how your system is to be used for each type of user. So you may have documentation that represents how your customers will use the system, documentation that describes how the business department uses the system, documentation that describes how senior management will view the system, and finally documentation that describes how the system will be operated and maintained.

You will implement the system or system part when it is ready. Once the system is implemented, it needs to be operated according to the description that you have documented. However, as the system is operated, your operations and business personnel may discover new advantages that were not perceived earlier. And so both your operations documentation and user documentation may need to be updated to reflect the actual uses of the system.

The Review

Once this cycle of your system has been put into place, you need to perform a review to discover new opportunities that were not obvious before. Your new opportunities that are discovered need to be taken back to Phase I and documented. These new opportunities may change the way the rest of the cycles will be implemented.

Your constant reviews provide the opportunity to rapidly improve the project. They help you find better ways of implementing the remaining tasks of the project. You catch major errors early while the cost of correcting is minimized.

Some Advantages of CS-PM

Early within each cycle of the project, you have an opportunity to discover new ways of satisfying business needs and technology alternatives. You will include all possible elements of the business for each alternative that could be supported. With correct design of the extended supported features and the selection of alternatives, you will not add project implementation time. Instead, your correct architecture will significantly reduce the amount of money and time spent on future projects.

For example, in the health care environment, I used a multitasking architecture with a high level of reuse. Our reuse reduced the amount of code and debugging that we needed to perform, and we were able to meet our time constraints with zero defects.

Your innovative process uses a minimal amount of work to satisfy the maximum amount of requirements. Your reusable business process and IT components are identified for reuse, thereby reducing future work. You will document, label, and index your processes in an easy, retrievable form.

In the same way, your architecture and technology provide new ways of supporting your business needs. In your processes, you should review all of the required business functions. Your specific technology functions can support several of your business functions.

Your review process forms the basis for your negotiation among team members and end customers. After your study, you may remove some tasks. Your new value components will be added to the project.

Build an Enthusiastic Team

Your team, which creates the system and completes the project, is of utmost importance. You need specific types of people to be in the forefront in all of the steps of your project. You, the innovative project manager, have ideas about how you want to implement your project. Your team members should have a different idea of how the project should be implemented, and all the team members need to be open to negotiation to construct the best possible system.

You can use several types of people to satisfy the business analyst function. Your first business analysts need to bring a library of experiences and a flexible, open mind. In large projects, you may also use other analysts with less experience. The other analysts should be open to new ideas and able to express their own ideas, and they should be skilled negotiators. Much of your work consists of identifying the critical business needs and alternatives. Your architecture and technology, when combined with creative business ideas, will empower the solutions.

Technical personnel are often hired after the business analysts have completed their work. In your innovative project, it is important for your analysts and technicians to co-exist and negotiate the chosen alternatives.

Your system structure is dictated by your architecture and not the structure of the business. Your technical architecture stands on its own and is extremely flexible and capable of changing as your business changes. Thus, your technical personnel need to be added at the same time as your business analysts.

Your first technical person needs to establish a valid technical architecture for the system, and must be able to negotiate with your business personnel, your business analysts, and possibly even with your customer. If your project is large enough, you may need more than one technical person of the highest caliber. Other technical personnel that you add later may have less experience, but they need to be eager to learn, able to discuss and present ideas, and be willing to negotiate for valid solutions.

For example, in the credit system, the technicians were added at the very beginning of the project. The technicians created the architecture that was to be used by the system. The business and technical architecture was combined, and business and technical alternatives were presented and negotiated to achieve the best of the potential solutions. This team completed their project ahead of schedule.

Your process of understanding your business and technology early, identifying alternatives, and discussing options helps to build an enthusiastic team. All of your team participates in presenting and making decisions. Your team identifies the best way to implement your business needs.

Each team member's voice is heard, and your entire team participates in the creation of the project. In order to make this work, however, you, the innovative project manager, need to be willing to place their jobs on the line. You bet your job on the results.

The best management comment that I heard came from one of my directors. I had made my presentation. I wanted an advanced system architecture.

When I was finished, the director said, "Would you bet your job on it?" My answer was, "You bet." My team was in place. We had already discussed the alternatives. I would have bet anything on my team.

Build a Network of Sponsors

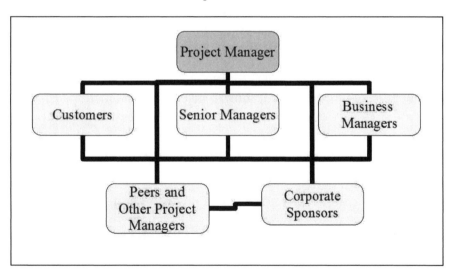

Figure 9.3
Building the network of sponsors.

In Figure 9.3, you see the people whom the innovative project manager needs as a network of sponsors. You need to create sponsors within management, the business areas, and even the customers. Your business department identifies the business needs.

You increase business benefits and add value through your robust systems architectures. To add benefits, you need to negotiate between the business people and the technical people. Your negotiation identifies the benefits and extra value that will be added to the project.

You have many different sources for sponsors, including managers and directors from other systems departments. In large corporations, rapid implementation can be attained reusing work from other project leaders. So it is important for you to network with other project leaders.

Your senior management aligns the project direction with management intent. Your senior management sponsors need to include both business and systems areas.

With the support of your senior managers, it is easy to convince managers, supervisors, and even project leaders on other projects that the support that you need is valid and would be to their benefit.

Express Gratitude

Your innovative project management process requires assistance from several levels of management and many different departments. You need to express gratitude each time you get help.

Your expression of gratitude builds good feelings between all of the personnel involved. You may need to use the good feelings to accomplish something that is a little bit tricky or difficult from either a business or technology standpoint. You may need support from many of the company personnel. You may even need to identify the personnel who support your needs from those who do not. When this occurs, you are more likely to get support from friendly personnel.

Following is an example from the city government environment:

> I wanted to use a new systems architecture to implement a system. The city needed to know if it was a valid selection.

> Our director created a debate with pro and con represented. I presented the pro while a friend presented the con. The director of the data center sat as a judge over the debate. At the end of the debate, the director decided to use the architecture.

> Even though my friend had presented the con, I needed his help to implement the architecture that I had presented. So together we immediately made plans for implementing this technical architecture. He needed to make special provisions to support this architecture. Each

time he implemented a part of the architecture, I thanked him for his assistance. When he took the time to help my team, I expressed my gratitude.

Use Cycles to Enhance Projects

Your innovative project management process implements business needs in cycles. At the end of a cycle, your new discoveries will allow more or different business functionality to be implemented at a later cycle than was understood at the beginning of the project.

I can never see much past where I have already been, and so when I reach a new plateau in business, I am better able to see new business and system uses. It is easy for me to determine a small part of the overall project. I can easily deliver on that part of the contract.

When I deliver a part of the system, people begin to use it. As people use the system, they find new applications that had not been anticipated. This is a new perspective. I often use the new perspective to determine the next system parts to be delivered.

In the retail environment, the team implemented a credit information system. The users of the system recognized that the information was usable for investigating specific credit problems.

When the team designed the system, this specific use was not described. But as the credit personnel worked with the system, they found that the credit information could be used to perform specific tests that simplified their jobs. The credit personnel wrote each other describing the new uses for the system. The project team had an extension of the initial system construct, and the future cycles were able to take advantage of the extended benefits.

Learn from Everything

You have learning opportunities at every step in a project. Your team members learn when the initial project goals are set. They learn from studying business processes. Business and architecture alternatives provide more learning opportunities. As the system is implemented and used, the synergy for new levels of understanding creates tremendous learning opportunities.

Embrace the Barriers

Project barriers provide knowledge that may be systematized. Your study of systems advantages and disadvantages reduces project risk and project barriers. Alternative studies help bypass non-optimal solutions.

Projects barriers are difficult to detect, and some potential good solutions have hidden implementation barriers. Alternative solutions are used when primary solutions encounter insurmountable barriers.

For example, I worked for a company that manufactured large manufacturing plants. They had a problem implementing their projects on schedule. They decided to implement a system to help them determine the cost of missing specific scheduled dates. There is the personnel cost that is related to the project overrun and there may be fines or lost contract fees for missing the schedule.

The design team decided to use the accounting system to track each expense for both material and personnel. If the material was not ordered and logged into the accounting system on schedule, there would be a project overrun. If the personnel did not fulfill their work on schedule and log it in the accounting system, there would be an overrun. The design team created complex formulae based on these accounting activities to calculate the cost of the overrun.

They created a monitoring system to review these complex projects and to forecast the overrun costs if the project appeared to be behind schedule. The project leader created an architecture to support the system.

Shortly before the system was to be implemented, both technical management and business management determined that the forecasts were incorrect. This appeared to be a major hurdle. The formula changes, as specified by the business, would have changed the system structure completely.

The technical team identified the types of requirements that needed to be changed. The architecture of the system did not follow the business requirements, but was able to stand on its own. The architecture was based upon a decision table structure. The technical architecture allowed the complex changes to be made within a few days.

Develop Business Judgment

If your team has good business judgment, then it adds a high level of value to the business. When your team negotiates to support good business processes, the members will begin to develop good business judgment. Your group business judgement will be enhanced when management, business, and senior management are involved in the negotiations. Your entire innovative process strengthens the bond of the people who work throughout the entire organization.

Decision Table Architectures

A decision tables provides a way of representing a complete set of requirements for a specific business function. It describes all of the possibilities that can occur within the business function and all of the different actions that can be taken based upon each possibility. Decision tables are usually constructed as follows:

Contains the list of each condition that needs to be investigated

Contains an indication of all the different combinations of the conditions being tested

Contains the list of actions that can be taken by the system

Contains an indication of the set of actions that will be taken under a specific set of conditions

A brief example of a decision table follows:

Conditions being tested

Condition Number 1	Y	Y	N	N
Condition Number 2	Y	N	Y	N

Actions to be taken

Action 1	Y	N	Y	N
Action 2	N	Y	Y	N

This is what happens in the decision table above:

When Condition Numbers 1 and 2 are met (indicated by the Y in their columns), then Action 1 is taken (indicated by the Y in its row).

When Condition Number 1 is met and Condition Number 2 is not, then Action 2 is taken.

When Condition Number 2 is met and Condition Number 1 is not, then Action 1 and 2 are taken.

When neither condition is met, then no action is taken.

Your business alternatives help further business goals and support technology or architecture. Your teams develop good business judgment through studying and understanding the alternatives. Your understanding and the team's understanding help you and your team to sell the business concepts to the business departments and to senior management.

Conclusion

In this chapter, I addressed the need to take moderate risks to create value and add competitive advantages to your business and to your project. Your salesmanship is used throughout the project to select the best combination of alternatives. Your salesmanship helps you to negotiate throughout the organization to obtain new project benefits.

I showed how architectures advance your project value. Your flexible architecture helps support continuous upgrades to projects, and you will provide early and continuous value improvements for the project and the corporation.

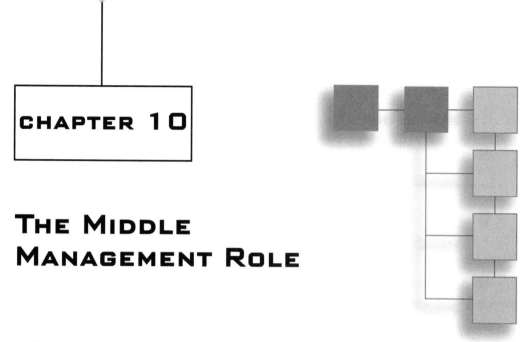

CHAPTER 10

THE MIDDLE MANAGEMENT ROLE

In this chapter, I show you how middle managers help to create the innovative project team. I describe how middle managers use all of the project participants to co-create valuable business advantages. I show how middle managers challenge and negotiate with their project teams to create projects with vision. This negotiated vision translates into business and technical advantages.

I show how the foresight of middle management inspires all of the project participants. The middle manager's mental picture can cross over many projects, and each project's advantages can come from many different projects. The middle manager's creativity inspires people throughout the entire organization. I'll show how the entire organization adds to business value over the original project charter.

I'll show how middle managers can become a focal point to help create project value throughout the entire organization. They can do this by inspiring project managers and project teams to have foresight and creativity.

Description of Middle Management Participation in Projects

The middle manager who understands innovation and intrapreneurship should easily accept Common Sense in Project Management (CS-PM) as a basis for his projects. It is important for you to know about the many similarities and differences between innovation and intrapreneurship. Intrapreneurs need the participation of all management, including middle management.

Note

> Innovation represents the creation of new products, or the enhancement of existing products. An innovative project manager finds new ways of creating new products, of enhancing existing products, or of implementing a project with less cost. An intrapreneur creates a new product, and potentially a new department to handle the product, and the intrapreneur remains in the corporation. Intrapreneurs are innovators.

The innovative project manager does not need the middle manager to participate in making a project successful. When the middle manager does not participate, the project is more complex, but it is still possible.

For example, in the insurance health care environment, I worked for a middle manager who was not innovative. He probably would have stopped the innovation within my project except that I had written authorization from senior management and participation from the business managers. He actually went so far as to hire a spy, but we were in the second or third cycle of our cyclic implementation by that time, and we had product up and running. So I managed to convert the spy to the innovative process.

A project manager with power and organizational connections can make an innovative project successful without middle manager participation. Some project leaders are able to run more than one project at a time. Usually, though, the projects are smaller. If the middle manager is not innovative, however, then the project leader can run only one major project at a time. Yet, few innovative project managers can survive in an environment where the middle managers are not supportive of innovation because their spirit would soon be broken.

In his book, *Intrapreneurship*, Gifford Pinchot says, "To a large degree, the culture of an organization is created by the actions of the middle managers." It is much easier to run an innovative project with the participation of the middle managers. A middle manager can control several innovative project managers at the same time, while creating an extremely productive environment involving several innovative projects.

In business today, the project leaders can handle several projects at the same time and not necessarily from the same middle manager. The middle manager can handle several project leaders at the same time.

The middle manager can help the innovative project managers reuse work from one project to another. I describe the process of interconnecting and reusing the work from one project to another later in this chapter, and I have placed forms in Appendix A that you can use to help identify potential reuse.

The middle manager can help project managers to assist and profit from one another. Project managers can use or reuse information from one active project to another, from completed projects or from completed project cycles.

For example, in the city environment each morning I held combined meetings with all of my project leaders. Each meeting covered the following topics:

- How critical items were handled yesterday
- What critical items their project needed to solve today
- How they intended to handle their critical items today

Project leaders from one project made suggestions to the other project leaders about how to handle their critical items. It also was a forum in which each project leader heard how specific critical items had been solved.

Vision That Inspires

Together the middle manager and the innovative project leader can negotiate an improved vision. The middle manager provides the basic resources for the project leader. With these resources, the project leader creates and runs a valid innovative project environment. Under the guidance and challenge of the middle manager, the project leader studies customer needs, determines organizational goals, investigates business departments, understands the functioning of the business department, and supports the customer.

The middle manager participates in determining the best technology to support the needs of the affected organizations. The middle manager can easily take advantage of innovative projects because the innovative projects create functions usable by other projects and other business departments. Innovative projects create and benefit from a high level of reusability.

The middle manager needs a proper identification of project functions and potential reusability. The middle manager takes advantage of the documentation that identifies the sources for reuse of elements and functions. The middle manager also takes advantage of these functions from one of his projects to another.

Note

Specific business and technical functions are identified using the critical project documentation of CS-PM. The description of each function provides the knowledge to create a matrix of requirements as a way of determining potential reusability.

The functions can be reused from one middle manager to another through senior management.

The middle manager can help identify potential reuse from the initial project leader identification of project requirements. This means that the middle manager obtains reuse information long before the design and implementation stage of an innovative project. The implementation stage is where systems personnel perform their system coding.

The innovative project manager begins reuse identification while planning a project and before designing it; the middle manager has reuse information as soon as it is identified by the innovative project manager. Identifying and reusing processes and code simplifies projects, but the reuse must fit within the needs of the business, customers, and systems.

The middle manager ensures that the innovative project managers satisfy the needs of the customer and oversees the negotiations between senior management, the business departments, and systems so that all the project requirements are satisfied. The middle manager benefits from the negotiations by setting the best alternatives for each of the projects. The middle manager takes advantage of the study of the business and architecture alternatives and concepts.

The middle manager requires, participates in, and challenges the study for combining the business structure, system architecture, and potential reusability. The study provides benefit for the customer, senior management, business managers, and systems. The middle manager may benefit from reusable functions for other projects, departments, and customers.

The middle manager challenges the project managers with his vision. His vision helps the project manager think about different business and technical alternatives, and ways of improving upon that vision. The alternatives support the project, and also help create competitive technical and business advantages. Middle managers help create new business advantages using their gathered knowledge and alternatives.

Here is an example from the credit project:

> The middle manager participated in the formulation of the team. The team was staffed in a different order than either waterfall or spiral development projects, because the technical architects and developers were added at the same time as the business designers.

> The middle manager encouraged and supported the project team during their negotiating process. The project team provided a better system through the negotiation process than was originally anticipated. Business

analysts, business management, senior management, technical architects, and designers developed the basic project requirements, and together they extended the basic requirements to provide an enhanced set of requirements.

The middle manager encouraged the creation of a better design that simplified the implementation while providing a customer oriented system. The system implementation was simplified by reusing existing systems parts, and alternatives were studied. The advantages and disadvantages of each alternative were also studied, including the combined business and technical alternatives.

Here is a thought that seems contra-intuitive, but the middle manager understood that the project implementation time would be shortened by the addition of extra studies. The project team used the EstimaX product to estimate the project implementation time, yet their project was completed in half the time of the estimate. Within the first month, the first parts of the project were demonstrable as production-ready code. The business departments increased their participation based on this success because they could see the added benefits.

In Figure 10.1, you can see the interrelationship between the middle manager, senior managers, and project leaders. The vision of middle managers is not always the same as that of senior managers. Middle managers may only have a portion of senior management goals and information.

In Figure 10.1, you can see that a middle manager may control more than one project leader. Each project leader should be controlling the business, as well as architectures, of the projects. The reuse in the project comes from the combined business and architectural functions. Middle managers should understand and promote this reuse among their innovative project managers, making reuse extend across several projects.

Co-Create Vision with Others

A middle manager takes advantage of handling several innovative projects. The middle manager can create an overall vision by incorporating the best features of each innovative project, and can bring that vision to each project environment. So it is the middle manager and the project leaders that create the vision.

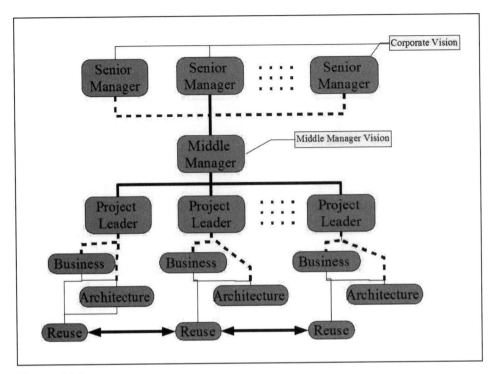

Figure 10.1
Middle manager relationships.

The middle manager can challenge her innovative project groups to work together to help create a common vision. The common vision is about the customers, senior management, the business departments, and the technology that supports the vision. The vision is an extension of the advantages of each of the projects. The middle manager supports the common vision, which is a combination of the goals of all of the projects.

The middle manager guides each project manager to take advantage of the benefits of the other project leaders. In this way, the middle manager creates an enhancement of the benefits for each organization and creates high level benefits for each project and for the company.

Here is an example from a large city:

> Within a large city environment, the middle manager was herself innovative and coached each project manager to become innovative. As each project manager became innovative, he was challenged to provide alternatives within his projects. The project managers learned to understand

the benefits for the customer, departmental system use, and the technology and architecture to use within their organizations to produce their systems.

The middle manager used the information that was created by each of the innovative projects. Each project provided a description of the alternatives for the business, the technology, and the advantages and disadvantages of each of the alternatives. Each project also described the advantages and disadvantages for the combination of business, technology alternatives, and architecture.

Each project manager understood the tasks to be accomplished that day. He or she understood the technical tasks and alternatives. If a selected alternative did not work, the project manager could decide to use another alternative. Each alternative was divided into the tasks critical for that day.

The project managers described their critical tasks for each day. They also described how they planned to handle their critical tasks for that day. Each team could build reusable tools for their specific project and for use on other projects and even other departments.

The middle manager directed each project team to understand the progress and project contents of the other projects. When a project created a tool, a tool usefulness assessment was made along with the tool documentation. The tool usefulness was investigated when the tool was being constructed. Part of the tool creation determined how the tool would apply to the different projects.

Note

The tools for reuse can come from your current project, other current projects, or from projects that have already been completed.

The middle manager directed all the project managers to work as a team. Some tools built by one group would be used by other groups. The project managers built a mutual trust level. This trust extended from the systems department to the business departments.

The process of being able to reuse functions brings up a number of questions. For example, which functions within a project should be constructed for reuse either within this or other projects? Then, as you are constructing a project, which of your project tasks should reuse functions that have been created for this or other projects? Need, timing, and production capability determine where and when a tool will be produced.

The middle manager directs her groups to discuss the actual tool production, features, and potential reuse. Object-oriented programming was supposed to provide a high level of reuse, but it is only the mechanism. Project groups need to provide specific, reusable business tools and need to describe and show how the tools are used.

Note

The forms found in Appendix A will help you to collect the required information.

For example, in the JAVA development language, there is an extensive support library for reuse. This library can be used to simplify project implementation. These are tools that are supplied by JAVA but not necessarily used by coders. The teams need to build their own business-oriented tools for reuse. For example, in the health care insurance environment, we built reusable tools for determining handling the payment of the claim. In the telephone company environment, we built reusable tools for handling telephone numbers within the system. This reusable code was used by projects within several different middle manager groups.

The innovative middle manager and project managers know that each business has common requirements. The common requirements are business processes and eventually reusable code. The teams create reusable business objects that simplify business projects. The project teams reuse the business and technical tool sets to implement their projects.

Again, there is a level of creating tools that makes sense. Making everything into an object does not always make sense. Making everything into a tool does not always make sense.

Co-Create Visions That Inspire

Middle managers and project managers have a hard time getting business department managers to participate in project construction. Business departments will participate when the innovative project managers continue providing successes for business departments. The successes are measured by simplifying the tasks of the business personnel, or providing new processes that enhance the job that can be performed by the business personnel. Successes entice business departments to participate in innovative projects.

Middle management enhances the project successes by selling the ideas to each department. Innovative project management successes entice business organizations to help create and enhance the projects that affect them. User department personnel participate because they see benefits immediately.

The middle manager sells the successes of his innovative projects to the business middle managers. In some organizations, the business middle managers are the first to participate.

Here is an example from a large insurance company:

> The middle managers from the business departments participated in finding the best solutions by helping to find the alternatives. They helped with the study and supplied analysis. The involved business managers continuously reviewed competition, the needs of their customers, and the needs of doctors.

> The business personnel knew how to improve the business. They did not fully understand how improving systems would enhance the business functionality, but they knew from early deliverables that the business would be improved. These facts made the business managers easy to approach. Networking gave the innovative project managers the knowledge necessary to approach each business manager.

In Figure 10.2, you can see all of the different departments and areas of a company that need to be focused on creating ideas. The ideas are formalized and made into parts of projects. These project parts alter the way that business works. This process is the way business and technical competitive advantages are created. The following describes a part of that process that deals with business managers.

Some business managers continuously analyze how their processes affect customers and their departments. These business managers normally will participate in the continuous and innovative discovery processes. These managers will help set corporate business goals.

When information technology personnel approach innovative business managers with innovative ideas, these managers are extremely excited and helpful. Business managers will accept the technically based business recommendations when stated in business terms and not solely from the technology. The business managers determine how these recommendations will affect customers, the business, and their departments, and they negotiate about the functionality and benefits needed.

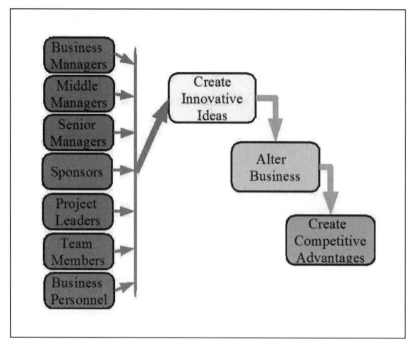

Figure 10.2
Co-creating competitive visions.

People directly involved with the business processes also need to be involved and excited about forward thinking ideas. The forward looking middle manager and project manager will network with these business people and other industry people to help them understand the potential business advantages.

Ask for Help

Middle managers are lucky when they encounter a business manager who is forward thinking. Innovative business managers accept recommendations and add their own. These business managers will negotiate to achieve their business goals and advantages.

The forward thinking business manager considers the future of the organization. This involves satisfying future customer needs and the future of the department. The innovative business manager will participate in discussions of business functionality and benefits. The middle managers and business managers negotiate, describe, and understand the advantages and disadvantages of each business proposal.

Over time, this business manager will begin to learn the advantages of applying technology through the middle manager and the progressive project manager, and will begin to formulate technology-based recommendations of new functions or benefits. They will discover new ways to apply technology. They may even begin to investigate new types of technology to significantly improve business.

These business managers would expend extra dollars to achieve a higher level of return. The innovative business manager accepts and furthers your own vision. This business manager will propose a new vision, which will help tune the overall corporate goals.

Here is an example from a health care environment:

> Again, in a health care insurance environment, an innovative business manager had been exposed to the innovative process. She used the process to improve her department and the business. Because of her abilities, she was transferred to another department. The systems services in her new department were not intrapreneurial. She continued to take advantage of the business and systems relationships that she already had.
>
> She found a way to use these services within the less developed department. She determined how to pay hospital claims using a doctor payment system. There were advantages for her. It took less time to modify the doctor payment system than it would have taken using the hospital payment system. This unusual situation was initiated because she asked for and received help from systems. She understood the capabilities supported by the systems department, and she applied these services to her current position.

Many business managers have lost any ability to be forward thinking. The innovative middle manager and the forward-looking project manager need progressive department personnel willing to advance this process. By working with advanced thinking people, the forward-looking tasks can be accomplished, and over time a non-innovative business manager may see the business advantages and allow and support the innovations.

Over time, the innovative middle manager can give business sales presentations to the business manager. This may help the business manager become forward-looking.

Become a Sponsor

There are two types of sponsors that we need to discuss. The first type of sponsor resides within the systems department, while the second type resides within the business department.

The systems management sponsor will have systems project leaders reporting to him or her. This manager conveys the need for the project leaders to become innovative. The project leaders need to take the time to learn and to practice being forward-looking. Each project leader learns to be innovative by applying the process to a project.

Following is an example from the city:

> A middle manager managed four project leaders, and guided each project leader through the innovation process. The middle manager project tasks included functions supporting the inspection of buildings, the city budget, personnel, and the comptroller functions. Each area required special attention. Personnel and comptroller functions used one project leader. The project leader responsibilities were described in Chapter 9, "Advice for Hands-on Project Innovators," and the interplay between the middle manager and each project leader is described here.

Building Inspections

The middle manager controlled the development of a building inspections system. The project had been started before the middle manager was assigned this responsibility, and the requirements documents had already been completed. The project team up to that point had not developed an architecture for the system, and had not been innovative in the creation of its requirements. The middle manager determined that architectural technologies would simplify the project and allow it to be completed.

The middle manager created a research project to study the application and to find an architecture that would simplify the project. The research team included a professor from a local university and an advanced thinking team member. Research documentation was gathered describing the potential architecture.

The research team prepared papers and reported the results and usefulness of the studied architectures, and provided a valid architecture for the building inspections project. The middle manager appointed a new project manager. The middle manager, the new project manager, and the team selected a short project for implementation to prove the validity of the research.

Budget Process

The governmental budgeting process is an extremely long process. The budget department starts the budget process at the end of March and completes the process sometime in January. Budget system changes had to be completed between January and March.

Planning a budget system needed to be extremely accurate. An innovative project manager would identify the alternatives and the advantages and disadvantages. Under the guidance of the middle manager, the innovative project manager searched for an architecture to support a fast way to implement the changes to the budget system.

A fourth generation language was chosen as the base architecture to rapidly implement a budget system from the existing information. The project manager tested the process to guarantee success. The system was designed around the high-level language.

The innovative project manager planned the base process with alternatives for recovery. The innovative project manager controlled the implementation, which worked smoothly using the primary business and technical alternatives.

Payroll

A payroll system was being implemented for personnel and the comptroller. Making payroll payments in the city is a complex process because the process has many facets. The city wished to purchase a system for payroll and a different system for personnel. This made the job of the project leader very difficult.

The middle manager used an innovative project manager to identify alternatives. The team defined a way to use distributive processing to gather payroll data. The innovative project manager found a way to use distributed data processing to allow the project to convert one department at a time.

The system allowed each department to be moved separately from the old payroll system to the new payroll system. The innovative project manager implemented this part of the system first. As the specific needs for each department were met, parts of the payroll system could be installed. This met the "implement early and often" criterion of innovative project management.

A forward-looking business manager will see the benefits of working with innovative project leaders and middle managers. From positive experiences, business managers will want their systems managers to be innovative. The business manager will request project managers to make forward-looking recommendations, and will negotiate with these project managers to achieve the best possible system. This negotiation will help the business become more advanced, and will entice the business manager to become a sponsor for innovative project management.

Business sponsors, systems sponsors, middle managers, project managers, and personnel will identify and negotiate for the creation and use of new ideas. These ideas will simplify the business and satisfy customer requirements. The innovative project leader will implement these new ideas.

The sponsors, middle managers, project managers, and interested personnel in each of the city departments discussed new ideas over coffee. This planning of ideas made the entire developmental process simpler. These informal sessions kept projects on target and on schedule. These informal sessions became planning sessions to advance each operation both quickly and efficiently.

Casual Time with the Team

The middle manager of CS-PM teams spends casual time with the team to make the team members feel comfortable with the manager and with each other. By spending casual time together, the team learns about you and your goals. The team also learns to feel comfortable proposing alternatives to complete a project.

When the middle manager meets casually with the team, this gives the middle manager a better perspective of its members. This helps the manager understand the people on the team and helps make the team as a whole easier to handle.

In small environments, middle managers find it easy to have breakfasts, breaks, or lunches together with their team members. These meetings provide an environment where the team can spend casual time together. Activities outside of work are another way to provide casual time with the team. Activities like sailing, tennis, golf, going to movies, or just out for coffee provide opportunities for casual time and increase positive team dynamics.

One of my project teams was ahead of schedule. We would select a special restaurant, have a long lunch, and then not return to work. By this tactic, I created very high morale within the work group.

Years later, I met one of my group members at a business function. That person told me that we had the most productive group in which he had ever worked. He also said that the time he spent there was one of the most enjoyable of his career.

A Network of Sponsors

When business managers and middle managers sponsor innovative project managers, the organization improves its work environment. As middle managers become innovative, they create competitive business and technical advantages through their forward-looking project managers who provide considerable benefit to the corporation.

As more projects become innovative, the ability of the systems departments to support and enhance the business grows exponentially. Project leaders continuously build one benefit on top of another. The atmosphere of the business also changes for the positive.

Usually, a systems department supports a specific set of business departments, but your sponsors can come from anywhere in the company. Many times, the work accomplished within one project has positive benefits in other areas of the company. Managers who work in a supported area have specific advantages for being sponsors. Sponsors are not restricted to supporting only one project.

In the examples that I have given, I have had many sponsors from different departments. I had sponsors throughout the company, and I sponsored people throughout the company. In the city environment, I had sponsors from many different departments, and I also sponsored other project areas.

In the health care environment, I had sponsors throughout the entire company. At times, I was able to ask and receive answers to important questions in a one-minute elevator ride. Sometimes, my one-minute elevator ride provided more information than a formal hour-long meeting might have gained me.

The forward-looking project manager can find sponsors anywhere in the company, including business departments, senior management, other systems areas, technical support, or operations. When all of these people were involved, I could select anyone from anywhere throughout the company to assist me. At the same time, I was willing to assist people anywhere throughout the company.

Faith in Your Innovators

As an innovative middle manager, you should develop innovators throughout the company. You need to make sure that project managers can perform their required tasks, and you need to show the forward-thinkers how to avoid the usual problems. Send your project managers to meetings to learn about the innovative spirit.

Bottoms Up Marketing from Ries and Trout teaches innovators to understand the customer. Innovators learn why the customer buys one product rather than another. Further, the advanced thinkers learn how to market the goals of the project. Innovators understand the buyer, the corporate goals, and the benefits and features to incorporate within a project.

I have used other books to help me fit system features and benefits into an organization. Changes should not cause problems to other parts of the business. *The Fifth Discipline* from Peter Senge is one of the books that I have used to help me investigate the effects of my changes.

There are other books of interest, which should be studied by the innovative project manager. These include:

> Michael Porter's *Competitive Advantage*
>
> *Works* by the Software Engineering Institute

In Figure 10.3 you can see all of the functions that a middle manager uses to make innovation work. The middle manager builds a network of sponsors, inspires his team, inspires other people, asks for help in furthering the vision, becomes a sponsor, and spends casual time with the team.

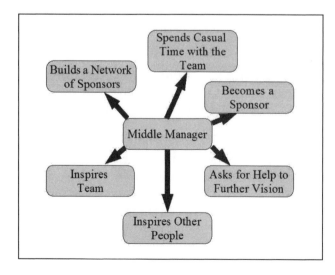

Figure 10.3
How the middle manager makes innovation work.

Conclusion

In this chapter, I showed how middle managers help the innovative project team create valuable business advantages. I showed how challenges and negotiations are used to create projects with vision, and I showed how vision translates into business advantages.

CHAPTER 11

THE SENIOR MANAGEMENT ROLE IN INNOVATIVE PROJECT MANAGEMENT

In this chapter, I will discuss senior management's role in delivering projects that help to improve the corporation's competitive value. Communication plays a big part in enhancing senior management goals. Through innovation, senior management can help create new corporate businesses and enhance corporate benefits.

You need to document your innovative projects for senior management so that they can justify the benefits to the board of directors and shareholders. Senior management wants to show the enhancement or extension of benefits for the corporation. Extended benefits often means large increases of profitability through new products or reduction of internal costs.

Senior Management Participation

Senior management participates in the role of innovative project management in two ways. They set the corporate goals and communicate the goals to the middle managers. Middle managers direct the organization toward attaining those goals. Senior management needs to set flexible goals so that more benefits can be delivered by the innovative projects.

Senior management holds the middle managers accountable for achieving or even improving on those stated goals. When senior management encourages the innovative spirit, the traditional downward flow of directions becomes bi-directional. With innovation, middle management passes innovative information upward from the innovators to senior management.

Senior management receives the innovative information, forms new insights, and alters or rejects goals. Senior management can reject goals because they do not fit within corporate goals. Senior management can take several different steps when an innovative recommendation does not fit the corporate directive. They can redirect or stop the recommendation.

When senior management accepts an innovative idea, they could decide to form a new corporation from the recommendation. Forming a new corporation is called a *spin-out*, and the personnel in the new corporation are called entrepreneurs. Senior management and the corporation will support the spin-out until the new corporation gains some foothold in the market.

The corporation will benefit from the spin-out by taking a piece (a share of stock) of the corporation. This senior management action is similar to that of a venture capitalist. Benefits will accrue to the corporation from the spin-out.

Note

A *venture capitalist* finances start-up or young corporations. The finances help the young corporation extend their market and become a profitable corporation. Venture capitalists like to have a good return on their financial investment.

Senior management could use the innovative recommendation as a spin-in to form a new division, create new products, or create new processes within the company. Benefits accrue directly to the corporation from the spin-in. The innovators that formed the spin-in within the company would be called intrapreneurs.

Note

A *spin-in* begins from an innovation of corporate employees. The innovation becomes a part of the business. The corporate employees, called intrapreneurs, are usually rewarded by the company for their creations.

Senior managers provide information about what the company intends to accomplish, and they set the corporate goal. This senior management communication expresses how the corporation positions itself within the market. This senior management communication may take the form of enhancing existing products or may extend their product base to better support their customers.

In Figure 11.1, I show the corporate potential gains from new innovative technology. The forward-looking project leaders and middle management form the new technology by understanding corporate goals. The motivated project leader investigates the goals from the aspect of business and technical alternatives. When the project leaders and middle management combine the alternatives, they can create new ideas and new business.

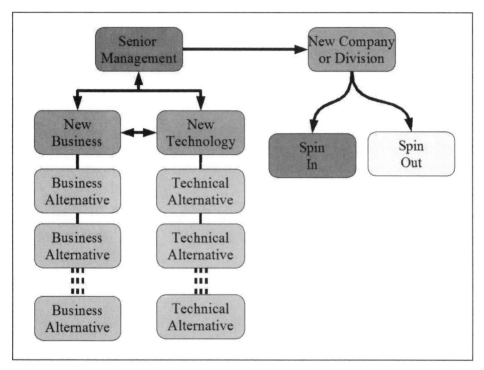

Figure 11.1
New technology creates new entities.

Together, senior management, middle management, business management, and the project leader decide that the enhanced design is sufficient to create a new entity. So the entire team forms a new business, which can be either a spin-in or a spin-out.

Senior management learns new ways of satisfying the customer when they participate in the innovative project management process. New technology, new products, and new services that are useful to the customer are provided.

Senior management may encourage an innovative company spirit. Their spirit guides middle managers, within the organization, to become sponsors of enhancing projects. As more middle managers support innovative projects, interconnecting information between projects becomes available. Each forward-looking project manager can take advantage of technology, products, or services from other project managers.

Senior managers guide innovative project managers to provide project documentation for and about the progressive technology, products, or services. Through the documentation, forward-looking project managers give examples of potential uses of each enhancement. They use examples that cross departmental lines and are good for the entire corporation.

Here is an example from a telephone company:

> I created a tool for the internal handling of telephone numbers. I had created this tool for a specific project. Middle managers understood the information, and they needed and used the same tool in their departments. Before my project was completed, this tool had been incorporated into 20 different applications. As senior management directs operational managers to become intrapreneurial, operational managers can take advantage of the developed new ideas.

Other innovative project managers or middle managers may identify opportunities in their area of responsibility. They could create new applications using the innovations. They may even extend the forward-looking enhancements. So senior management participation with intrepreneurial management carries the highest level of benefit to the corporation.

Increase Discomfort with the Status Quo

Senior management needs to be uncomfortable with the current processes used in the projects that advance the company. Computer technology projects are seldom implemented on schedule or within budget. They seldom accomplish the functions and benefits needed by the business departments or customer. According to the Standish report, only a small percentage of projects (about two percent) are successful. Few accomplish what was needed.

Unfortunately, senior management, middle management, and even project leaders accept these failures. This acceptance is unfortunate because it reflects the lack of advanced thinking in the development of projects. Senior management needs to understand and show discomfort with the status quo of project development.

The poor implementation track record is an accepted fact, which means that the systems development processes are not working. The same development processes have been used for over 40 years. New systems have only automated the tasks that we have performed poorly. We can now make the same mistakes using diagrams rather than words, and we now refer to the basic processes with new names.

Much of the work that has been put into the development of project methodologies and the development of systems did not really break new ground. Only the names have changed. So the procedures that we used 40 years ago are much the same as the procedures that we use today. They did not work 40 years ago, and they won't work today.

How do senior managers stop this unsuccessful behavior? Some senior managers now require full documentation of everything needed, which, unfortunately, just adds red tape to the process. It provides a level of documentation that does not contribute to the success of a project. Excessive documentation needs to be avoided at all costs.

Spiral development does not provide the enterprise-wide view necessary to successfully control project implementation. It does not handle negotiations to select the best of alternatives to implement a project because it lacks investigation into both the alternatives and architectures. It also does not collect sufficient knowledge about reuse to simplify the projects being implemented.

Some senior managers and middle managers restrict development to only small projects. Project leaders implementing only small projects is much different than implementing small cycles within a large project. Project leaders restricted to implement only small projects are prohibited from making innovative advances. Senior managers with the limited vision of small projects give their competitors an opportunity to create business and technical competitive advantages.

All of these behaviors and tactics do not solve the problem. So how do senior managers stop this unsuccessful behavior? They stop it by changing the environment from bureaucratic to innovative and forward-looking. Innovative senior managers change the way that projects are selected, designed, and implemented, and therefore they eradicate the problems that cause projects to be late.

Senior managers request their middle managers and project managers to be progressive by having them follow specific, innovative steps. The middle managers and project managers must be aware of the needs of the customer, the business department, and the goals of the corporation. They must also be able to identify the needs of the business that are critical and the needs of technology for a valid and flexible architecture, and they must be able to identify alternatives, select the best alternatives, and satisfy new business needs.

When senior management requires these recommendations, they are breaking the mold of doing project development in the same old way. They take a new look at ways of making the entire business work better. This makes their corporation enriched and enlightened.

Senior management needs to create the progressive process with negotiations between departments. In an innovative systems department, the business requests will change. Business requests will be challenged by the advanced use of technology and simplification of business. The business departments will negotiate with systems to find solutions superior to the initial request. These will be supervised by senior management.

Create a Stretch Vision or Strategic Intent

Senior managers need to require a continuous negotiation with each progressive project. The negotiations help find better ways to deal with the customers, set the corporate goals, and perform business functions. Some processes will be continuous enhancements and others will be break-through innovations.

Here is an example from budgeting in a city environment:

In a large city, the budgeting process is extremely difficult. The city needed to make the process simpler and quicker to shorten the time spent by departments in creating their budgets. The city needed a different procedure. Senior management was open to and supported these changes.

Aldermen could have problems budgeting for their neighborhoods using a different procedure. The aldermen would take too much time creating their budgets. When the aldermen were slow, it would be an extremely difficult task for the city to balance the entire city budget.

The project manager used an available technology to automate the budget manipulation. With the automated budget process, the budget department could play "what-if" to help determine a proper budget funding level. The budget personnel would have a better understanding of their budgets.

The budget department could use the "what-if" scenarios to study the budget dynamically. The budget department could react rapidly to disasters like major snowstorms. So when events change capital needs, the budget department could reallocate funds dynamically.

For example, a major snowstorm would cause the city to greatly exceed the budgeted funds for snow removal, causing a budget shortfall. The budget department could dynamically reallocate budgeted funds to cover the budget shortfall. The excess use of funds could be studied. "What-if" scenarios would help balance the budget under the altered monetary constraints.

Ask for Help

Senior management needs company-wide participation to make innovative project management work exceptionally well. Middle management participates and makes suggestions for improvements. Information technology and project managers make suggestions about their potential project improvements.

Forward-looking project management and information technology can enhance business benefits by increasing business functionality through their enhancements. Different systems architectures may simplify the business process or make a new business process. Senior management needs to support all these improvements.

Senior management asks each department for the specific help that they need; they need to see how the new customer interfaces and interactions work, and how the customer benefits. Senior management then begins to understand the new business environment and how technology impacts business.

Each business and technology area has different ideas about how the business should be improved. Each area must be able to present its ideas to senior management. Senior management reviews the ideas and identifies results to see if they meet company goals.

Senior management, business management, middle management, and the innovative project manager form a team. The team enters into a valid negotiation where the negotiation ensures that the recommended approaches will work together. The approaches should advance the company in the desired direction.

Senior management selects paths that contribute to the business goals based on the team discussions and negotiations about the future. Some discussions will uncover new business alternatives. Senior management will require a market assessment to identify the validity of a recommended alternative.

The team will not always be able to make a valid market assessment. Senior management will set future goals from the choices and alternatives presented by the team. These choices fit senior management's understanding of the marketplace and fit the goals of the corporation.

Remove the Blocks to Innovation

Companies sustain themselves through innovation. Unfortunately, in many companies, much of the innovation is considered to be "rabble-rousing" or "troublemaking." It is difficult to determine the difference between innovation and troublemaking.

Forward-looking project managers are always requesting information, knowledge, and ideas from their management and senior management. The forward-looking project managers are also trying to sell their ideas and looking to see if some of their ideas could be useful. To a busy senior manager, this is an interruption in her day. For example, I have heard comments stated in a derogatory manner like, "What are you selling today?" Or they could even feel that you are challenging their ideas.

If the company thrives on innovation, then progressive thinking is shown in results and competitive advantages. For non-innovative companies, innovators seem like troublemakers. Senior managers in companies sponsor forward thinking by sponsoring people who change the way the company operates. Companies change through their projects, and innovative companies change through innovative projects.

Innovation within projects can be blocked. Senior management needs to know that the enhanced design within the company is being blocked, they need to understand the cause of the blockage, and they must take action to remove it.

There are many forms of blockage. A few different cases will help to understand the potential source of the blockage.

- A blockage occurs when the project manager does not include architects in the project design.
- When the entire team, including architects, is not involved at the beginning of the project, then the project does not have a good opportunity to be innovative.
- The project manager may not take the necessary steps to identify and investigate alternatives.
- When senior management sends positive directions with no flexibility, demands that the project be done in one and only one way, and does not accept any recommendations, then the project may have an innovation block.

Middle management and progressive project management must clearly define their changes to senior management. Their description needs to include how the business deals with the customer, and how technology usage will support the business, the customers, and senior management goals. With this understanding, senior management decides how the project will be implemented and then can resolve any conflicts.

Here is an example, again from a health care insurance company environment:

> A technical system alternative identified a logical solution for a specific need. However, business issues indicated that the technical alternative would not work for business.

> The proposed solution from the innovative project manager would not have supported the long established health care documentation structure and practices. Senior management worked with the business department to set the design requirements for the system. The process satisfied the long established health care practice and was flexible enough to work with a valid system architecture.

Here is a second health care example.

> In another health care project, senior management commissioned an outside consulting company to investigate the creation of a new health care system. The outside consulting company interviewed the technical designers of the existing systems, and they designed a new replacement. The consulting company used this innovative project manager to help in the design of the new system. Their new design extended the progressive concepts used by the innovative project manager and bypassed problems that had been encountered within the existing systems.

> In yet another health care example, senior management transferred the progressive project leader to lead one of the non-innovative groups. The innovative project leader's task was to make this other group innovative.

> Senior management needed the second team to be more forward-thinking to extend their current product. The progressive project manager studied the group and identified a procedure to make this group innovative. The innovative project manager challenged the team members with specific tasks and documented the results for senior management to see.

> This initial step took about six weeks. The team provided large drawings of all the parts of their existing system and hung them on the walls. They studied potential enhancements to their system and showed how they would help the business. The team described these to senior management.

> Senior management could see the difference in the attitudes of the personnel, and could see the progressive thinking with the potential business enhancements. Senior management responded by rewarding the team and the project leader.

Search for and Reward Sponsors

In one of the preceding examples, senior management hired an outside consulting company to search for an innovative project manager. A vice president sponsored the investigation. Senior management rewarded that vice president with control over development of the new system.

The consulting company identified the business departments that needed to work with the project manager. Senior management rewarded both the business department and the systems department for being innovative. Senior management's rewards were beneficial because these were the people who would be responsible for creating and supporting the new business of the corporation.

When business and systems departments work well together, there are signs of compatibility. One such sign is that they often have lunch together. The people at many lunch meetings are trying to solve business problems, or they may be streamlining business functions.

Here is a retail credit example:

> The innovative project manager and team members met with credit department personnel over many lunches. During those lunches, the team discussed different technical topics to improve business processes. They identified a solution to some of the problems faced by the business people. The business people presented this solution to their management. As a result, an AI (artificial intelligence) system was used to determine and extend credit to credit-worthy customers. The solution was subsequently implemented and the participants rewarded.

Reward Continuous Innovation and Breakthrough Innovation

There are two types of innovations: incremental and breakthrough. Incrementally improving functions or products is an important facet of improving business. Senior managers understand and can help incremental improvements. The improvements are built upon improving what is already known about the business to make it better.

Incremental innovation is a continuous process. Management keeps track of the corporate areas that create incremental enhancements. Business management and middle management document the enhancements and uses. Senior management rewards the creating departments.

Breakthrough innovations are more difficult to create. Senior management has a more difficult time understanding breakthrough innovations when they are first proposed because they are quite different from what is already known. The breakthroughs do not follow the standard business path because they are not a change to an already understood process.

Breakthrough innovations have the potential of creating entirely new product categories. Examples of breakthrough innovations are products like sticky notes and the photocopier machine. How valuable were sticky notes? Well, sticky notes languished within its company.

Here is a quote taken from notes about Art Fry and his invention.

> …and, of course, there was the market research which is extremely difficult with revolutionary new products. Who would pay for a product that seemed to be competing with cost-free scrap paper? Despite the initial "kill the program" efforts, Nicholson convinced Joe Ramey, the division vice-president, to come with him to Richmond, Virginia, and walk up and down the streets on "cold" calls to see if they could sell the product…they did, and this almost-killed program was resurrected.
>
> The result is, as they say, history. In 1981, one year after its introduction, Post-it Notes were named the company's Outstanding New Product. Fry was named a 3M corporate scientist in 1986.

The Web location for the full quote is:

http://www.3m.com/about3M/pioneers/fry.html

The creators of breakthrough innovations almost need new departments for spin-in or new companies for spin-out innovations. New departments could be led or supported by the inventors of the breakthrough. If the creators are interested, this could be a proper reward for having created the breakthrough.

When senior management determines that the breakthrough product or process may not fit within the company, they may decide to create a new company. This breakthrough would then find its own market. Creating a new company is a spin-out from the existing company. If successful, the people who are spun-out would be properly rewarded through the success of their new company.

When innovators have created a new product, they should help to decide whether the production of that product stays with the existing company as a spin-in, or a new company is created as a spin-out.

Create a Mutable Architecture

Corporate structures are usually based upon a hierarchical structure. The hierarchical structure looks like a tree structure with senior management at the top and the worker bees throughout the remainder of the tree. In corporations, many innovations will come from the worker bees. This puts pressure on the corporation to change to accept the forward-looking ideas of the worker bees.

Along with the formal organization of a company, there is an informal organization. People attending churches, sailing clubs, golf clubs, exercise organizations and others allow senior management to meet and discuss many topics with others throughout their corporations.

Peter Drucker suggested that an orchestra is the best structure for a corporation. Every player in the orchestra has a task and performs that task under the director's guidance. There is, however, a structure within the orchestra. For example, there is the first violinist, followed by other violinists. There is no business environment involved, however. The first violinist does not direct the second violinist as a manager directs employees.

In Figure 11.2, I show a flexible business structure. All participants are responsible for satisfying changing customer needs. Senior management still directs the company. Senior management, business, and technical personnel negotiate to provide customer and company advantages.

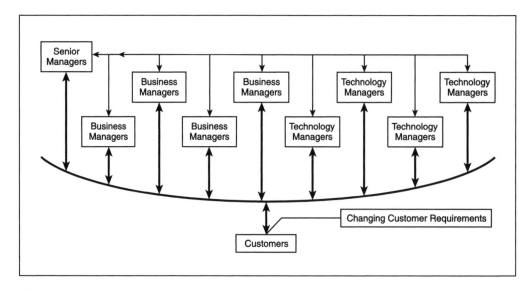

Figure 11.2
All participants are responsible for customer benefits.

A corporation may not be ready to form a flexible business structure. Senior managers can coax employees to participate in an innovative process without full senior management participation.

Business and systems personnel support corporate ideas through progressive architectures. So the systems meet the needs of the business and advance flexible architectures.

The forward-looking project manager needs to construct systems that are just as flexible as the nature of the company. An innovative corporation will quickly change its structure and supporting procedures. Systems that specifically support the old corporate structure will soon be out-of-date. Systems must change rapidly with the mutable structure of the company.

Build Choice into the System

Innovative companies do not run with hard and fast rules. These companies use alternatives to achieving goals. Specific alternatives to achieving a goal may not always be the best way. However, given the circumstances, a specific choice may be the best available.

The forward-looking project manager and team study each alternative for potential use. Through studies, the team selects the best alternative choices at the time. The progressive project manager may change the alternatives that are available at each step of a project.

As companies change, their information changes. The documentation created by the innovative project manager must support the information changes. Senior management will guide a company from its current state to a state where innovation works. This requires a senior manager to be astute.

The visionary project manager changes corporate documentation as the corporation changes. Senior management will need new applications as the corporation changes. So senior management will guide the corporation through continuous changes. These changes need to be reflected in flexible systems that are capable of supporting the corporation through its changes.

Here is an example from the city budget system.

> In the city budget department, the aldermen and city business departments used the changed system interfaces. The project manager changed user interfaces as the budgeting process continued to be enhanced. The project manager made the process more powerful and made the budget process simpler.

Budget personnel could easily review and revise their budgets and could look for budget overruns. Once the budget was revised, the budget department could use new "what-if" scenarios to determine the best dynamic budget.

As the budget department and the project manager understood the new requirements, new budgets could be easily presented for an aldermanic vote. This system simplified the process for the budget department. The flexible system allowed budgeting to be performed dynamically in order to deal with variable issues of city budgets.

Build Community: Be Intolerant of Selfish Politics

In most companies, managers tend to protect their business interests instead of the company interests. In many cases, the protection of self-interest is detrimental to the company. It may also be detrimental to the managers who are protecting their interests.

Here is an example of selfish politics from a retail environment:

I have observed selfish politics within a corporation. The project crossed departmental boundary lines with many departments participating in the project. The project manager of one of the departments used policies of self-interest.

Some needed tasks were designed and written in the department with selfish politics. These tasks were not completed when required. To complete the project, other project managers working on the same project needed to finish some of the tasks of the selfish project manger.

When performing the testing, the tests were not performed by the selfish manager when they were needed. The tests were always delayed by one, two, or more days. This delay made it extremely difficult to complete the project on a timely basis. Unfortunately, in this company these selfish politics were not observed and they continued.

Here is a second example of selfish politics, this time from an insurance company environment:

In another organization, the selfish politics were initially demonstrated by a power game. I call this game "Power grabbing through space accumulation." A systems department had file cabinets in a front hallway. A business department took control of the file cabinets and space.

This same business department did not provide information when needed by the systems department. The systems department needed the business requirements in order to complete the system design.

The systems department was judged to be behind schedule. The business department was responsible for supplying the information. The business department appeared to have the power and appeared to be in the correct position. Again, in this instance, senior management did not notice the selfish politics.

When senior management notices selfish politics, it should be stopped quickly. In this way, senior management discourages selfish politics. The process of innovative project management works with the cooperation of all involved departments. Middle managers and project managers need to bring valid issues to the attention of senior management for resolution and guidance.

Measure the Rate of Innovation

As previously stated, there are two types of innovation: incremental and breakthrough. Senior management needs to measure these types of innovation differently. I will describe them separately.

You can use existing measurement processes to measure incremental innovation. Your procedures for making changes will be used to document the incremental changes. Senior management measures each of the changes based upon the existing process or procedure.

I have provided forms and procedures in Appendix A, "Forms," to guide the enhancements. Senior management can observe the method of achieving the enhancement through reviewing the alternatives and negotiations used and documented by these forms. Your documentation identifies the different business and technical alternatives studied and used because your documentation of the negotiations identifies your specific innovations.

Your rate of enhancement should be easy to measure. Your documentation identifies the decisions of project managers and business departments. Your enhancement speed is measurable.

Over time, your innovation should become shorter or more productive. Project managers continue to build the business and technical tools that speed the enhancement. You also need to measure your rate of tool creation for implementing innovative ideas.

Visionary or breakthrough innovations are much harder to measure. However, you will use the same documentation of alternatives and negotiations to determine the rate of innovation. It takes much longer to create breakthrough innovation. Your breakthrough still needs documentation.

You still follow specific progressive processes. Most likely, your breakthrough innovation will require business or technical research and planning. Your research tasks need documentation, and your research requires both business processes and technical functions. It is difficult for senior management to measure whether the research was meaningful because there is little basis for comparison.

Here is an insurance company example:

> Health insurance companies have long required investigations into potential fraud. I made breakthrough innovations to provide a fraud detection process for them. Their fraud detection process required research covering both technical and business processes.
>
> I formed the idea from my understanding of artificial intelligence (AI) and my knowledge of the business. I needed to find the correct architecture to support the idea and to allow the business to define the types of investigations that needed to be performed. After an initial study, I found an architecture and technical structure that I thought would support the business requirement. I presented my ideas to our senior technical management, and they said, "If you can find one in the United States, then the project is yours."
>
> I searched the U. S., and I was not able to find any project that was similar. However I found an AI practitioner on sabbatical at Massachusetts Institute of Technology who believed the idea had merit. He offered to present the reasons to our senior manager. I described this to the senior manager, and he decided that I could spend half my time implementing this process.
>
> The AI practitioner provided guidance during the technical research. He was facing similar technical investigations for the field of AI. We seemed to encounter the same type of problems throughout the year that it took to complete this research. For my part, I used business process research covering the types of criteria needed to guide the computerized fraud determinations.
>
> I documented both the business and technical concepts. It was only after I performed the research that the business senior management became interested in the process.

Measure the Climate for Innovation

As the senior manager begins the innovative process, little exists as a good innovative or intrapreneurial climate. Senior managers run most organizations in a more or less dictatorial fashion. For innovation to flourish, this is not a good style of operational behavior. Project manager innovation requires a participative climate.

Business and technical departments working together increase the climate for progressive thinking. Sufficiently large companies require several business and technical departments to innovate together. As departments progressively extend their ideas more, they produce more useful tools. These tools can be used by many departments. As these tools are built, the speed of the enhancements increases, decreasing innovation time.

Senior management needs to help innovative information to cross from one department to another. The ideas for enhancing business need to flow from one department to another. But the language spoken by one department is not the same language as spoken by the other.

If a tool is created by one department, then the language used to describe the tool needs to be understood by the other department. You need to describe potential tool usage so other departments can use the tool. As a part of your documentation, you describe the potential tool uses that could occur in another department. As you discuss the tool usage topic, the language differences will erode, and the communication between the two departments will improve.

Through your description and interdepartmental communication, the description of tool usage and applicability becomes clearer. The specific processes within the two departments have different descriptions, but much of the content of the processes is the same.

Your process needs to be described in the abstract. Your abstract description helps understanding without the hindrance of names. Your abstract description contributes greatly to the reuse of the tools. Your process of creating tools for use within another department will become commonplace.

The innovations from one technical department need to cross into other technical departments. The innovations from one business department need to cross into other business departments. The information must cross freely to either business or technical departments. This is how tools created in one department are used in other departments.

You describe the potential tool in abstract terms. The second department reads your potential tool use and determines if there is a potential use within their department.

As the abstract application topic is discussed, the language differences will erode. The communication between the two departments improves. The tool usage and applicability between the two departments becomes clearer.

Note

You normally describe a process or tool in the terms that you understand from within your department. For an *abstract description*, you need to remove the departmental concepts. It also helps if you can give abstract examples of the process or tool.

The specific processes within the two departments have somewhat different descriptions and yet much of the process is actually the same. Examples of tool use contribute greatly to the ability of a department to reuse a tool.

Senior management measures the enhancement climate by the activity between the business and technical departments and between different departments. If there is a lot of reuse, then documentation will help different departments to help create advantageous end results.

In Figure 11.3, I show the multiple departments involved in the innovation process. I show an interconnection between all of the departments involved.

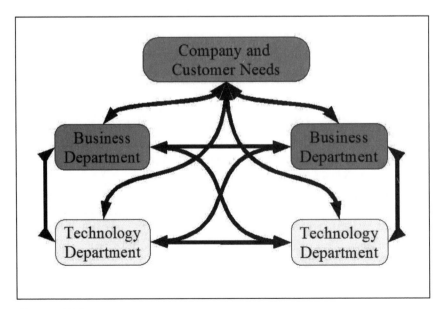

Figure 11.3
Interdepartmental innovation.

Your customer and your company need you to drive the innovation. Each of your business departments can use innovations from your other business and technology departments.

Each of your technology departments can use forward-looking enhancements from your business and other technology departments. These combined innovations should help speed the creation of business and technical competitive advantages.

Conclusion

In this chapter, I showed senior management's role in delivering projects with added competitive value. The potential is great for senior management and includes improving business and even creating new business. Your senior management will require proper documentation in business terms to keep informed. Proper documentation reduces the costs of implementing projects.

Senior management challenges those who report directly to them to create new corporate benefits. These department heads, presidents, and vice presidents pass that challenge on to the project leaders and department managers. Senior management creates and implements a stretch version of their corporate strategic intent.

PART FOUR

INNOVATIVE PROJECT MANAGEMENT WITH BEST PRACTICES

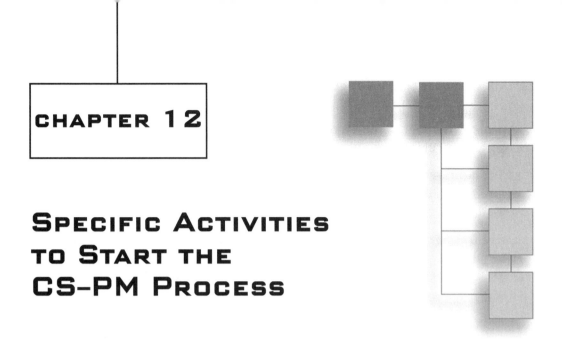

CHAPTER 12

SPECIFIC ACTIVITIES TO START THE CS-PM PROCESS

In this chapter, you will learn the specific activities that you will use to start a Common Sense in Project Management project. You begin the process with the original project charter. Since CS-PM is an innovative process, the project charter needs to be flexible so that it can be enhanced.

In this chapter, you will study how to begin the process. You will identify the features and functions that your business needs to create its competitive advantage. You will also identify the different alternatives that would satisfy the needed business requirements and features.

You can use different technical architectures to satisfy the business requirements. You will identify the architectures that are critical to supporting both the business and the technology.

Common Sense Project Management projects are implemented in cycles. You will determine the cycles that are critical and that will provide value early as a prototype in production. You will gain knowledge from exposure to business and technological reality.

Note

Instead of making a prototype that someone just looks at, you need to take your concept to production so that everyone is confronted with the reality of what has been accomplished. This is a *prototype in production*. This ensures that any problems are exposed and corrected early.

Specific Activities That Start the Process

When a company begins a project, everyone assumes that they know the solutions. Companies assume that the software structure, the business functions, the business departmental use, and the way of implementing the software are all known.

For a CS-PM project, you begin project implementation from the unknown rather than the known. You begin with a discovery process, and you try to understand the business for which the system is being implemented.

You need to know if the corporation intends to satisfy a specific customer need, a specific business goal, or specific functions or processes within a business department. Sometimes, your project will satisfy architecture or technical support needs. By finding solutions, you may shorten the system implementation time.

Your intrapreneurial project begins at an earlier stage than does a standard project. You will concentrate on both business and technology advances. You will start your technical architecture at the same time as your business study. You will support both technology features and business functionality while you hunt for business breakthroughs.

Cycles of the Process

You will implement your innovative projects using a cyclic methodology using several cycles for a full implementation. In Figure 12.1, you can see a project with several cycles.

The first cycle is nearing completion and is ready for production implementation at Phase IV. The second cycle is nearing completion at Phase I. The remaining cycles have not yet started. Each cycle consists of several steps.

You will use several cycles to control and implement specific elements of a project. You will reduce the amount of time needed to implement a project through your cycles. You will reduce your implementation time because your initial steps are designed to find implementation shortcuts and reusable functions.

You, the innovative project manager, will search for existing features or functions to simplify project implementation and to reduce your implementation time. You will identify and align customer needs with overall corporate goals. You will match these needs with simplified business processes. It is easy for you to match needs with processes and with potential architectures.

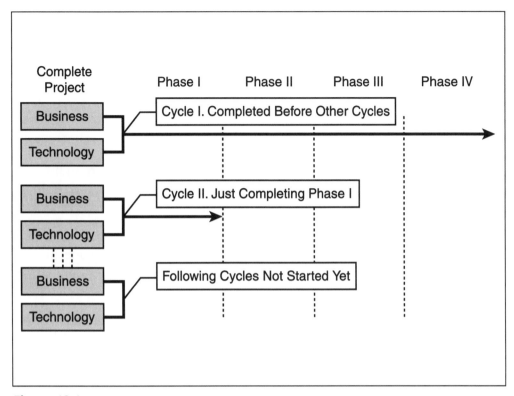

Figure 12.1
Cyclic development process.

You will match needs with goals to help form a system architecture. Your architectural structure will support business well into the future. You will support business in a flexible way through your architecture. Your flexibility allows business to change easily. Your systems can change to support business as it changes, and do it without having the change cause a delay.

You will require only a few days to complete your first tasks. You will identify requirements as tasks and project studies. You will select and implement portions of the requirements that are critical to the business, while you spin off other portions to follow-on project cycles. Your first cycle is not a prototype but is production ready.

For your early implementation, you will require all the people and tasks to make the process work in the production environment. You immediately will correct any problems that you encounter with making the process work.. When you create a prototype, people may believe that a process will work when, in fact, it may not. When you prototype for production, you will create a production system as rapidly as most people take to create a prototype.

Prototypes usually receive a cursory review from the involved parties. These parties may accept the prototype. People do not have to use the prototype, so they are not overly critical of the prototypes.

Parts of the prototype may not be workable, but those parts often remain undiscovered. Personnel may not discover that a prototype does not meet the needs of the customer and may not meet the needs of senior management or the business department.

In your innovative project, your early production implementations are significant parts of the project. You will satisfy the requirements of the customer and business goals with your project parts. The business departments use your project parts.

Once implemented, your team reviews and corrects the project parts in production. Once corrected and implemented, you can further simplify your project development from your existing project parts. You have built a solid foundation for the remainder of the system.

In a CS-PM project, you select parts that are critical to the business and to the technology for early implementation. Your innovative system parts, which have been implemented early, are critical to the business and the technology.

You implement your project process in cycles, implementing the most critical cycles first, rapidly and early in the project. Implementing early helps to identify the misunderstood requirement descriptions and helps you to clarify both business and technical concepts.

You find your mistakes early in the process. You complete a cycle early, place it in production, review the results, identify mistakes, and repair the mistakes. The cost of correcting the mistakes is low when you find your mistakes early. Project mistakes are costly to repair at the end of a lengthy project.

Here is an example from a large retail environment:

> The credit process was started as a study in the large retail environment. The team selected specific alternatives for early system implementation. For one of their alternatives, the team used database functions from an existing system. They needed to make only minor adjustments to make it work.

> The database handling was changed and immediately implemented. The team showed the business department these implementation results. The business department requested only minor changes.

The project manager planned this cycle in one week. The team made modifications from the existing system, which took two weeks. The team spent the fourth week testing and showed the results to the business department at the end of the fourth week.

Meanwhile, the team was investigating other technical and business functions and planning other early stages for the project. The team used the same forms that are contained in Appendix A, "Forms," to identify and study alternatives.

From the study, the team selected alternatives for system implementation. They used the waterfall developmental methodology for each implementation cycle. After the team implemented a cycle, they made reusable tools for future system development.

Building and Using Tools

You make an innovative project successful by building business and technical tools and fitting them into an architecture. Michael Porter introduced the concept of a competitive technical advantage, and you make the technical advantage with your architecture and technology. With innovative project management, you build both the business and the technical advantages.

Its business advantage is a critical foundation of your business. You build your technical tools around the critical business advantages. You build your technical tools around creating a technical architecture.

You merge business and technical critical items to form a formidable business and technical competitive advantage. I have depicted the high level procedures in Figure 12.2. Your team technologists review critical business requirements. You need to create a workable technical architecture to support your requirements.

Technologists review your requirements and propose different support architectures. Each of your proposed technical support architectures would support business in a different way. Some technical architectures would provide business opportunities not supported by other architectures.

Your business designers and technologists will negotiate to choose the best potential implementation for both business and technology. You will have merged critical business and technical processes.

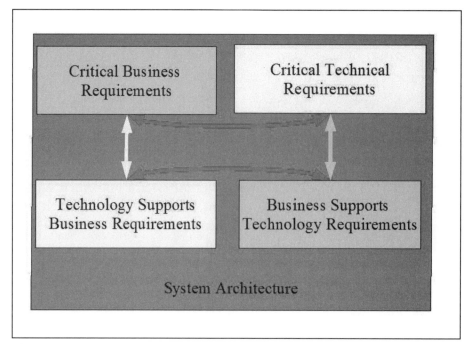

Figure 12.2
System architecture.

Merging critical business and technology processes helps you to form a competitive barrier, making it harder for a competitor to enter your market space. You form a solid competitive advantage, supporting future business expansion through your merged critical business and technical advantages.

Usually, you start projects to satisfy a specific need. Usually, the processes and systems that satisfy these needs are assumed to be known. Using CS-PM, you will instead look at the specific need and determine how to do it better, or you will find other functions that can be supported with the same construction and implementation effort.

You start your innovative projects with an investigation followed by negotiation. You will have merged few business and technical processes at that point. You start your large projects by selecting business and technical processes, and combining them. Once they are combined, you bring a critical portion of the project to production as a first cycle of a project.

You place a business element of the project into production early. Once in production, your business takes advantage of this new function. Once your function (potentially a process) is being used, all of your limitations in the design and implementation are exposed. With this knowledge, you enhance your function to make it better. You improve your remaining project cycles through your knowledge about enhancing the exposed function.

Once you have implemented the initial functions, it becomes easier to schedule the remainder of the project. You will know more about the functions and requirements within the project.

Here is an example from the health care environment:

> In the health care insurance payments project, we gained advantages from building tools. The team created a technical architecture to support the required business functions. My technical systems team easily created the architecture.

> The technical team used the architecture to achieve specific business goals. We used the architecture to help gather historic claim information. Through the architecture, we simultaneously ran many tasks (or threads). We used specific technical functions for each subtask or thread.

> The team created reusable processes, which were reusable simply by making a one-line macro call. Macros helped the team reuse parts of the system. Today these macros would be called abstract objects and would be the basis for new objects. Macros and abstract objects form a basis for reuse.

> The team created business functions through the macros. The system used these business functions and health care contract usage to make payments. One specific business function determined whether any personal benefits remained by contract and benefit type. The team reused these business functions by writing macro calls or abstract object calls.

Note

A *macro* is a system function that creates a program call simply by placing the macro call within a program. A macro call causes the code to be created within the program. An abstract object is code that can easily be modified to perform a specific task.

Each macro was a tool. Team reuse of tools was automatic through the macro or use of the abstract objects. The team documented usage and reuse examples so that others could easily reuse the code. In the documentation, they described the purpose and use of each macro or object.

Java is one of the languages in wide use today. A team using Java provides this documentation with standard Java documentation. The team described the order in which the macros needed to be used. They described usage order and macro usage, forming a high level specification (which is like a running scenario). Technicians were assisted by this description and running scenario.

Identifying Critical Business Elements

The term *"critical to the business"* identifies something that a business cannot live without. For example, your competition is breathing down your throat, and in order to compete, you need some business function that will help you to compete. You and your project team need to understand what the necessary business functions are.

Necessary business functions are those that your business must have to succeed. Your business has, or desires, many functions. Your business can ignore some of the business functions because they are of little benefit to the company, and your company would not miss them.

Your company needs other functions that are so elemental to the business that if they were not performed, the business would lose customers or might run afoul of some government regulation. Some missing functions might cause your company to fail to provide required documentation or any of several other requirements critical to the success of the business.

I will discuss some techniques used to identify critical business functions. You can easily identify and document critical business processes because these processes become the foundation for creating or changing your business. Analysts use documentation to determine how to control your business change.

You need to access your documentation easily. You need access to any of your corporation's business or technical concepts, and you could use an intelligent access of information.

You should capture your business and technical information in an intelligent database system. You will find and use your captured information more easily when you use an intelligent database system. You also need knowledge about primary and fallback procedures.

Your intelligent documentation accessing process should help direct your project toward the ultimate implementation. Your accessing of the recorded information ensures that important information will not be lost or forgotten.

Here is an example from the food processing industry:

> In a food business, a company that produces mayonnaise, candy, salad dressing, and cereals, senior management needed product volume information to better run their business. They needed information to determine business issues critical to running the business. Senior management reviewed reports to help determine future product quantities for production. If the company produced too much product, there would be spoilage. If the company produced too little product, then sales would be lost to competitors.
>
> Senior management needed this critical business information to support the profitability of the operation. This company needed to control production plants for each time period. These reports helped management decide what to produce, where, and in what quantities. This is critical to the business.
>
> The technical team produced these technical functions to create these critical business reports. The team housed the technical functions in a technical architecture.

Satisfying Business Issues

Companies use systems to address specific business issues. Sometimes, a business begins a project by stating the business issue as a solution. In many cases, that solution statement becomes the architecture for the system. Systems architectures that follow the business structure are difficult to keep current as the business changes.

You must carefully describe your business issue in business terms. You describe your ideas in terms of the marketplace. Note that the description of the business need is not the description of the system architecture.

Here is a description from the insurance industry:

> Many insurance companies are composed of only one company that serves the physicians, hospitals, clinics, and more. This insurance company was composed of different parts. One part pays hospital claims, another part pays physician claims, and a third part pays the remaining portion.

> In order to be competitive, these parts of a company must appear to the public as one company. The company can achieve this objective by informing the patient about the entire health care coverage at one time. The company will convey all of the appropriate information to the customer in one envelope. One document describes the insurance coverage.

Senior management begins the project by describing a specific goal. Senior management passes this goal description down through the ranks of business managers. The senior management goal description is stated in terms understood by those involved. Eventually, the goal description is given to systems. This last description usually becomes the architectural structure of a system.

You need to modify your work process slightly so that senior management state the goal to business management in business terms. In turn, business management states their understanding of the business goal or business need and gives it to systems. Business also needs to determine the different alternatives that could be used to satisfy their goal or need.

Business management, systems management, and an innovative project manager can define different ways to handle the business alternatives. The project manager can add new alternatives to satisfy the business needs through the application of technology.

In the system environment, the project manager defines a valid supporting architecture and alternatives. Your architecture must be flexible and able to support several different business alternatives. You, the innovative project manager, and your team will study business issues and technical architectures. The project team logically combines the business and technical alternatives and selects the best solution for the combination of business, technology, and architecture.

Figure 12.3 contains a guide for each cycle of a complete innovative project management process. You begin the process by determining the business, technology and architecture alternatives, and your team identifies critical business and technology issues.

Your team identifies the business and technology alternatives and the benefits of each. Your team combines the business, technology, and architecture and continues with the process within a development cycle for a part of the project.

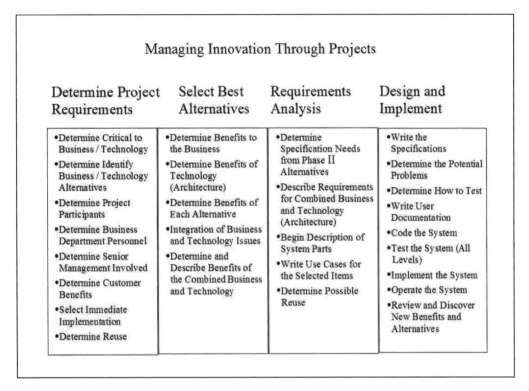

Figure 12.3
Managing innovation through projects.

Why Is This Issue Critical to the Business?

Successful businesses handle the issues that keep their customers returning. Business issues are critical if they can help the company forge a competitive business advantage.

Many business issues are not critical to the business. Many are issues of convenience. Issues of convenience may not be strategic to running the business, they may not help to keep customers, or they may not satisfy the working needs of the business department.

For example, the layout or appearance of a business report is not a critical business issue. It is more an issue of clarity and not one of competitive business advantage. Specific business issues are not critical if they have little impact on the business or if there are other issues that have a much larger impact on the business. Critical issues affect the customers, benefit senior management, or benefit the business department.

Business personnel could believe that a specific issue is critical to the business. When the innovative project team reviews the issue, it may determine that the issue is not critical. You will use a review by peers, middle managers, senior executives, and even technical architects to help determine if a specific issue is critical to the business.

The review team identifies a critical issue with specific documentation, describing its need in the marketplace. The review team identifies the potential business gains and losses, and determines whether an issue is resolved. I have placed forms in Appendix A that you can use to help determine issue criticality.

Business people document the impact of issues on the business and the ability of the business to deal with its customers. There are times that your description of the impact of the problem is sufficient to define workable alternatives. It is possible that the business issue may not be critical.

Here is an example from a health care insurance company:

> Many times, businesses believe that specific issues are critical to their operation when, in fact, they are not. For example, in a health care claims area, a process automatically determined claim payments. Management felt that specific claim types should be automatically paid more often. At first, this seemed like a valid request. Each claim not paid automatically required a person to determine whether the claim should be paid.

> The company needed to consider a new type of health care. This change provided the project manger with the opportunity to enhance the architecture and simplify the system. If the project team enhanced the architecture, then the business and system was easier to perform and to modify, and the cost for maintenance was lowered.

> The project team could implement the change directly, or it could enhance the architecture of the system. Of the two business alternatives, the second would provide a much higher return on investment, so the company chose the second alternative. The project team upgraded the architecture by having the system perform a simpler claims process.

Alternative Business Processes

Companies use business processes to satisfy one or more business issues. The company may use several business alternatives to satisfy a critical business issue.

Here is an example from a large manufacturing company:

> The billing process in a large manufacturing company needed to be simplified. An innovative project team performed the study. There were two different business processes. These processes illustrate this point.

> The manufacturing company manufactured bulk product. Most of the customers were repeat customers. The shipping location for most of these companies was constant or was limited to a few locations. The billing location for most of these companies was also constant.

> Here is the first alternative:

> The project manager proposed two different solutions. The first was a distributive solution. Each division could perform its own billing. There were a limited number of customers. To bill the business department, personnel would select the customer, product, and other information, and the system would prepare the bill; the captured information would be forwarded to the centralized accounting system.

> The team performed and prepared timing studies determining the amount of time personnel would need to complete the information entry. Once the distributed information was entered and validated, it would then forward this information to the central processing system.

> Here is the second alternative:

> The project manager proposed a centralized solution for the second alternative. The centralized system would gather the customer information, product, billing address, and other sales information. Timing studies were performed to determine the time centralized personnel needed to complete the entry.

> The study indicated that it would take twice as many people using the centralized alternative. The obvious selection is to use the distributive entry alternative.

Within any project, there are many business alternatives. You must investigate each different alternative for its ability to satisfy business needs. The solutions must fit within the business and within the projects.

It is possible that the solution might be exceptionally good for the business, or there may be no way that the solution would work within the project or company.

The project manager should conduct a short study to determine whether a solution fits the business or ongoing projects.

All organizations run multiple projects simultaneously, and this includes innovative organizations. You will have business and technical functions in some stage of development in each of the projects. The project team documents these ongoing projects. Each project team investigates each business or technology segment for possible reuse. You investigate past and current projects.

The project team should reuse business functions and processes from other projects. A project team may have specific business functions or processes in development in one project, and may use the business function or process in another project. The developing project may even benefit from some assistance from a potential user project. The assistance may help the project teams make the business function and process more reusable.

Your project team may use a completed business function, may need to change the function, or make it more abstract before using it. You need to make business functions into tools, thereby making business tools.

You will find that tools are usually abstracted to make reusable functions. If the business function is not a tool, then you must abstract it to form a tool. Each of the functions must be properly documented to be found and reused within a project.

Note

A *process* or a *tool* consists of a series of steps. We tend to think of the series of steps specifically as performing a task for a specific need. The process is abstracted by preserving the series of steps without the specific need. For use, the uniqueness of the specific need is added back to the tool, and the tool is then used to perform that specific task.

Your projects must satisfy the goals of the corporation. Your project must also be directed toward the customer, because it is the customer who buys the products and thus drives the corporation. It is the customer's perception that causes him or her to buy your company's products.

The customer either chooses your products or those of a competitor. One of your goals is to shape the perceptions of the customer, so you need to describe your company's goals as related to customer perceptions. You filter out goals that do not satisfy the customer needs.

You do not satisfy all of the company's goals with a single project of the company. You need to set goals that are clear and easy to understand in order to satisfy this project. Your project documentation must provide a clear description of how a project enhances a specific company goal. Your description identifies how this project fits into the goals of the other projects.

The goals of one project may dovetail with the goals of another project. Corporations can create breakthrough business processes and breakthrough technical functions by adding to and reusing the existing set of reusable tools. These topics would add considerably to the length of this book, and they would not add significantly to your understanding and use of the practices contained herein. I am reserving these topics for a later discussion.

Identify Critical Technology Elements

The system architecture should not be taken directly from the business process. You will find it hard to change a system architecture that is derived directly from the business process. Business changes, business processes change, and so your systems need to be flexible enough to change.

There are two types of technically critical functions:

1. A related business process is critical.
2. It forms the system architecture.

A critical business function and its critical, supporting technology relate to an application function and not to the system architecture. The health care insurance process, which I have discussed before, is an example. The project had critical business processes, and the applications depended upon their working. The project also had critical architecture questions. The architecture required the system to be multithreaded. Both of these technologies were separate and needed to be combined and tested together.

Your project team investigates critical technology issues that are at the heart of the business application. If your business application were not satisfied, then your business would lose many customers. You support the business application with your technology issues.

Issues are critical to the technology if they can help a company forge a competitive technical advantage and a business competitive advantage. You will forge business competitive advantages through your critical business issues. You will occasionally forge technical competitive advantages through your critical business issues.

Many of your systems issues are not critical to business or technology; they are issues of convenience. These convenience issues are not strategic to running the business, and they are not strategic to technology evolution. Issues that follow the structure of the business process are not critical to technology. You provide the flexibility required for the business processes to change through your technology. When you provide issues for clarity, you do not create a competitive technical advantage.

Sometimes, people believe that a specific issue is critical to the technology. A review by a team of peers, middle, and senior managers may show otherwise. The team can tell if a described issue is really critical by reviewing the documentation. The technical advantages that you provide by your technical issues will indicate whether an item is critical.

Business and technical people can tell if an issue is really critical when there is sufficient information about the impact on business from your technology. You reflect your business issue on the ability of the business to deal with its customers, which ability you sometimes determine from the description of the problem. At other times, your description helps determine that the problem is not really critical.

Alternative Technical Processes

Processes satisfy technical issues, and each of your processes will need to satisfy one or more technical issues. You may have several technical alternatives to satisfy critical technology or architectural issues.

Your project may have many technical functions and many alternatives for each technical function. You will investigate each technical process and alternative to determine how well it satisfies business, technology, or architecture needs. Your technical functions must fit within the business, and architecture within the projects.

Your solution might be exceptionally good as a piece of technology but may not work within the project or business. You will demonstrate the technology fit for ongoing projects with your short studies.

Your organizations run many projects at the same time, and your company may have many technical functions at some stage of development in other projects. You must investigate these technology functions for reuse in the innovative project.

You may find a technical function that is in development for another project, and it may need some assistance to make the technical function more reusable. You may reuse the completed technical functions directly.

You may need to abstract your technical functions for use. You may find technical functions which are technical tools that have already been abstracted for reuse. You must have a clear understanding of how technology satisfies specific company goals and a clear description about how a specific goal is enhanced by this technology.

Initial Study of Business Alternatives

You have already described the business approaches. For each approach, you described how the approach meets the business requirements and how your business alternatives provide ways to bypass problems that you encounter during your project. You have already described the advantages and disadvantages of the business alternatives. You will combine business and technical requirements for the best possible business implementation.

Corporate data processing environments usually make the business process the design structure of the business systems, which is a business-oriented architectural structure that is difficult to change. Your business processes need to change to meet the requirements of your customer. It is better if you make your technical approach the architectural structure of the system.

Your technical approach should be an abstract control process capable of supporting the business structure and requirements that allow the business to be flexible. You satisfy your business goals with your business approach and technical architecture.

You will assess each combined business and technology alternative to find the alternatives that give the best, reasonably priced business support, and you will use them to implement the system. You perform a trade-off analysis for the combined business and technical approaches.

As in all projects, you need to know your time frames and costs. Your management, business personnel, and technical personnel have many questions such as:

- How much will it cost?
- When and how can you prove that what you propose will work?
- What happens if your primary design does not work?
- What can you do immediately that will improve my business process?

As the last part of this process, you prepare budgets for the overall project. Your budgets cover the implementation that will be done in cycles. You will implement some tasks immediately.

You will also prepare the timeline and milestones for both the overall project and for the immediate project. Your immediate project becomes the focal point and will be taken through a full project cycle.

Prototyping Immediately for Production

Your intrapreneurial project combines critical business and technical elements, and it studies their use for implementing the business functions. Because you use a cyclic implementation, you create benefits for the new system as rapidly as possible.

Your critical elements are implemented first. Your critical elements are the ones most likely to cause the project to fail. If your critical elements are unworkable, you will use an alternative. With your alternatives, you reduce the risk in projects.

Note here that your critical element is different from your critical timeline. The critical timeline is described in the Critical Path Method. In most project methodologies, the critical time element is used and closely observed.

Note

The tasks within a project can be divided into several, separate groups for implementation. Each group forms a line. If one task (task A) must be completed before another task (task B) then task A is placed before task B. Task B is dependent upon the completion of task A. A project divided this way will have several different lines required for completion. The line that takes the most time is called the *critical path*.

There is a problem with the critical timeline. The problem is that your critical timeline could be satisfied, but your critical element (which had a shorter timeline) may not work and could cause project time problems. You may have other problems outside the critical time path that might be dependent upon either technical or business critical items. Either business or technical criticality most often cause projects to fail.

You need to implement the critical element of the project as early as possible. Critical elements within the project complete a full cycle before other tasks start. You will find that all of the studies that help you determine alternatives, criticality, and time criticality precede the phases of a typical project plan.

In Figure 12.4, I show the steps that you take to create both business and technical competitive advantages.

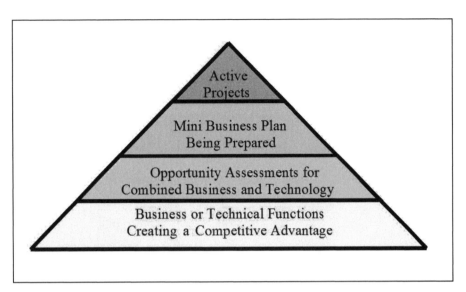

Figure 12.4
Determining business and technical criticality.

Conclusion

I have shown organizations how to begin their projects. The CS-PM process is an extension to your existing project management processes. CS-PM helps you and your team identify business and technical critical items, and it provides for the negotiation to find the best way to implement your projects.

It also provides for negotiation with all interested parties to identify and add value to projects. The procedures include identifying and supporting business requirements that add a high value to the project, and helps you and your team find and describe alternatives to the critical business requirements. They also help you and your team identify and describe critical architectures and alternatives to support these critical business requirements.

You will create tools that simplify current and future business and architectures. You will implement your project using a cyclic development process with early delivery of your project. This makes the process easy to adopt. The cyclic implementation process helps add value to your project.

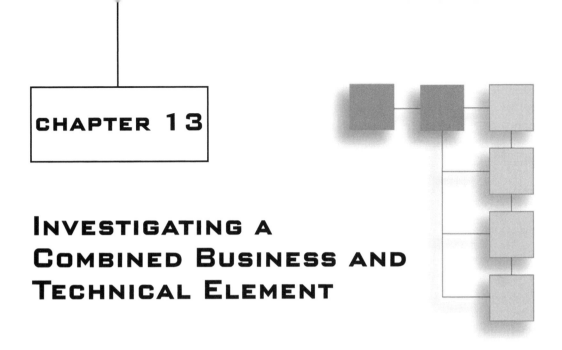

CHAPTER 13

INVESTIGATING A COMBINED BUSINESS AND TECHNICAL ELEMENT

In this chapter, I show organizations how to combine the business and architectural elements to create a more competitive value than promised in the original project charter. I show you how to add innovation throughout the life of the project by adding elements that can be used and reused. Reuse reduces time, minimizes risk, and increases current and future value.

I demonstrate how available personnel can alter the way a project is implemented. You may choose specific implementation alternatives based on personnel availability. I make specific recommendations about significant portions of the project. My recommendations ensure that you will add considerable value for each part of the project.

The concepts in Common Sense in Project Management are easy to adapt because they extend your existing project management processes. You will continue to negotiate between business teams and technical teams, and your business and technical teams learn from each other.

A Short Review of the Process

You studied business, technical, and combined business and technical solutions as you began your innovative project. Your solutions satisfy the needs of the customer, senior management, business departments, and systems departments.

In your first phase of CS-PM, you determined the most likely alternatives to satisfy the project needs. In your innovative project management process, you will combine two or three business and technical elements to provide you with alternatives or options for implementing the project. These options were passed to Phase II for your further review.

You combine business, technical, and architecture alternatives to form a complete solution. You study these combinations in Phase II. You select the best combined solutions for an early implementation.

The solutions that you have selected consist of business and technical critical elements that will fit into an architecture. Your combinations are used to solve business issues and also provide a technical architecture. You selected your best combined solutions for early implementation: the solutions that are critical to the business and to the technology or the architecture.

You place other alternatives on hold. If your primary alternatives will not work, then you will use the secondary alternatives. In extremely critical projects, you will study and pass the alternatives from Phase II to Phase III. You will select project elements from your study results. You will advance these elements to the next phase to be implemented.

Study Process for Business and Technical Solutions

As part of your study, you will examine each particular combined business and technical issue. You will study your combination in relation to the total system so that your solution fits within the project. It must benefit the business department, senior management, and the customer. You must fit your solution into the system architecture.

You will describe the fit of your combined selections for each of the combined business and technical issues. You will indicate how each alternative relates to the fully integrated system and which alternative best supports the goals of the corporation.

As you did in Phase I, you will have a cost associated with the Phase II performed studies. Your project leader determines the cost of combining business and technology solutions. If your cost is acceptable, this combination will be passed forward to the requirements study of Phase III. Management uses your cost estimates to help determine the solution validity and financial viability.

You will need to make your systems satisfy all of the needs, including customer, senior management, business management, and information technology. You will implement your innovative project in phases or cycles. As you implement each cycle, you need to know how well the needs are satisfied. Did the implemented part satisfy the needs of the customer, senior management, business management, and information technology? Your integration and your changes must be well understood.

You will combine business and technology solutions as system parts for your overall system. You will select systems parts to pass to Phase III for requirements analysis and Phase IV for implementation. You will supply information from Phase I and II that contains enough information to support your existing project management processes.

You can use the waterfall, spiral, or any other methodology to complete Phases III and Phase IV. The waterfall and spiral methodologies are well known. Your business and technical combinations contain sufficient information for you to proceed to Phase III for requirements analysis.

You will study your business and technical combinations, which will satisfy the known needs of your business. You will study your combination of benefits in Phase II, and these results are also known. You will know early the difficulty that you will face in implementation of your project. Your Phase I and Phase II studies help reduce and mitigate your risks throughout the project.

You will implement your project in phases. The scope of this part of your project phase is small. When you have completed this study and it has been approved, you will pass this part to Phase III and Phase IV for implementation. This part of your project consists of the best selection of your alternatives and backup alternatives.

Remember that if your primary alternative does not work, then you will use a backup alternative. You selected your primary alternative because it provided the best advances for the business and/or for the technology and architecture. Your primary alternative is usually not the simplest one to implement. There is a chance that this primary alternative may fail, and you will need to use the backup alternative, thereby reducing the project risk and possibly some of the benefit of the primary alternative.

Here is a health care example:

> In the health care insurance environment, claim personnel use the health care claim as the document for the administration of payments. The claim personnel use standard, industry wide codes (CPT4 or ICDA9) to describe the procedures and actions that were used for the health care process. The automation of a claim could be made far easier by using a completely different coding structure. This primary alternative was rejected based on sound business reasons. The coding structure used throughout the industry could not be changed to meet our internal needs.

Note

> CPT4 and ICDA9 are health care codes that are common in the health care industry. CPT4 describes the procedure that a doctor performs on a patient. ICDA9 is a code used primarily by hospitals to identify the illness.

Looking for Part Reuse within the Solutions

Architects have tried to create a systems environment that provides a high level of reuse. If you can reuse parts of a system, you will lower your cost of systems implementation. You need to plan your reuse, rather than have it be discovered accidentally.

Here is how you look at finding reusable processes. You break down each process into a series of steps. Each step is written describing the specific process and without business-oriented vocabulary or jargon. This makes an abstract series of steps. You compare the series of steps from a number of processes that you have documented. If your series of steps satisfies several documented processes, then it is reusable, and you can create reusable programs. When you reuse a program, that program does not need to be written a second time.

You should identify reuse at the design level. You should not leave the identification of reuse to the programmers. When you leave the discovery of reuse to programmers, then reuse does not happen as often as when you design reuse into your project and plan for the program to be reused.

For example, in the health care environment, the project team identified both technical and business functionality that could be reused. We were making a multitasking, multithreading system. In order for the programmers to create an application that would be threaded, they only needed to code two macros; those macros took care of the multithreading.

Note

> To create a reusable program, you create an *abstract series of steps*. You turn the abstract series of steps into a program. To use the abstract program, you call that program with data unique to your current need.

We also had common business processes that we needed to code, such as making the payment. We created an abstract payment program. The programmer coded a macro that called the payment program and gave it all of the unique information that it needed to handle the payment. These two features, technical- and business-oriented, fit within our architecture.

Your reuse should be supported by the system architecture. You include and plan your reuse needs to fit in the system architecture. System and program reuse has not worked as well as it should because project leaders have not made reuse a part of the architecture or design process.

You design your reuse and don't let it happen by accident. Your study of the systems structure helps to identify reuse. You select your system's architecture to support reuse. You identify reuse at every opportunity during Phase I and Phase II. Reuse must start with your initial studies for system implementation.

In Figure 13.1, I show the concepts of reuse beginning long before the requirements analysis. I have identified reuse in the first phase. Reuse is important and belongs with understanding what is critical for the business and technology.

You begin creating programs for reuse in the initial project studies. You continue your concepts of reuse through the selection of alternatives and into the study of requirements.

You will create new reuse items in the last phase. You will create reuse because it has been designed. You implement the design with reuse. You perform all of the work of creating reuse during the implementation phase.

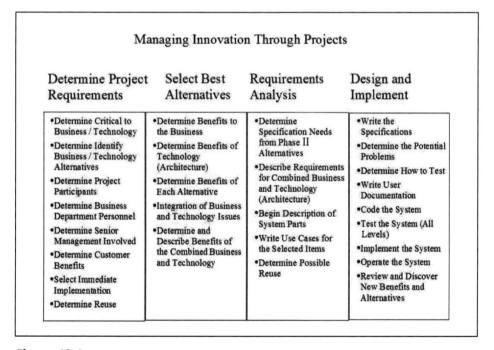

Figure 13.1
Managing innovation through projects.

In Phase I, you study business and technical elements for your production system. In Appendix A, "Forms," you will find forms that are designed to guide your early design and creation of reusable objects. When you begin your project, there may not be existing, reusable functionality. Your study also helps to determine the business and system complexity.

You need to review each element for the creation of reusable, abstract objects. You will consider some reusable functions and benefits as critical, and you will produce these early. You will have passed these functions into Phase II for investigation.

Here is an example from a large telephone company:

> The handling of telephone numbers needed to be reused, and yet I was not able to find a good example of telephone number handling. I prepared a reusable design to handle telephone numbers. The team programmed the process, debugged it, and made it ready for reuse. This process was quickly reused 25 times. Project managers reused it before it was installed in the system for which it was required.

Use of Available Talent

How you use the abilities of personnel is extremely important. How well will your personnel carry out the required functions? What are the capabilities of your personnel?

Your personnel design the system, study the business requirements, and program. They test the business and technical requirements, and they produce the objects and modules required by the system.

You create resource estimates that encompass all of the activities. Where possible, you will include the capabilities of your personnel in your estimates. Your requirements need to include the work for the primary and secondary alternatives; they need to include your preliminary testing plans and testing requirements to take the project to the implementation.

You need to consider the ability of your staff to implement specific alternatives. In the past, I have rejected the best of the alternatives because the correct personnel were not available. The alternatives you choose need to be the best possible given the personnel involved.

Here is an example in the health care environment:

> I had a design alternative, which would have integrated several different types of health care that belonged to specific processing groups. If I could implement my system using the primary processing groups, I would have shortened development considerably. Unfortunately, the one person capable was in the hospital and her absence forced me to use an alternative.
>
> The technical personnel did not have enough experience to create the architecture required. I used a simpler architecture. The team determined the level of architecture to be used.
>
> If this capable person had been present, I could have provided reusable functions to handle 50 types of health care with just four application modules. With this person absent, I was forced to handle each type of health care separately. I was, however, still able to use reusable functions within each of the modules.

Conclusions and Recommendations

In this section, I present the sets of actions that you should use at the end of each project phase. Your specific business or technical solutions may be passed from one project phase to another. Or your specific solutions may be stopped at the end of the current phase.

Your potential solution may be stopped because it will not work. In the health care example discussed earlier in this chapter, I changed my implementation recommendation based upon the available personnel. I used the skills of each person on my team, and yet I combined business and technical solutions in my approach.

At each phase of the cycle, I made a "continue or terminate" recommendation. The conclusion of your study of combined business and technical approaches helps you to determine whether to make a continuation or a termination recommendation.

You must satisfy the customer with your selected approach. You, the project manager, understand how your approach satisfies the customer. You, the project manager, understand and know how the customer will react to recommended project changes.

You initiate some of your business recommendations through the architecture and technology, and you initiate some of your architecture recommendations through business requirements. As your study progresses, you will highlight competitive advantages with your new knowledge. You communicate these advantages as new project recommendations. Your recommendations are made during the study of combined business and technology.

You, the project manager, also investigate how your approach will affect the company. Your selected approach must have benefits for both the company and the customer. Your approach is good if it benefits the customer, enhances corporate profitability, or enhances productivity.

Your current implementation should simplify future system implementations with reuse being one of the simplifiers. Your system should be easy to maintain with little downtime, and it should be easy to use. Being easy to use and maintain makes your system more able to satisfy new needs for business, the company, senior management, and the customer.

Your project began with an understanding of your business. You identified and understood what was critical to your business. You identified what was critical for technology to support your business.

If you use a specific technology, you will support business in one manner. If you use a different technology, you will support business in a different manner. You have paired a business process with an element of technology as an alternative. If your primary combination is rejected, you would use your secondary combination of business and technology.

You identified alternatives for both business and technology. From your understanding of the alternatives, you drew conclusions about the usefulness of each alternative, and you used your conclusions to form your recommendations.

For each of your alternatives, you recommend either to reject or continue this study as part of your project. Your decision to continue means that the project will continue. You will use your gathered knowledge in the next phase. In the next phase, you will perform a requirements analysis. This requirements analysis is Phase III of the innovative project.

Normally, for a specific business benefit or technical approach, you will recommend two alternatives. You will select one alternative for the requirements analysis. Your other alternative will be held in reserve.

If your project is extremely critical, you will select both the primary and secondary alternatives and pass them forward into the requirements analysis in Phase III. When you work on more than one alternative simultaneously, you reduce the risk and guarantee a successful conclusion.

Your first alternative may be successful, meaning that your secondary alternatives are not needed. On the other hand, if your first alternative does not work, you have a second alternative in reserve. If this part of the project were critical, your alternative would be already in process; otherwise, it is in reserve and ready to be completed. This mitigates the risk of causing the project to fail or to be behind schedule or excessively over budget.

Sometimes, you can only determine the usefulness of your alternative when it is implemented. At other times, you discover your alternative success during your alternative study. Sometimes, usefulness of your alternative is discovered during your requirements analysis. Remember that if your first alternative does not work, then your secondary alternative is used.

Here are examples of use and non-use of alternatives:

In the large retail environment, most of the primary alternatives were used and the secondary alternatives were eliminated. For example, using the database handling from an existing system was the primary alternative, while creating the database handling specifically for this system was the secondary alternative. The primary selection worked, so the secondary alternative was not used.

In another case, the amount of credit information for a specific customer could be voluminous, requiring more than one screen to display. The first alternative provided a slider bar to control the access of the information. The secondary alternative scrolled full pages. The first alternative worked, so the second was not used.

In the health care insurance environment, I used most of the primary alternatives. However, business requirements forced us to use our secondary requirement. The CPT4 codes, the description of doctor services, are used to administer all health care claims. Doctors use these codes to identify the procedure performed on a patient. It would have been difficult to abandon this industry standard code for one created for internal company usage.

In the large telephone company environment, we established secondary alternatives, and the secondary alternatives replaced the primary project alternatives. The primary alternatives had been set prior to the use of CS-PM. The project manager determined that he was having trouble with the project and needed to find a solution.

We initiated CS-PM and quickly identified alternatives to the initial project plan. One of the critical tasks was divided into two parts. Each separate part was assigned to a different designer and technologist. Separate technical alternatives were used to implement each part.

Another segment was simplified through designed reuse. The reusable functions were advanced to Phase IV and were implemented early. The reuse simplified the implementation of a large part of the system.

These two major changes allowed this system to be implemented on schedule.

In all of these projects, the project manager made specific recommendations to management for project continuation.

When you search for alternatives to implement a project, you can more easily create business and technical competitive advantages. Your alternatives reduce the project risks.

You will implement parts of your project early. Early implementation reduces risks and helps you to create competitive advantages. The knowledge that you gained from your studies and your early implementation helps you to create competitive advantages.

Your alternatives, your early implementation, and your knowledge help your project participants to create reusable parts. Your reusable parts provide alternatives, assist with your early implementation, and help you create competitive advantages.

Conclusion

I have shown organizations that combining their business, technology, and architectures adds value to their projects. The functions that I have shown in this chapter help projects to combine their critical business and technical or architectural requirements. Your combination precedes your current project management processes and introduces procedures for innovation. You also learn to negotiate to identify business and technical advantages that add value to your projects.

I have identified how the creation of reusable parts adds value to your project and to your future projects. I have shown how you use available personnel and how it plays a large part in the alternatives that will work within your project.

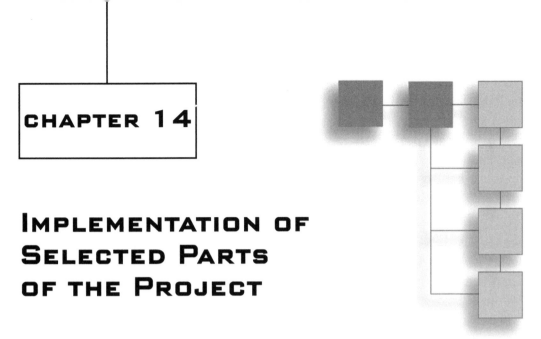

CHAPTER 14

IMPLEMENTATION OF SELECTED PARTS OF THE PROJECT

In this chapter, you will learn how to deliver and complete projects and project cycles. You will discover more competitive value that can be delivered. Your value can be above the value promised in the original project charter. Your project can be delivered in cycles. At each cycle, you will add value to your business.

You should implement the most beneficial alternatives at each cycle of your project. Your benefits are both current and future. You will simplify your future projects because of discoveries you make in your project. I will also show you how to understand and create tools for reuse.

Review of Prior Steps

I extended the basic structure of the innovative project management process from NASA's Phased Project Planning (PPP) process. PPP provided an initial project investigation phase. Next, NASA used a phase for the study of alternatives. They followed the alternative study by the requirements analysis of what would have been a waterfall process. In their final phase, they implemented and operated the product of the project.

In Chapter 12, you addressed the first phase of PPP. From the functional side, you performed your initial investigation and creation of alternatives. You determined what was important to your business and to the architecture of your system by the identification of your critical business elements and of your critical technology.

You reduced and mitigated the risks in your project by creating alternatives, and you shortened your overall process by investigating tool usage. You investigated further to see if you could find any existing tools that you could put to use, and when you did not find any, you determined how to create new tools. From an operation standpoint, you identified project personnel for your team, including sponsors, management, business department participants, technicians, and system architects.

In Chapter 13, you dealt with the combination and study of alternatives for tasks within the project. Alternatives are for both business and technology. You combined and created several business and technical alternatives. You can use some of these alternatives to implement your system. You select your best apparent combination of business and technical alternatives. Alternative combinations, which you will use for further development in Phase II, are recommended at the end of Phase I.

In the first two phases, you worked through your flexible design and created alternatives. You selected at least two alternatives for your combined business and technical objective. In Phase III, you will perform standard development methodology processes, starting with requirements analysis, where you design and continuing through to planning for development.

As you start Phase III, you have prepared business and technical alternatives from Phase I and Phase II. You brought your implementation plan with your primary selections to Phase III for requirements analysis, implementation, and production. You also brought your combined alternatives to reduce and mitigate your project risk and to ensure that your project will work.

Your early implementation cycles contain critical project parts. When you implement the early cycles of your project with critical issues, you leave less critical issues for future project cycles. If the early phases of your project work, then the remainder should be a cakewalk because each remaining part is less critical.

In this chapter, I will be discussing both Phase III and Phase IV. In Phase III, you will perform your requirements analysis. In Phase IV, you will develop and implement your project.

These phases are similar to a standard project. Thus, there is no need for me to spend an enormous amount of time on them. You probably understand these processes well.

From Alternatives to Implementation and Operations

You begin your requirements analysis in Phase III by using your combined alternatives from Phase I and Phase II. The amount of analysis that you performed during Phase II depended upon the funding that you were provided. If you have any remaining alternatives that were not studied in Phase II, you will need to complete their study.

After you have completed the study of your alternatives, this brings you to requirements analysis. You can use most of the material for your requirements analysis from standard project management books.

Typical titles for your Phase III and Phase IV tasks include:

- Information planning
- System definition study
- Global design
- Detailed design
- Implementation
- Installation
- Operation and control
- Future state process mapping

The standard developmental process contains no method or controls for creating new tools or common functions. You simplify business processes and the implementation of systems when you create tools and common functions.

Common functions are processes that you can use to perform more than one specific task because these tasks are usually reusable. Your tools are processes that make your specific job easier to accomplish.

Phase III completes your study of alternatives and creates requirements for your system. In the last part of Phase III, you identify new functions and tools that you could use to simplify this current project as well as future projects. Your tools make your systems implementation easier. Your tools are for reuse.

In Phase IV, you write specifications for your system, code, and debug it. You test it against business requirements, you install it, and you operate it. You produce special code for your reusable tools where needed.

You have documented the possibilities for reuse in Phase I, Phase II, Phase III, and Phase IV. Your documentation of reuse makes it easier for your future projects to reuse the code and for you to reuse code for this project.

Many practitioners are not able to define reusable functions or processes until a project has been completed. Other practitioners never define any reusable functions. Your creation of tools and documentation at the end of your project simplifies the design and development of future projects and future cycles of this project.

Your project team creates far more useful information while designing an innovative project than you would create for a standard one, because you take advantage of your extra information to improve your development process. Your extra information becomes knowledge, and you use that knowledge to create competitive advantages. Your knowledge is also used to handle early implementation and to reduce risks.

So you have no reason to redevelop documented processes, existing processes, or tools. Existing tools provide for reuse within the innovative project management process.

You have been exposed to the innovative project management process called Common Sense in Project Management. I have shown you some examples of how you use the process. I have shown where CS-PM fits in your development process.

Appendix A, "Forms," contains forms that I have used in the past to control my innovative projects. Paper forms are not the most ideal way of controlling projects, so I am providing automated versions of the forms and of the tasks for inclusion in your project plans. On these forms, I have provided interesting information for controlling your projects.

Check Appendix A to see the different types of information that I have used in creating my innovative projects. You can then use these concepts to shorten the amount of time it takes you to implement your projects. Finally, have fun while you make implementing your projects shorter and more profitable.

Creating Tools for Reuse

One of your primary functions of the Phase III and Phase IV processes is your creation of tools for reuse. In Phase I, you identified existing tools that could be reused, and you identified the potential to create tools that could be reused. In Phase IV, you create those new tools.

Your new tools consist of reusable code and reusable processes with full documentation. So your process or code gets created for your specific project, and it is adaptable for reuse for other projects. You make the implementation of current and future projects easier with your reusable code.

I show one of the ways in which you can identify and build tools in Figure 14.1. Programs perform many steps within business systems, most of which are the same series of steps, only using different names so programs perform the series of steps with different data. The data could look quite different, while the series of steps is the same.

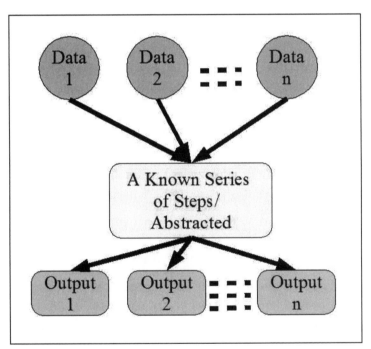

Figure 14.1
A concept behind reuse.

For example, posting data to an account or placing a new salary for an employee really amounts to the same series of steps. You know your [account | employee]. You know the data layout [amount | salary]. The specific record is obtained from the database. The information is posted. Then the [account | employee record] is placed back into the database. Notice how only the names within the steps are different while the steps are the same.

You create either abstract objects or macros so that your code can be reused. You use your abstract object as a basis from which the code will be reused. When you reuse the object, the reusable object handles different information than the original use. In each use, you handle different information.

If you use macros, then you create the macro. If you use objects, you create abstract objects, which will perform your abstract function. In each application, you make an abstract call that uses your macro. You use this style with languages like LISP, which has macro support.

You use abstract objects and macros to support either the creation of business functions or technical architecture functions. Your reuse creation should not be used to create standard "if-then" or "perform" structures. Rather, your abstract business functions should be the processes that are created for reuse. Your abstract business functions are unique to your company and can become the basis for your creation of a business and technical competitive advantage.

Obtaining Insights from an Implementation Phase

Cyclic development helps you better understand your needed business processes. Here are two different viewpoints. The first is from the business, and the second from the technical standpoint.

In business, you used a specific required procedure. At your project start, your business personnel understood the business functions that could be added. When your process is complete, you observe what was really needed.

You look for those things that seemed correct when you planned the project. You determine if different processes could better support your business. You can only make this determination once your process is being used by business personnel.

Did your business implementation provide the needed benefit? We now have a clearer picture of the needed benefit. Did we have a misconception about the needed benefit? Is the benefit we envisioned really what was needed? Possibly the process accomplished more than was anticipated. We now can experience an insight about the requested business process.

From your new business understanding, you need to review other open processes. You need to apply your gained knowledge to the remaining parts of your project. In many cases, this process will change.

Potentially, the change to the remaining parts or cycles of your project could be drastic. You will determine how to implement the remainder of the project. This is a benefit of the cyclic implementation process.

On the technology side, your team planned to implement a specific procedure or architecture. Your technician or architect understood the technical functions to be added. Now that the process is complete, you can observe what is really needed.

We look for technical functions that could have been more easily completed, and we look for alternatives for handling these technical functions. You may have some alternatives that could have been simpler or may better support business.

Did your technical implementation provide the needed benefit? Did you have a clear picture of the needed benefit. Did you have a misconception about the needed benefit?

Did you accomplish what you had in mind? Was it what you needed? Possibly your provided technology or architecture accomplished more than you anticipated, so you now can experience an "ah-ha" about your requested technical process.

Using your technical insight, you need to review other open and required technology, and you need to apply your gained knowledge to the remaining parts of your project. In many cases, you may change your technology or architecture. Potentially, your change could be drastic, causing you to change the way you implement the remainder of the project. Again, this is the benefit of your cyclic implementation process.

Conclusion

Your CS-PM process is an extension to your existing project management processes. I have adapted the standard project management processes and extended them to discover new business and technical advantages. Your new advantages will be implemented in one of your next project cycles.

You have also discovered reusable functions. You can use these reusable functions in your follow-on project cycles and in other projects.

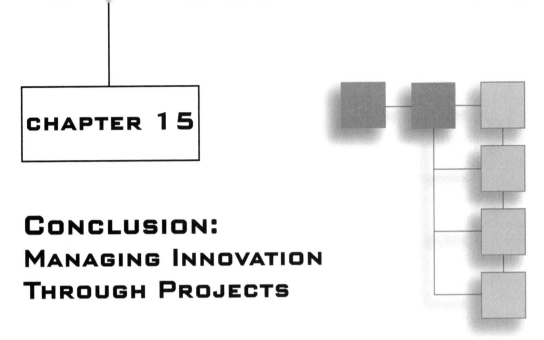

CHAPTER 15

CONCLUSION: MANAGING INNOVATION THROUGH PROJECTS

You have seen how your organization adds value to your projects. CS-PM is a common sense extension of existing project management processes. It helps to make an intrapreneurial project manager of every project manager. You saw checklists for innovation.

In CS-PM, you negotiate with senior management, business management, your business team and technical teams, and even customers to identify and add value to projects. Your innovation creates value within your business and combines the benefits of business and technology.

You added value to your project through a cyclic or phased implementation, through the team members, and through negotiation.

You delivered competitive value in your project by identifying and using your innovative skills, using processes that help create innovative ideas, and recognizing the importance of people who are idea generators. The ideas included different alternatives to satisfy the business needs and different architectures to support the business. Through negotiation, you enhanced the new business and architecture ideas of all of your team members, including senior management, business management, your business and technical teams, and even customers. You learned how to find and identify your innovative sponsors, those people who supported your searches and negotiations to help create a better project. You learned to have your business people challenge your architects and your architects challenge your business people to create enhanced requirements for your project.

You created new value-based ideas for your business and your architecture. These new ideas made your products easier for your customers to use, simplified how business handled its tasks, or reduced the cost of implementing your project. You gained and used these new skills and negotiations to create competitive project value. You found that there were ways to make your systems more flexible through different architectures, and you used these architectures to reduce the cost of creating projects and maintaining systems.

You studied the different missions of each of the participants. Senior management sets your initial project goals. Business personnel and technicians extend the initial ideas of your senior management by searching for better ways of performing business or system architectures to support the business, and to make the systems flexible enough to help business create both business and technical competitive advantages. You have gained innovative skills that support both business and your technology and architecture.

You build your innovative project, extending the business that you are able to perform, around your flexible architecture, which will support not only this project but other and future projects. You now know how to obtain both business and technical competitive advantages while minimizing your risks.

You identified your business requirements and used your business alternatives to add value to the project. Your architecture shortened the implementation time for the project and made it easier for you to implement your projects faster. You also used your architecture and your technical alternatives to enhance your potential project value and to create technical competitive advantages. Your alternatives helped reduce risk and create competitive advantages.

You used a cyclic or phased implementation to immediately provide value to your project, and you gained and used knowledge from your early implementation to create more competitive advantages for your corporation.

From Basic Concepts to a Working Project

You can create a project from the basic concepts using innovative project management techniques. You move through your initial project concepts, finding what is critical to the business and what is critical to the architecture of your project, while you gather support from all your corporate stakeholders. You identify, address, and extend the capability of your business by supporting the technology that makes it easier to implement your system.

You need to understand the benefits of team participation. Your team identifies and extends the business aspects of your system, those technical innovative ideas that support your business or provide your architecture, and you network these ideas throughout your participating company divisions. This entire team searches for improvements to the business. Your networking helps discover innovative, business, and technical competitive advantages. You uncover new knowledge through these advantages, which leads you to discover new business and technical value.

You build a project plan for cyclic or phased implementation. You implement your critical business and technology or architecture needs, thereby adding value to your project. When you have completed a cycle of the project, you review what has been accomplished, asking the questions:

- What worked well?
- What could we have done better?
- What are the new advantages of what we accomplished?
- What do we need to repair now?
- What business should we implement next?
- What technology or architecture do we need to implement next?

Answering these questions gives you new knowledge for your next cycles. You made new knowledge available by your early implementation. When you continue to the next cycle of your project, you will be able to add new competitive value through your new knowledge. You reduce project costs and mitigate risks through your new knowledge.

You incorporate your new innovative ideas into your projects to create competitive value. You learned how to identify and control the inhibitors to change incorporating flexible business and technical, architectural, structures to make changes easier. Your architectures supported your needed business flexibility. Your flexible architectures also support business competitive advantages, reduce project costs, and mitigate risks.

You learned how to identify the different types of project participants and how they help create new competitive value, to recognize the new insights that add value to the project, and how to use architectures to reduce risk and add project flexibility.

You learned techniques to avoid the common mistakes while creating innovative enhancements to your project charter. You incorporated flexible business and technical structures to make future change easier without adding to the current costs, and you learned the importance of architectures to support needed project flexibility. I introduced methods to demonstrate how your cyclic or phased implementation can provide early project value.

You discovered how innovation is created within and after each project cycle. Within the project, you negotiated to find the best possible solutions for the needs of the project. After the project, you studied the results and determined new tasks that could be satisfied. You learned how to identify and eliminate needless tasks. You found new goals and alternatives to reduce project cost and risk. Your new goals also add value to the project.

We described the important attributes that make a project team successful:

- Using business and technical alternatives, the project team creates project value.
- Continuously communicating and reviewing creates value.
- Continuously investigating and identifying new project benefits adds value.
- Innovating allows the project team to lower project costs.

Tricks of the Trade

With CS-PM, you take moderate risks that create value and add competitive advantages. You use salesmanship throughout the project to select the best combination of alternatives, and your salesmanship helps you negotiate new project benefits.

With CS-PM, you select specific flexible architectures to advance your project value, to support continuous project upgrades, and to provide early and continuous project value improvements. Your middle managers help your innovative project team to create valuable business advantages, and they challenge and negotiate with you to help you create projects with vision, which helps you create business advantages. Your vision and the vision of your middle managers inspire people across projects and throughout the entire organization and in each of the projects with which they are connected.

Your vision is contagious. It inspires people to contribute positively to achieving new value within their projects. Your middle manager assists the project team to add business value to projects.

Senior management helps the CS-PM team define ways to improve business. Senior management even helps create new business based upon the knowledge gained through the CS-PM team. Either way, your corporation gains competitive advantages.

You need documentation so you can keep senior management informed and to help reduce costs associated with implementing projects. Documentation also helps meet governmental reporting requirements, such as Sarbanes-Oxley.

Senior management challenges its middle managers to create new corporate benefits and creates a stretch version of the corporate strategic intent. Your project teams and middle management extend corporate strategic intent through innovation.

Innovative Project Management with Best Practices

You begin your project from a known goal. From that goal, you discover new value that could be added to a project and architectures to increase the value of the project and mitigate risks. The added goals and architectures create competitive advantages.

Your architectures enhance business and business enhances architecture. You tune your architecture usage through your enhanced business competitive advantages.

You learned how to remove unimportant tasks from your project while keeping the tasks that are most critical. You added alternatives that enhance business value, reduce project cost and time, and mitigate risks. You used project alternatives to enhance the project.

You learned how to use cycles and phases to implement a project, thereby creating early project value. You implement your difficult issues early, thereby mitigating risks and creating early knowledge. You remove unimportant tasks by using the knowledge that you gained early in your implementation. You use the knowledge that you gained early to identify new competitive advantages and project values.

Architectures simplify projects and help identify alternatives. With CS-PM, you identify business and technical alternatives for study and delivery of the project.

You provide knowledge to identify and negotiate the best benefits for your company. You identify the critical business and architecture elements, and you combine business and technology benefits so that you can implement your project early.

You learned how organizations select and combine their alternatives and create more competitive value than promised or outlined in the original project charter by using alternatives.

You select the right architecture choice, reducing project costs while increasing the overall project value. When you use CS-PM, you use the full capabilities of your project staff, putting their abilities to practical use. You also seek business and IT benefits, and create new competitive advantages.

Your journey in CS-PM illustrates how to make innovative processes core to standard development practice and inject competitive value in early project phases. You create extra value throughout your CS-PM project life cycle.

With CS-PM, you design an approach with reuse in mind. You reuse before, during, and after each project implementation cycle. You identify the documentation needed to create reuse.

When you use the techniques in this book, you will create the innovative project team with each of the listed benefits.

PART FIVE

APPENDICES

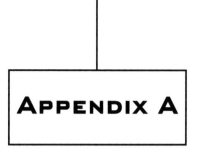

APPENDIX A

FORMS

Identify Critical Business Problems

Form CDPI01CB02 (on the next page) identifies critical business problems. They are addressed by the implementation of a system. Quite often, business functions are considered critical by the business departments when they are not critical, or conversely, they are not considered critical when they really are. Consequently, systems departments spend a lot of time implementing business functions that are not actually critical and bypassing the implementation of business issues that are critical to the business. Defining the elements of the business that are critical is the first step in making a determination about whether a function is critical or is not critical. As the business functions are defined, the descriptions will make it obvious which of them are in reality critical.

These forms are studied to describe and then to determine the critical business functions that will be implemented within a project. Some of the critical business issues will be implemented early during the project.

Common Sense in Project Management—Control Form

Phase: _____   Index Number: _____

CRITICAL BUSINESS CONTROL FORM

TITLE OF BUSINESS PROBLEM:

Describe why this is a critical business problem:

Date Created: _____   Created by: _____

Date Changed: _____   Changed by: _____

Form CDPI01CB02

Describe Why the Business Issue Is Critical

Form CDPI01CB3 is further used to help define the criticality of specific business issues. The form requires a description of the end result of implementing or not implementing a specific business function. The business department and systems personnel need to describe the process that is involved within the business department. By following the process, the results of implementing it can be clearly defined.

Common Sense in Project Management—Control Form

Phase: _____   Index Number: _____

CRITICAL BUSINESS CONTROL FORM

TITLE OF BUSINESS PROBLEM:

What is the impact of this problem on corporate business?

      What happens if the problem is solved?

      What happens if the problem is not solved?

Date Created: _____   Created by: _____

Date Changed: _____   Changed by: _____

Form CDPI01CB03

Critical Tool Control Form—
for the Creation of Reusable Tools

Form CDPI01TL01

Tools are used to simplify business processes and procedures, as well as by systems to simplify their implementation. One of the objectives of the Common Sense in Project Management process is to create tools that are reusable. By having tools that are reusable, the business process will be simplified and the implementation of projects will be simplified. But for tools to be useful, they need to be known. There are several processes that need to be used in describing tools. First, the tool needs to be named and described. A description of the use of the tool needs to be provided. Then examples of the use of the tools need to be provided. Further examples of the use of the tool in production need also to be provided. Then future uses of the tools need to be provided. None of this information will be sufficient because the actual use of tools will change over time as people discover new ways of using the tools. In many cases, our initial desire for the use of the tools was greatly expanded when people actually began using the tools for purposes other than our original intention. This is why a continued log of examples of tool use is important.

Common Sense in Project Management—Control Form

Phase: _____   Index Number: _____

CRITICAL BUSINESS CONTROL FORM

Tool Control Form—Name of the Tool:

Summary description of the tool created:

Date Created: _____   Created by: _____

Date Changed: _____   Changed by: _____

Form CDPI01TL01

Critical Technology Control

Form CDPI01CT01

Tools are used to simplify business processes and procedures, as well as by systems to simplify the implementation of the systems themselves.

Two types of critical technical processes need to be described. The first is critical because it supports a business critical process. The second is critical as a part of the architecture that allows the technical part of the system to be supported on its own. The technical critical architecture is not derived from the structure of the business or structure of the business process. Each of these processes will be described separately.

There is the technical process that is critical because the business process is critical. The technical description describes how the business needs will be satisfied through this specific process. In the common sense project, there may be more than one technical alternative that can support the business requirement. Each of the technical processes needs to be described. If there is more than one technical process that supports the business process, then the technical alternatives will be studied, and the best of the technical alternatives will be selected to implement the business requirement.

There is the technical critical process that is used for the architecture of the system. There may be many different parts of the architecture of the system that are critical. Each of the different parts of the technical architecture needs to be described. Further, there may be several alternatives that describe each of the technical architecture requirements. These alternatives will be studied to determine the best alternatives to use in implementing the technical architecture.

Common Sense in Project Management—Control Form

Phase: _____   Index Number: _____

CRITICAL TECHNOLOGY CONTROL FORM

Title of Technical Problem

Provide cross-index information to the critical business functions.

Describe how this technical function helps solve the critical business function and provide cross-reference information:

Date Created: _____   Created by: _____

Date Changed: _____   Changed by: _____

Form CDPI01CT01

Summary of Critical Technical Process

There are two types of critical processes that need to be described. The first is critical because it supports a business critical process. The second is critical as a part of the architecture that allows the technical part of the system to be supported on its own. The technical critical architecture is not derived from the structure of the business or structure of the business process. Each of these processes will be described separately.

There is the technical process that is critical because the business process is critical. The technical description describes how the business needs will be satisfied through this specific process. In the common sense project, there may be more than one technical alternative that can support the business requirement. Each of the technical processes needs to be described. If there is more than one technical process that supports the business process, then the technical alternatives will be studied and the best of the technical alternatives will be selected to implement the business requirement.

There is the technical critical process that is used for the architecture of the system. There may be many different parts of the architecture of the system that are critical. Each of the different parts of the technical architecture needs to be described. Further, there may be several alternatives that describe each of the technical architecture requirements. These alternatives will be studied to determine the best alternatives to use in implementing the technical architecture.

Common Sense in Project Management—Control Form

Phase: _____   Index Number: _____

CRITICAL TECHNOLOGY CONTROL FORM

Title of Technical Problem

Summary of technical critical process:

Date Created: _____   Created by: _____

Date Changed: _____   Changed by: _____

Form CDPI01CT04

Describe Why the Technology Is Critical

Many of the processes, both business critical and architecture critical, may not actually be critical. Some of the processes will be critical to the initial person making the decision, but will not be critical to the person who will need to implement the process. The level of criticality can only be discovered through the explanation of why something is critical. By reading the explanation, the people who need to implement the critical element can determine how that critical element needs to be implemented.

Common Sense in Project Management—Control Form

Phase: _____   Index Number: _____

CRITICAL TECHNOLOGY CONTROL FORM

Title of Technical Problem

Describe why this piece of technology is considered to be critical:

Date Created: _____   Created by: _____

Date Changed: _____   Changed by: _____

Form CDPI01CT05

Summary of Technical Alternatives

Each of the technical critical requirements will have been described. In order for the common sense project management project leader to make the decisions necessary for the project, each of the alternatives needs to be described. This description will make it easier for the parties responsible for the project to make proper decisions about the alternatives of the project.

Common Sense in Project Management—Control Form

Phase: _____   Index Number: _____

CRITICAL TECHNOLOGY CONTROL FORM

Title of Technical Problem

Summary description of technical alternatives:

Date Created: _____   Created by: _____

Date Changed: _____   Changed by: _____

Form CDPI01CT06

Technology Recommendation

At each step of the common sense project, decisions must be made about the ability of business and technical elements to satisfy the needs of the project. There are many factors that are used in the decisions. For example, the decisions may be made based upon cost, amount of time to implement, amount of research that needs to be accomplished, and even the personnel available to perform the work. These decisions need to be documented. Information about the acceptance or rejection of projects or project steps is very important. This information may be used in making future decisions.

Common Sense in Project Management—Control Form

Phase: _____   Index Number: _____

CRITICAL TECHNOLOGY CONTROL FORM

Title of Technical Problem

Technical Recommendation

     Terminate

     Defer

     Further Study Required

Pass Project to Phase _____ for Further Work

Date Created: _____   Created by: _____

Date Changed: _____   Changed by: _____

Form CDPI01CT07

Detailed Description of the Total System

As decisions are made, it is very important to know how all of the information about the project fits together. The project is a combination of many different elements. These are described as the combined business processes, procedures, and technical functions. This represents a description of all of the elements of the project, how those elements fit together, and how they will work together when the project is complete.

Common Sense in Project Management—Control Form

Phase: _____   Index Number: _____

DESIGN ACTIVITY CONTROL FORM

Title of Design Description

Detailed description of the total system:

Combined business processes, procedures, and technical functions:

Date Created: _____   Created by: _____

Date Changed: _____   Changed by: _____

Form CDPI01DA01

Required Refinement of Selected Alternatives

Within the common sense project, there are many different types of information that need to be brought together. The descriptions in this part of the project include a description of the business approach that will be used to implement the project. There could be many different business approaches, but as the project progresses, the number will narrow down to one or two.

Further, there could be several critical technical control forms representing the different critical elements of the project. Each of these will be described.

Some of the elements of the long term project will need research. The type of research will be described.

There may be other special requirements related to the project that could require special control or special interest. These will be described here.

Finally, it is possible that tools will be constructed from information that is gathered here. The tools that will be created will be described here.

This form provides the mechanism for controlling much of the functionality of the overall project, including the business approach being used, the control for the critical technical elements, the control for the research that will need to be performed over the long term for the project, control for any special requirements that need to be satisfied for the project, and finally, control for the tools that will be constructed for the project.

Common Sense in Project Management—Control Form

Phase: _____   Index Number: _____

REQUIRED REFINEMENT OF SELECTED ALTERNATIVES

Business Approach

Critical Technical Control

Research Description Control

Special Requirements Control

Tool Control

Alternate combined business and technical approaches to be studied:

Date Created: _____   Created by: _____

Date Changed: _____   Changed by: _____

Form CDPI01RR01

Schedules for Each of the Pieces

Schedule and costs need to be tightly controlled for all phases of the Common Sense Project. This set of forms handles the schedules for understanding the various parts of the project. The schedule involves the control of each of the different parts and includes schedules and controls for:

Management

Critical Business Study Schedule

Critical Technical Study Schedule

Business Analysis Schedule

Technical Solution Schedule

Research Schedule

Special Requirements Study Schedule

These forms are not much different from forms found in other project control processes. However, the topics are slightly more encompassing than other topics. The study of the critical elements of both the business and technology is prominent. There is a further study of the business analysis and technical solutions. Again, the amount of time that needs to be devoted to research is estimated, along with the estimates for special requirements that would be handled within the project.

Common Sense in Project Management—Control Form

Phase: _____   Index Number: _____

SCHEDULE AND COST CONTROL FORM

TITLE OF BUSINESS/TECHNICAL PROBLEM:

Management Schedule

Critical Business Study Schedule

Critical Technical Study Schedule

Business Analysis Schedule

Technical Solution Schedule

Research Schedule

Special Requirements Study Schedule

Title	Time	Sched	Sched	Actual	Actual	Var
Total this page						

Date Created: _____   Created by: _____

Date Changed: _____   Changed by: _____

Form CDPI01SC01

Costs for Each Part of the System

The costs for each of the different types of processes need to be made. Included in the study of costs are the following topics:

Management Costs

Critical Business Study Costs

Critical Technical Study Costs

Business Analysis Costs

Technical Solution Costs

Research Costs

Special Requirements Study Costs

Again, all of these costs are similar to the costs that most project management methodologies estimate. However, some of the topics are primarily relevant to the studies that need to be performed for the Common Sense in Project Management process. The costs provided are summary costs. The detailed costs need to be estimated and then rolled up to provide the costs for each of the categories.

Common Sense in Project Management—Control Form

Phase: _____   Index Number: _____

SCHEDULE AND COST CONTROL FORM

TITLE OF BUSINESS/TECHNICAL PROBLEM:

Management Costs
Critical Business Study Costs
Critical Technical Study Costs
Business Analysis Costs
Technical Solution Costs
Research Costs
Special Requirements Study Costs

Costs for specific aspects within the overall project

Gross Cost of Hardware Required	$ _____
Gross Cost of Software Required	$ _____
Cost to Create the Model	$ _____
Cost to Test the Model	$ _____
Cost for Management Support	$ _____
Cost for Operations of the Model	$ _____
Cost of Funds	$ _____
Costs for Manpower	$ _____
Cost for Facilities	$ _____
Total Costs	$ _____

Date Created: _____   Created by: _____

Date Changed: _____   Changed by: _____

Form CDPI01SC03

Topic List of Brainstorming Ideas

You need to capture your brainstorming ideas. You will have created many different ideas during the brainstorming process.

You will brainstorm for ideas, trying to find anything that might be different or might apply to the basic project requirements. You will ask yourself questions, trying to find yet another angle that would be good for the project or possibly something entirely different that could help the project. You will scan across many different fields of interest to find something that might be useful to your project or to the business.

This form is intended to capture your brainstorming process. First, put the basic topic of the idea as the title of this form.

Common Sense in Project Management

Brainstorming Control Form

Phase: _____   Index Number: _____

Topic of the brainstorming idea:

Field from which this idea was taken:

Description of the brainstorming idea:

Describe how this idea fits with the customer:

Describe how this idea fits with the company:

Describe how this idea fits with your project:

Date Created: _____   Created by: _____

Date Changed: _____   Changed by: _____

Form CDPI01SC03

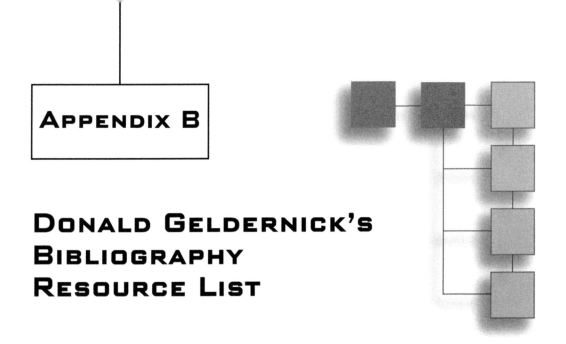

APPENDIX B

DONALD GELDERNICK'S BIBLIOGRAPHY RESOURCE LIST

1. *Software by Numbers: Low-Risk, High-Return Development*
   Mark Denne and Jane Cleland-Huang
   Prentice-Hall, ©2003

2. *Earned Value Project Management*, Second Edition
   Quentin W. Fleming, Joel M. Koppelman (Paperback)
   Earned value project management/Quentin W. Fleming, Joel M. Koppelman.
   Edition: 2nd ed.
   Published: Newton Square, Pa., USA: Project Management Institute, ©2000.
   ISBN: 1880410273 (alk. paper)

3. *The New Project Management: Tools for an Age of Rapid Change, Corporate Reengineering, and Other Business Realities* (Jossey Bass Business and Management Series)
   J. Davidson Frame
   Series: The Jossey-Bass business & management series
   Edition: 2nd ed.
   Published: San Francisco, CA: Jossey-Bass, ©2002.
   Related URL: http://www.loc.gov/catdir/toc/wiley022/2002001909.html
   ISBN: 0787958921

4. *A Guide to the Project Management Body of Knowledge* (PMBOK Guide) — 2000 Edition
   Project Management Institute (Paperback—December 2000)
   Published: Newtown Square, Penn., USA: Project Management Institute, ©2000.
   ISBN: 1880410222 (alk. paper)
   1880410230 (pbk.: alk. paper)

5. *PMP Exam Prep* (4th Edition)
   Rita Mulcahy (Paperback)
   Published: [Minneapolis, Minn.]: RMC Publications, ©2002.
   ISBN: 0971164738

6. *Project and Program Risk Management: A Guide to Managing Project Risks and Opportunities*
   (PMBOK Handbooks)
   R. Max Wideman (Paperback)
   Publisher: Project Management Institute (May 1, 1998)
   ISBN: 1880410060

7. *Managing Multiple Projects*
   Michael Tobis, Irene Tobis (Paperback)
   Series: A briefcase book
   Published: New York: London: McGraw-Hill, ©2002.
   ISBN: 0071388966

8. *The Fast Forward MBA in Project Management: Quick Tips, Speedy Solutions, and Cutting-Edge Ideas*
   Eric Verzuh (Paperback)
   Series: The fast forward MBA series
   The portable MBA
   Portable MBA series.
   Published: New York: J. Wiley, ©1999.
   ISBN: 0471325465 (paper)

9. *Project Management: A Systems Approach to Planning, Scheduling, and Controlling*
   Harold Kerzner (Hardcover)
   Edition: 8th ed.
   Published: Hoboken, N.J.: John Wiley & Sons, ©2003.
   Related URL: http://www.loc.gov/catdir/bios/wiley044/2002028892.html
   http://www.loc.gov/catdir/description/wiley036/2002028892.html

http://www.loc.gov/catdir/toc/wiley031/2002028892.html
ISBN: 0471225770 (cloth: alk. paper)

10. *Balancing Agility and Discipline, A Guide for the Perplexed*
Barry Boem and Richard Turner, Addison-Wesley, ©2003

11. *Peopleware: Productive Projects and Teams*, 2nd Ed.
Tom Demarco, Timothy Lister (Paperback)
Edition: 2nd ed.
Published: New York: Dorset House Pub., ©1999.
ISBN: 0932633439 (softcover)

12. *Project Management ToolBox: Tools and Techniques for the Practicing Project Manager*
Dragan Z. Milosevic (Hardcover)
Published: Hoboken, N.J.: Wiley, ©2003.
ISBN: 0471208221 (cloth)

13. *Fundamentals of Project Management: Developing Core Competencies to Help Outperform the Competition*
James P. Lewis
Edition: 2nd ed.
Published: New York: AMACOM, ©2002.
ISBN: 0814471323 (pbk.)

14. *Project and Program Risk Management: A Guide to Managing Project Risks and Opportunities (PMBOK Handbooks)*
R. Max Wideman (Paperback)
Published: Drexel Hill, PA: Project Management Institute, ©1992.
ISBN: 1880410001 (10 vol. set)
ISBN: 1880410060 (vol. 6)

15. *Identifying and Managing Project Risk: Essential Tools for Failure-Proofing Your Project*
Tom Kendrick (Hardcover)
Published: New York: AMACOM, ©2003.
Related URL: http://www.netLibrary.com/urlapi.asp?action=summary&v=1&bookid=86794
An electronic book accessible through the World Wide Web; click for information
Other Name: NetLibrary, Inc.

Notes: Electronic reproduction. Boulder, Colo.: NetLibrary, ©2003. Available via World Wide Web. Access may be limited to NetLibrary affiliated libraries.

ISBN: 0814427138 (electronic bk.)

16. *Advanced Project Management: Best Practices on Implementation*
Harold Kerzner (Hardcover)
Edition: 2nd ed.
Published: Hoboken, N.J.: Wiley, ©2004.
Related URL: www.loc.gov/catdir/bios/wiley047/2003053805.html
http://www.loc.gov/catdir/description/wiley0310/2003053805.html
http://www.loc.gov/catdir/toc/wiley032/2003053805.html
ISBN: 0471472840 (acid-free paper)

17. *Project Management: A Systems Approach to Planning, Scheduling, and Controlling*
Harold Kerzner
Edition: 8th ed.
Published: Hoboken, NJ: Wiley, ©2003.
Related URL: www.netLibrary.com/urlapi.asp?action=summary&v=1&bookid=104136
An electronic book that is Internet accessible.
Other Name: NetLibrary, Inc.
Notes: Electronic reproduction. Boulder, Colo.: NetLibrary, 2004. Available via World Wide Web. Access may be limited to NetLibrary affiliated libraries.
ISBN: 0471476307 (electronic bk.)

18. *Agile Project Management: How to Succeed in the Face of Changing Project Requirements*
Chin, Gary
Published: New York: AMACOM, ©2004.
Physical Description: x, 229 p.: ill. ; 24 cm.
ISBN: 0814471765

19. *Agile Project Management with Scrum (Microsoft Professional)*
Ken Schwaber (Paperback—March 10, 2004)
Microsoft Press
Published 02/11/2004
ISBN 0-7356-1993-X

20. *Rapid Development*
Steve McConnell
Published: Redmond, Wash.: Microsoft Press, ©1996.
ISBN: 1556159005

21. *Effective Project Management: Traditional, Adaptive, Extreme*, Third Edition
Robert K. Wysocki (Author), Rudd McGary (Contributor)
Published: Indianapolis: Wiley Pub., ©2003.
Related URL: http://www.netLibrary.com/urlapi.asp?action=summary&v=1&bookid=91819
An electronic book accessible through the World Wide Web
NetLibrary, Inc.
Notes: Electronic reproduction. Boulder, Colo.: NetLibrary, ©2003. Available via World Wide Web. Access may be limited to NetLibrary affiliated libraries. Excludes data from the CD-ROM which accompanied the original book.
ISBN: 0471481084 (electronic bk.)

22. *Agile and Iterative Development: A Manager's Guide*
Craig Larman (Paperback—August 15, 2003)
Series: The agile software development series
Published: Boston: Addison-Wesley, ©2004.
ISBN: 0131111558 (pbk.)

23. *Earned Value Project Management*, Second Edition
Quentin W. Fleming, Joel M. Koppelman (Paperback—June 1, 2000)
Published: Newton Square, Pa., USA: Project Management Institute, ©2000.
ISBN: 1880410273 (alk. paper)

24. *Value Stream Management: Eight Steps to Planning, Mapping, and Sustaining Lean Improvements*
Don Tapping, Tom Luyster and Tom Shuker
Published: New York, N.Y.: Productivity, ©2002.
ISBN: 1563272458

25. *The Deming Management Method*
Mary Walton (Paperback—September 1, 1986)
Published: Dodd, Mead & Co. 1986
Deming, W. Edwards (William Edwards), 1900-1993
ISBN: 0399550003

26. *Project Management*
    Gary R. Heerkens.
    Series: A Briefcase book
    Published: New York: McGraw-Hill, ©2002.
    ISBN: 0071379525 (acid-free paper)

27. *The Product Manager's Field Guide: Practical Tools, Exercises, and Resources for Improved Product Management*
    Linda Gorchels
    Published: New York: McGraw-Hill, ©2003.
    ISBN: 0071410597

28. *Data Modeling Essentials,* Third Edition (Morgan Kaufmann Series in Data Management Systems)
    Graeme C. Simsion, Graham C. Witt
    Published: Amsterdam; Boston: Morgan Kaufmann Publishers, ©2005
    ISBN: 0126445516 (acid-free paper)

29. *Oracle E-Business Suite Manufacturing & Supply Chain Management*
    Bastin Gerald, *et al.*
    Published: New York: McGraw-Hill/Osborne, ©2002
    Notes: at head of title: Oracle; Oracle Press.
    "Implement Oracle's internet-based manufacturing and supply chain management products"
    —Cover.
    ISBN: 0072133791

30. *Construction Operations Manual of Policies and Procedures*
    Andrew M. Civitello (Hardcover—July 11, 2000)
    Edition: 3rd ed.
    Published: New York: McGraw Hill, ©2000.
    ISBN: 0071354956 (set)

31. *The Complete Idiot's Guide to Knowledge Management*
    Melissie Clemmons Rumizen
    Published: Indianapolis, IN: Alpha, ©2002.
    ISBN: 0028641779 (pbk.:alk. paper)

32. *A Guide to the Project Management Body of Knowledge: PMBOK Guide*
Manufactured by Project Management Institute
Edition: 3rd ed.
Published: Newtown Square, Pa.: Project Management Institute, ©2004.
Notes: "An American National Standard; ANSI/PMI 99-001-2004."
Also available on CD-ROM.
ISBN: 193069945X (pbk.)
ISBN: 1930699506 (CD-ROM)

33. *Lean Thinking: Banish Waste and Create Wealth in Your Corporation*
James P. Womack, Daniel T. Jones
Edition: 1st Free Press; ed.; revised and updated.
Published: New York: Free Press, ©2003.
ISBN: 0743249275

34. *The Lean Six Sigma Pocket Toolbook: A Quick Reference Guide to Nearly 100 Tools for Improving Process Quality, Speed, and Complexity*
Michael L. George, *et al.*
Published: New York ; London: McGraw-Hill, ©2005.
ISBN: 0071441190 (pbk.)

35. *Principle-Centered Leadership*
Stephen R. Covey, Reynolds
Edition: Free Press
Published: New York: Free Press, ©2003.
ISBN: 0671792806 (pbk.)

36. *Critical Chain*
Eliyahu M. Goldratt
Published: Great Barrington, MA: North River Press, ©1997.
ISBN: 0884271536

37. *Effective Project Management: Traditional, Adaptive, Extreme* (DUPLICATE)
Robert K. Wysocki, Rudd McGary
Edition: 3rd ed.
Published: Indianapolis: Wiley Pub., ©2003.
Related URL: http://www.netLibrary.com/urlapi.asp?action=summary&v=1&bookid=91819

Notes: Electronic reproduction. Boulder, Colo.: NetLibrary, ©2003.
ISBN: 0471481084 (electronic bk.)

38. *The Six Sigma Way Team Fieldbook: An Implementation Guide for Process Improvement Teams*
Peter S. Pande, Roland R. Cavanagh, Robert P. Neuman, Roland R. Cavanaugh
Published: New York: McGraw-Hill, ©2002.
ISBN: 0071373144

39. *Lean Thinking: Banish Waste and Create Wealth in Your Corporation*
James P. Womack, Daniel T. Jones
Edition: 1st Free Press ed. ; revised and updated.
Published: New York: Free Press, ©2003.
ISBN: 0743249275

40. *The Goal: A Process of Ongoing Improvement*
Eliyahu M. Goldratt, Jeff Cox
Edition: 2nd ed.
Published: Aldershot, Hampshire: Gower, ©1993.
ISBN: 0566074184 (pbk.)
ISBN: 0566074176 (cased)

41. *Extreme Programming Explained: Embrace Change* (DUPLICATE)
Kent Beck, Cynthia Andres
Edition: 2nd ed.
Published: Boston, MA: Addison-Wesley, ©2005.
ISBN: 0321278658 (alk. paper)

42. *Peopleware: Productive Projects and Teams* (DUPLICATE)
Tom DeMarco, Timothy Lister, Timothy R. Lister
Edition: 2nd ed.
Published: New York: Dorset House Publishing, ©1999.
ISBN: 0932633439 (softcover)

43. *Winning at New Products: Accelerating the Process from Idea to Launch*
Robert Gravlin Cooper
Edition: 3rd ed.
Published: New York, N.Y.: Basic Books, ©2001.
ISBN: 0738204633 (pbk.: alk. paper)

44. *Agile and Iterative Development (Agile Software Development Series): A Manager's Guide*
Craig Larman
Series: The agile software development series
Published: Boston: Addison-Wesley, ©2004.
ISBN: 0131111558 (pbk.)

45. *Rath and Strong's Six Sigma Team Pocket Guide: How to Be an Effective Team Leader or Team Member*
Mary Federic, Mary & Beaty, Renee
Published: Hoboken, N.J.: J. Wiley, ©2003.
Related URL: http://www.loc.gov/catdir/toc/wiley031/2002014035.html
ISBN: 0471251240 (Cloth: alk. paper)

46. *Waltzing with Bears: Managing Risk on Software Projects*
Tom DeMarco, Timothy Lister
Published: New York: Dorset House Pub., ©2003.
ISBN: 0932633609 (pbk.)

47. *The Data Warehouse Lifecycle Toolkit: Expert Methods for Designing, Developing, and Deploying Data Warehouses* with CD Rom
Ralph Kimball
Published: New York: Wiley, c1998 (Norwood, Mass.: Books24x7.com)
Related URL: http://ezproxy.gl.iit.edu/login?url=http://library.books24x7.com/library.asp?
Available also in a print ed.
Digitized and made available by: Books 24x7.com.
ISBN: 0471255475

48. *Six Sigma for Green Belts and Champions: Foundations, DMAIC, Tools, Cases, and Certification*
Howard S. Gitlow, David M. Levine
Published: Upper Saddle River, NJ: Pearson/Prentice Hall, ©2005.
ISBN: 013117262X

49. *Project Management: Processes, Methodologies, and Economics* (2nd Edition) (Prentice-Hall International Series in Industrial and Systems Engineering)
Avraham Shtub, *et al.*
Edition: 2nd ed.
Published: Upper Saddle River, NJ: Pearson Prentice Hall, ©2005.
ISBN: 0130413313

50. *Project Management Methodologies: Selecting, Implementing, and Supporting Methodologies and Processes for Projects* (Youth Communicates)
    Jason Charvat
    Published: New York: Wiley, ©2003.
    ISBN: 0471221783 (cloth: alk. paper)

51. *Extreme Project Management: Unique Methodologies—Resolute Principles—Astounding Results*
    Shaun H. Ajani
    Series: The Jossey-Bass business & management series
    Edition: 1st ed.
    Published: San Francisco, CA: Jossey-Bass, ©2004.
    Related URL: http://www.loc.gov/catdir/toc/ecip0419/2004015788.html
    ISBN: 0787974099 (alk. paper)

52. *Research and Development Project Selection* (Wiley Series in Engineering and Technology Management)
    Joseph P. Martino
    Series: Wiley series in engineering management.
    Published: New York: Wiley, ©1995.
    Research—Methodology.

53. *LIMS: Applied Information Management for the Laboratory*
    Richard Mahaffey
    Published: New York: Van Nostrand Reinhold, ©1990.
    ISBN: 0442318200

54. *Introducing Riskman: The European Project Risk Management Methodology*
    Bruce Carter, *et al.*
    Published: Oxford, England: NCC Blackwell, ©1994.
    ISBN: 1855543567

55. *Management Projects: Design, Research and Presentation*
    Paul Raimond
    Edition: 1st ed.
    Published: London; New York: Chapman & Hall, ©1993.
    ISBN: 0412468107 (acid-free paper)

56. *Research and Development of Vaccines and Pharmaceuticals from Biotechnology: A Guide to Effective Project Management, Patenting and Product Registration*
Jens-Peter Gregersen
Out of Print—Limited Availability
Published: Weinheim ; New York: VCH, ©1994.
ISBN: 3527300597 (alk. paper)

57. *Environmental Methods Testing Site Project Data Management Procedures Plan: Project Summary*
E. H. Barrows
Out of Print—Limited Availability
Published: Research Triangle Park, NC: U.S. Environmental Protection Agency, Environmental Monitoring Systems Laboratory, [1988]
Physical Description: [2] p. ; 28 cm.
Subject (LCSH): Environmental monitoring—Methodology.
Other Name: *Environmental Monitoring Systems Laboratory* (Las Vegas, Nev.)
Notes: Microfiche. [Washington, D.C.]: U.S. Govt. Print. Off., [1991]. 1 microfiche ; 11 x 15 cm. "EPA/600/S4-87/023."
Other Identifying Number: EPA/600/S4-87/023

58. *Radical Project Management*
Rob Thomsett (Paperback)
Series: Just enough series
Published: Upper Saddle River, NJ: Prentice Hall PTR, ©2002.
ISBN: 0130094862

59. *Agile Project Management: Creating Innovative Products* (Agile Software Development Series)
Jim Highsmith
Series: The agile software development series
Published: Boston: Addison-Wesley, ©2004.
ISBN: 0321219775

60. *eXtreme Project Management: Using Leadership, Principles, and Tools to Deliver Value in the Face of Volatility* (Jossey Bass Business and Management Series)
Douglas DeCarlo, *et al.*
Series: The Jossey-Bass business & management series
Edition: 1st ed.
Published: San Francisco, CA: Jossey-Bass, ©2004.
Related URL: http://www.loc.gov/catdir/toc/ecip0419/2004015788.html
ISBN: 0787974099 (alk. paper)

61. *Agile Management for Software Engineering: Applying the Theory of Constraints for Business Results*
    David J. Anderson
    Series: The Coad series
    Published: Upper Saddle River, NJ: Prentice Hall PTR, ©2004.
    ISBN: 0131424602

62. *Project Management*
    Gary R. Heerkens
    ISBN: 0071379525
    Date Published: ©2002
    Publisher: McGraw-Hill

63. *New Dynamic Project Management, The*
    Deborah S. Kezsbom, Katherine A. Edward
    ISBN: 0471254940
    Date Published: ©2001
    Publisher: Wiley-Interscience

64. *Effective Work Breakdown Structures*
    Gregory T. Haugan, PMP
    ISBN: 1567261353
    Date Published: ©2002
    Publisher: Management Concepts

65. *Effective Project Management: Traditional, Adaptive, Extreme* 3rd Edition (DUPLICATE)
    Robert K. Wysocki and Rudd McGary
    ISBN: 0471432210
    Date Published: ©2003
    Publisher: John Wiley & Sons
    FFD List:

66. *Agile Project Management*
    Gary Chin
    ISBN: 0814471761

67. *Agile Project Management with SCRUM*
    Ken Schwaber
    Microsoft Press
    ISBN: 0-7356-1993-X

68. *Agile and Iterative Development* (DUPLICATE)
    Craig Larman
    ISBN: 0131111558 (Pbk)

69. *Agile Project Management, Creating Products* (DUPLICATE)
    Jim Highsmith
    Addison Wesley, ©2002
    ISBN: 0321219775

70. *Agile Management for Software Engineering*
    David J. Anderson
    Prentice Hall, ©2004
    Upper Saddle River, New Jersey
    ISBN: 0131424602

71. *Description of the Extreme Programming Process*:
    http://www.extremeprogramming.org

72. *The Agile Manifesto*
    http://www.agilemanifesto.org

73. *Extreme Programming Explained: Embrace Change* (DUPLICATE)
    Kent Beck
    Addison-Wesley, 1st Edition, ©1999

74. *Lean Software Development: An Agile Toolkit for Software Development Managers*
    Mary and Tom Poppendieck
    Addison-Wesley, ©2003

75. *User Stories Applied For Agile Development*
    Mike Cohn
    Addison-Wesley, ©2003

INDEX

projects/project management *(continued)*
- parallel construction, 95-97
- planning, 103
- retail example, 98-100
- return on investment, 116
- technical requirements, 98-100, 211-214
- top down construction, 94-95
- senior management, 196-198
bureaucracy (common mistakes), 118-120
business tasks (critical), 6, 59-61
- food processing industry example, 215
- identifying, 214-215, 217-218
- innovation, 152-153
- insurance company examples, 218
business competitive advantage, 63, 66-69, 74-75
business judgment, 164-165
business opportunities, 10-11
business processes (alternatives), 218-221
business requirements
- architectures, 98-100, 211-214
- critical business requirements, 17, 78
- cycles, 66-69, 76
business strategies (cycles), 65
business tools
- building, 211-214, 240-242
- insurance company examples, 213
business/technical solutions, 228-232
- insurance company examples, 229-230
- telephone company examples, 232
communication. *See* communication
competitive advantage, 44-47
- business competitive advantage, 63, 66-69, 74-75
- innovation, 149
- technical competitive advantage, 63, 66-69
competitive value, 83
critical business requirements, 17, 78

critical business tasks, 6, 59-61
- food processing industry example, 215
- identifying, 214-215, 217-218
- innovation, 152-153
- insurance company examples, 218
critical elements (avoiding mistakes), 105
critical issues (cycles), 71-74
Critical Path Method (prototypes), 224-225
critical technical requirements, 78
critical technical tasks, 6, 59-61
- identifying, 221-222
- innovation, 152-153
CRM (Customer Relationship Management), 123-124
CSRs (customer support representatives), 123-124
customer needs. *See* customer needs
cycles. *See* cycles
differentiation, 84
examples. *See* examples
flexibility (projects/project management)
- architectures, 98, 196-198
- charter, 6-9
- innovation, 6-9
- requirements, 6-9
- senior management, 185, 196-198
goals
- business teams, 53-55
- communication, 215-217
- implementation, 208
- innovation, 141-142
- overview, 49-50
- senior management, 50-53, 185-188
- technical teams, 55-56
implementation. *See* implementation
innovation. *See* innovation
insights, 163-164
- avoiding mistakes, 110
- implementation, 242-243

Leadership Mastery
in Turbulent Times

A personal training program for career advancement...

■ Understand the changing role of a leader in today's workplace and master the skills needed to be an effective leader

■ Uncover the three basic building blocks of leadership: self-development, strategic thinking, and energized performance

■ Learn how to fuel creativity and productivity within an organization

Herb Kindler, Ph.D.

ISBN: 1-59200-934-4 ■ $19.99 U.S.

Leadership Mastery in Turbulent Times is a powerful guide to the changing roles and new skills required to be an effective and ethical leader. Master these skills as you learn how to fuel creativity and productivity within an organization and how to energize performance.

"...*a wonderful tapestry, almost poetic in its articulation.*"
—**Ken Shepard, Ph.D.**
President, Canadian Centre
for Leadership and Strategy

"...*provocative, wise, and stimulating.*"
—**Susan Nero, Ph.D.**
Organizational Management Chair,
Antioch University

"...*eminently readable, and alive with personal reflections...*"
—**Dr. Beverly Kaye**
CEO/Founder, Career Systems International
and author of *Up Is Not The Only Way*

A personal training program for career advancement...

Understand the changing role of a leader in today's workplace and master the skills needed to be an effective leader

■

Uncover the three basic building blocks of leadership: self-development, strategic thinking, and energized performance

■

Learn how to fuel creativity and productivity within an organization